Agile Portfolio Management

Agile Portfolio Management

A Guide to the Methodology and Its Successful Implementation
"Knowledge That Sets You Apart"

by
Klaus Nielsen, MBA

Fully aligned with the global standards for project portfolio management, major agile portfolio management frameworks and agnostic

Routledge
Taylor & Francis Group
A PRODUCTIVITY PRESS BOOK

First published 2022
by Routledge
600 Broken Sound Parkway #300, Boca Raton FL, 33487

and by Routledge
2 Park Square, Milton Park, Abingdon, Oxon, OX14 4RN

Routledge is an imprint of the Taylor & Francis Group, an informa business

© 2022 Taylor & Francis

The right of Klaus Nielsen to be identified as author of this work has been asserted by him in accordance with sections 77 and 78 of the Copyright, Designs and Patents Act 1988.

ISBN: 9780367650933 (hbk)
ISBN: 9781032059761 (pbk)
ISBN: 9781003200406 (ebk)

Typeset in Garamond
by Deanta Global Publishing Services, Chennai, India

Contents

Preface

It is good to see you. Today my memory is more blurred, however I still remember the day back in 2016 when I ran my first course at the IT University of Copenhagen in Agile Portfolio Management for professionals. Before that, Agile Portfolio Management played a minor part in our master course. I was a novice but had a great co-worker who is a top researcher in the field of portfolio management. After a day of lecturing, it was clear then than this topic was a keeper.

Many excellent books have been written on agile software development on the team level, agile frameworks on the portfolio level, project portfolio management, and such topics; however, I have never witnessed a combined and diverse content such as this. Some topics or fields of research are clearly more mature than others, however the work encompasses most of what we know and hopefully most of what you need to know. Agile development methods were originally designed for small and co-located teams, but changes of times require changes of solutions. Today more than ever, agile development methods are popular in large scale and complex software projects involving multiple teams spread across different geographic locations. Now is time for the age of agile portfolio management.

One of the motives for writing this book was to build upon strong academic research on the topics and combine them with best practices and knowledge from the many commercial frameworks. Also, to include all the good work done in the industry. It has been important to cover all you need to know from project portfolio management to agile portfolio management, the reality of scaling, the various frameworks, and all the things in-between.

I know you are busy and no matter what, I do not want to waste your time. That is why it is important this book is effective and includes all relevant content. I call this combination "Knowledge That Sets You Apart".

I hope you will enjoy being part of this journey and would love to hear from you.

Best regards, Klaus Nielsen

Acknowledgements

Acknowledgement is the recognition or favourable notice of the acts or achievements which are numerous in creating this work. My only plea is forgiveness for all not mentioned but not by any means forgotten. First, I would like to extend my thanks and gratitude to the people who have helped make this work a reality. By doing so, I need to acknowledge all the leaders, practitioners, participants, students, and academics within these fields of knowledge. Writing this book has been a research process standing on the shoulders of giants while learning and at the same time witnessing what is happening in a fast-growing and highly innovative industry. The work has been supported by a wide range of research, articles, global standards, frameworks, academic sources from ACM digital library, IEEE, and a range of trade, business, and academic sources.

Writing this work in the dark shadows of COVID-19 has been a strange situation. Nightmare situations, but isolated, and with time to wonder about better days to come again.

Many people have contributed over the years to the evolution of this work as many of the ideas in this work has been formed, sharpened, and aired at meetings, trainings, debates, and lectures around the world.

Also, thanks to all the wonderful people at the Taylor & Francis Group for making this dream possible and a wonderful experience. This work would not have been possible without the support of all the people who have taken part, one way or another ensuring the content and quality of this work. Thank you. I owe you my greatest gratitude.

My deepest appreciation goes to all my loved ones at home – Nina, Molly, and Julie.

Finally, my family has put up with my absence, while writing this book, for more birthdays and evenings than I like to think about.

Any errors, of course, are mine. Klaus Nielsen.

"With grandiose resolve a man endeavors to soar above all obstacles, but thus encounters a hostile fate. He retreats and evades the issue. The time is difficult. Without rest, he must hurry along, with no permanent abiding place. If he does not want to make compromises within himself, but insists on remaining true to his principles, he suffers deprivation. Never the less he has a fixed goal to strive for even though the people with whom he lives do not understand him and speak ill of him."

(**The Book of Changes**, Darkening of the Light)

About the Author

Klaus Nielsen holds a master's degree in Ecommerce from the IT University of Copenhagen which was supplemented with a year in Cambridge (UK) and later dual MBAs (HRM and Technology) from the U.S. He has worked in project, programmes, and portfolio management, plan-based and agile, for more than 20 years, still does, and has been embracing many of the international best practices for years.

He is the author of the books, *I am Agile* (2013), *Mastering the Business Case* (2015), *Achieve PMI-PBA® Exam Success* (2015), *Agile Certified Practitioner Exam* (2016), and writer of several industry articles published worldwide. He has been subject matter expert (SME) on various publications from PMI and Axelos, recently PMI core team member on the *PMBOK Guide* 7th edition.

Mr. Nielsen is the co-founder of Global Business Development (gbd.dk), a PMI Authorized Training Partner (ATP) and Scrum/DevOps training company, where he trains, e.g., PMI Authorized Training Partner Instructor and consults to businesses ranging from small start-ups to top 500 companies worldwide.

Since 2012, Klaus have taught part-time at the IT University of Copenhagen as faculty lecture and is a frequent speaker at events, conferences, and tradeshows. Klaus holds a wide range of certifications from varies Scrum organizations, PMI, Axelos, DevOps Institute, LeSS, Disciplined Agile, Kanban, SAFe, and others, many of which he has trained in for years.

For a complete listing on Klaus Nielsen's programmes, products, high-profile clients, and speaking schedule, visit the Global Business Development website at www.gbd.dk.

To book Klaus Nielsen for your next conference, event, or in-house training, please contact us at LinkedIn or the company website.

How This Book Is Organized

I also learned a lot, although I did not always realize it at the time, from the world-class educators at the University of Cambridge and fellows of Trinity College. Hard times spent come back tenfold. In Cambridge, Chinese was my major and some are perhaps familiar with the phase *"Di Ren Tian"* which is the Chinese expression of the Japanese term *"Shu Ha Ri"*, which was coined by Alastair Cockburn and applied to the development of agile learning. In Chinese *"Di"* may mean "Earth", which represents the basics and following the instructions to the letter. I hope this publication can provide you with a solid "Earth" foundation. *"Ren"* in Chinese may mean "Human" and represents the process of breaking out of a well-known process and making changes which should be possible soon after reading this work. In Chinese, *"Tian"* may have a meaning of the "Heaven" and represent that the sky is the limit and agile learning and knowledge arise from within and are at the highest level of agile mastery, with no limits.

The way the book is organized follows the *"Di Ren Tian"*/*"Shu Ha Ri"* concept approaches to learning. Each section introduces the background and core concepts which are equal to the first level of training or *"Di"*/"Shu". Each section goes deeper into the concepts and combines content in new ways which represent the *"Ren"*/"Ha" concept. Mastery ("Tian"/"Ri") of agile portfolio management requires right use of frameworks, maybe hybrid approaches, understanding differences between PPM and APM, learning from others/case studies, and some degree of tailoring, which is supported by the final sections of the book. The reference list will provide you with plenty to read next.

Chapter 1 Project Portfolio Management

Project portfolio management is vastly different from agile portfolio management, but we can learn from it and some of the overall concepts are similar, so it is helpful when working with agile portfolio management to know the financial approach before diving deeper into how it is done in software development.

Chapter 2 Agility@Scale

Agile portfolio management implies scaling. Scaling comes with consequences and new concepts we need to embrace and consider, some more than others, but it a part of agile portfolio management we need to consider.

Chapter 3 Agile Portfolio Management

This section explains what agile portfolio management all is about, what you need to know, and all the core concepts you need to master. This is kind of the generic approach to agile portfolio management, before you need to consider what to do.

Chapter 4 Agile Portfolio Management Frameworks

Most organizations perform agile portfolio management based upon a framework. Several frameworks exist, and with a framework come strengths and weaknesses. This section illustrates what this is all about, what you can use, and some of the considerations in the making.

Chapter 5 Project Portfolio Management vs. Agile Portfolio Management

This section compares project portfolio management and agile portfolio management to highlight how they work and the many differences and the few similarities. This will help create the big picture.

Chapter 6 Hybrid Portfolio Management

Project portfolio management and agile portfolio management are different approaches, but what if it is not that simple. We may need both. This section shows how this can be done and what to consider to make it work, and what would not work.

Chapter 7 Implementing Agile Portfolio Management

It is not a trivial task to implement agile portfolio management in any organization. Pitfalls and challenges exist in abundance, but this section will help you navigate your way through.

Chapter 8 Tailoring Agile Portfolio Management

Any off-the-shelf approach, framework, global standard, or one's own creation requires some degree of tailoring before being used and for this to be done continually to gain the most out of the approaches. This section gives you the theory, concepts, and concrete examples on how to tailor agile portfolio management approaches to your need.

Chapter 9 Case Studies on Agile Portfolio Management

This section goes beyond theory and concepts, and describes what real companies have done in different situations which is useful to illustrate some of the problems, challenges, possible solutions, and to give you the opportunity to apply critical thinking when discussing and analyzing the case studies.

Key Features:

- Covers *all* subjects addressed on agile portfolio management
- A full portfolio management course in a book
- Reduce costs with all you need in just one book covering both project portfolio management *and* agile

- Portfolio management
- Guide to tailoring your portfolio
- How to implement an agile portfolio and what not to do
- Several case studies from leading companies on agile portfolio management where *you* can test your critical thinking
- Latest research included with comprehensive reference list
- One book covering *all* the agile portfolio management frameworks from giants such as SAFe to newcomers like XSCALE
- Save time with accelerated learning in an easy-to-use format created by an experienced trainer and subject matter expert
- Have fun with activities and exercises throughout the book
- Tips and tricks of the trade and tools to improvement the outcome of the book
- Excellent reference material on the global standards
- Delivers a comprehensive and time saving self-study programme without the need for additional reading materials

Chapter 1

"Financial" Project Portfolio Management

Figure 1.1 Overview.

1.1 The Short History of Project Portfolio Management (PPM)

Humans have worked with projects since the dawn of civilization. Just think about the wonders of the world – the Hanging Gardens of Babylon were probably built around 605 BC. Going forward in time to the 1605 premiere of the play *The Merchant of Venice*, William Shakespeare's Antonio understands that the portfolio principle of "diversification" makes his business more robust against temporary and local fluctuations.

> Believe me, no. I thank my fortune for it.
> My ventures are not in one bottom trusted.
> Nor to one place, nor is my whole estate.

Upon the fortune of this present year.
Therefore my merchandise makes me not sad.

(Act I scene 1)

Shortly after World War II, the literature began to recognize the contextual structures of what we describe today as project portfolio management, or simply PPM. In the 1940s project portfolio management was relatively simple; some might argue it was underdeveloped and straightforward. The classical project management perspective covers the thinking emerging in the 1950s, e.g., technically oriented project management which was encouraged by the US Department of Defense because it was needed to control the development of the Polaris submarines. At that point in time, project portfolio management was mainly applied in the military and in defence, where it was used mostly for project selection. In 1952, portfolio research that focuses on financial portfolios rather than being directly applicable to project portfolios was developed by Nobel prize winner H. M. Markowitch (in the *Journal of Finance* and later in the book *Modern Portfolio Theory*). Markowitch talks about taking risks into account, the importance of diversity, and balancing the financial portfolio. Markowitch's thinking shaped the thinking about project portfolio management for generations to come, which sometimes leads us to think about, or label, project portfolio management as "financial" project portfolio management. This thinking continued until the 1980s when Cooper's Stage-Gate model was introduced and became the de facto standard for project portfolio management for years to come. Work by Cooper and others has given rise to modern project portfolio management theory where projects as components of the portfolio play a major part. In the 1990s the Stage-Gate model developed further: the basic idea is that an organization has several gates, and a project is required to provide some pre-specified information before proceeding to the next gate. As Western societies become increasingly more project-oriented, organizations are experiencing ongoing challenges in managing their project portfolios, since projects constitute a major part of the organizational budgets and strategic development.

The first scaled agile approach on the market was Crystal, in 1992, introduced by Alastair Cockburn. However, scaling agile had to wait another 15 years for a breakthrough. Most people may remember the dot-com implosion of the 2000s and an awareness of international maturity models (e.g., OPM3 and P3M3) that assume that there is a positive correlation between adoption of the defined practices of those models and the success of organizations' project portfolio management. Nolan and McFarlan (2005) document with the IT strategic impact grid how portfolios driven by IT/IS-related research due to the emerging need for managing portfolios of IT projects – The IT strategic impact grid.

In the 2010s the importance of internet technologies (IT) and their relation to project portfolio management was clear, and with the increased agility on the team level with frameworks such as Scrum, the research agenda shifted toward agility of business. Agility is no longer just a buzzword. Within the last ten years, the market has witnessed a range of scaled agile frameworks being introduced into the market and applied in organizations to some degree, e.g., the scaled agile framework (SAFe®), large-scale scrum (LeSS), dynamic systems development method (AgilePfM), disciplined agile delivery (DAD), and many others. The various agile frameworks for agile portfolio management are discussed in detail in Chapter 4. The literature/research shows, however, that there has been little experimental validation of these scaled agile frameworks to date. Indeed, the little research that does exist highlights problems with their application. Furthermore, most of these frameworks are also based on the assumption that the issue of managing a portfolio of agile projects can be addressed by simply scaling agile practices to the portfolio level.

Exercise 1.1 Starting from Zero or a Lot – What Do You Know?

What do you know about project portfolio management? Write it down or share it with the people in the room.

_____
_____
_____
_____
_____

Answers: No right or wrong answers.

1.2 The Definitions of Project Portfolio Management (PPM)

The literature does not have just one common definition of project portfolio management but several, all pointing us in the same direction; however, each definition contains its own emphasis and details. Archer and

Ghasemzadeh (1999) define the portfolio as "a group of projects that are carried out under the sponsorship and/or management of a particular organization". Years later, Clegg et al. (2018) define the portfolio as "the overall organizational ability to manage project portfolios strategically and holistic to support the success of the organization". The frameworks/global standards from the project management organizations, Axelos (2011) and PMI (2017) introduced new definitions of portfolios as

> a portfolio is the totality of an organizations' investment (or segment thereof) in the changes required to achieve its strategic objectives. Portfolio Management is a coordinated collection of strategic processes and decisions that together enable the most effective balance of organizational change and "business as usual".

And

> "a portfolio is a collection of projects, programs, subsidiary portfolios, and operations managed as a group to achieve strategic objectives".

Whether one prefers, or agrees with, one definition rather than another, it is clear the organization with a portfolio is managing a range of programmes, projects, and operations which are strategically aligned and need to be managed in a coordinated manner. Figure 1.2 illustrates how the project portfolio is driven by the vision/mission/strategy of the company and applies components such as programmes, projects, and operations to deliver on the organizational strategy. It also highlights that projects may or may not be part of a programme.

However, as some organizations are shifting toward agile, the definitions of portfolios change slightly as illustrated by Thompson (2013) as he defines the portfolio as the following: "We define a portfolio as a grouping of work

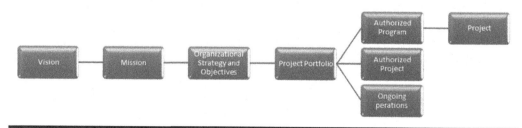

Figure 1.2   Project portfolio management – high-level view.

under consideration (which may or may not be related) and that aligns to investment strategies". The sum of these definitions neatly sums up the core of project portfolio management. Project portfolio management having been defined, we move on to what it entails. Blichfeldt and Eskerod (2007) define the managerial activities of project portfolio management as:

(1) The initial screening, selection, and prioritization of project proposals
(2) The concurrent reprioritization of projects in the portfolio.
(3) The allocation and reallocation of resources to projects according to priority

Project portfolio management (PPM) is a well-established topic in today's literature and has gained a central position in project management. We need to be clear that project portfolio management, as illustrated, is based upon financial management, in the thinking of the likes of Markowitch; while agile portfolio management, as the main topic of this work, is based upon agile software development. They may sound similar, and, to some degree, have similar goals and techniques, but agile portfolio management is a vastly different ballgame, as the following chapters will illustrate.

However, we still need a bit of basic project portfolio management knowledge to fully understand, appreciate, and master agile portfolio management.

1.3 The Main Goals of Project Portfolio Management (PPM)

Empirical research on project portfolio management has traditionally focused on measuring three to four main aspects of the project portfolio to evaluate the project portfolio success levels:

■ Maximize the value of the portfolio (value maximization).
■ Ensure balance among initiatives.
■ Achieve strategic alignment of the portfolio.
■ Pick the right number of initiatives.

Recent research by Ahmad et al. (2017) illustrated how the main goals of project portfolio management are tied to the application of various project portfolio tools and techniques (Table 1.1). It also highlighted the discrepancy

Table 1.1 Main Goals of Project Portfolio Management and the Applied Tools and Techniques

Main Goals of Portfolio Management	*Tools and Techniques Reported in Literature and Company Practices*	*Tools and Techniques Only Reported in Literature*	*Tools and Techniques Only Reported in Company Practices*
Maximize the value of the portfolio	Financial models Multi-criteria models	Financial models	Multi-criteria models
Ensuring balance among portfolio offerings	Strategic buckets	Portfolio matrix	Cumulative flow diagram, Kanban, and suchlike
Achieve strategic alignment of the portfolio	Strategic buckets	Strategic alignment	Key performance indicators
Pick the right number of offerings	Capacity analysis	Resource capacity	Work in progress

between literature and practices on the application of tools and techniques within project portfolio management.

1.4 The New Challenges for Project Portfolio Management

With the modern project portfolio management theory came management by programmes and projects; the project portfolios were filled with programmes and projects which were the means to deliver on the strategy. Now, most organizations find themselves operating in what some label a multi-project and programme environment where multiple projects and programmes are carried out simultaneously. This gives rise to a range of management challenges in a multi-project and programme environment which are illustrated in Table 1.2.

1.5 The Main Challenges of Project Portfolio Management

Some organizations do not have project portfolio management. These companies were researched by Carvalho (2010) who found the following concerns:

Table 1.2   Management Challenges in a Multi-Project Environment Adapted by Fenech (2014)

Demand exceeds capacity	• "[T]here are usually more projects available for selection than can be undertaken within the physical and financial constraints of a firm" (Archer and Ghasemzadeh, 1999) • When organizational capacity is exceeded in these circumstances, "each active project blocks the progress of other projects … [it] is like having the organization's arteries clogged" (Kendall and Rollins, 2003)
Competition between projects	• "Survival of the fittest is a concept that belongs to this mindset and competition and battles were exactly what I found in my empirical studies. Battles to get the highest priority among the projects, battles to get specific employees on projects, struggles to get attention from top management and so on. The concept of battle gives us a better understanding of the mechanisms in a multi-project environment" (Eskerod, 1996)
Complex interdependency	• Outputs and objectives which together contribute to the overall development objectives of the parent organization • Shared resources include people, capital investment pool, information, materials, equipment, and technology • Direct dependencies between projects
Autonomy and control	• Project management implies independence, decentralization, and delegation of authority • The widespread use of projects has brought with it the need to marshal project-based activity in some coherent and beneficial way (Pellegrinelli, 1997)
Innovation and predictability	• Innovation requires risks to be undertaken and investment in exploratory activity to generate new solutions • Project management can be classified as one example of what Leonard-Barton described as "core rigidities"
Accessing project knowledge	• While projects are especially suited to learning knowledge and experiences gathered are not systematically integrated into the organizational knowledge base • Self-contained, idiosyncratic, and finite nature of project tasks • Project knowledge is multi-disciplinary but in the broader organization people are segregated by function
Disruption of traditional structures	• Traditional organizations cannot handle the transactional overload of intensified communications • A rigid division of labour is contradicted by the empowerment of self-organizing units and facilitation of collaboration within multi-disciplinary teams

(Continued)

Table 1.2 (Continued)   Management Challenges in a Multi-Project Environment Adapted by Fenech (2014)

Project knowledge management issues	• However, the evidence suggests that projects cannot readily share knowledge • Schindler and Eppler (2003) – knowledge and experiences gathered in different projects are not being systematically integrated into the organizational knowledge base • Challenges stem from the relatively self-contained, idiosyncratic, and finite nature of project tasks
PPM Tools Implementation issues	• Limited Information • Product maturity • Product complexity • Change management effort • Cloud computing

■ Clarity about the availability of resources for management and implementation of projects

■ Evaluation, selection, and prioritization of projects by category

■ Comparison and competition for resources for the same project category

■ Information from the ongoing projects is considered when assessing, selecting, prioritizing projects, and allocating resources

■ Projects that are running are reassessed periodically and may be paralyzed so that resources can be directed to other projects when necessary

Many of the problems highlighted above might be expected with proper project portfolio management. Another group of organizations are those organizations which have project portfolio management but do not include all projects or programmes in the portfolio. Based on a research project comprised of 128 in-depth interviews in 30 companies, Blichfeldt and Eskerod (2007) propose that a key reason why companies did not do well in relation to project portfolio management is that not all projects were included in the project portfolio. The research finds that project portfolio management often only covers a subset of ongoing projects, while projects that are not subject to project portfolio management also tie up resources that initially were dedicated to project portfolio management projects. This results in major resource management challenges for these organizations as projects may cannibalize the resources, and all projects may suffer as the amounts of resources are just not enough to cover all the projects. This highlights the dilemma of wanting to include all projects and programmes in project portfolio management and aiming at keeping the resource and cognitive burden of doing project portfolio management at a reasonable level.

Then there are organizations that do have project portfolio management and try to include all the project and programmes; they still tend to face many of the problems illustrated in Table 1.3 by various researchers.

1.6 The Global Standards Approach to Project Portfolio Management

The global body of knowledge within project portfolio management consists mainly of academic research, company practices, and international best-practice global standards from organizations such as the Project Management Institute (PMI), Axelos (MoP), and the International Project Management Association (IPMA). International global standards are commercial products often containing what is generally recognized by some as good/best practice. The Project Management Institute updated the *Standard for Portfolio Management* to the fourth edition in 2017 and received the ANSI (American National Standard Institute) standard, while the *Management of Portfolios* (2011) from Axelos is long overdue. Both works are referred to in this section. The International Project Management Association (IPMA) does not have a global standard for project portfolio management. An international standard is a bit like a cookbook. It can show you the way from A to B; however, a big part of it is tailoring it to your organization's needs or to your flavour pallet, if we are still using the cooking terminology. Read Chapter 8 for more inspiration on the tailoring efforts. The global standards give organizations an easy-to-use approach to an area of application, e.g., project portfolio management, and support these standards/publications with certifications which support a range of consultants who can give advice and guidance on the application of the global standards. For a start, global standards are useful in many organizations because they provide a common framework which can be tailored to the organization, so you do not have to start from scratch; but, more importantly, the global standard can provide the organization with a common terminology.

The global best-practice standards from the Project Management Institute and Axelos are illustrated in Table 1.4. The standards contain the life cycles and principles to make the project portfolio run smoothly.

Table 1.3   Problems with Project Portfolio Management

Elonen and Artto (2003)	• Inadequate project-level activities (e.g., through improper implementation of pre-project stages and infrequent progress monitoring) • Lack of resources, competencies, and methods (e.g., through inadequate methods for portfolio evaluation, lack of resources, or extensive composition of steering groups and teams) • Lack of commitment, unclear roles, and responsibilities (e.g., at project level, but also between portfolio managers and other organizations, as well as a lack of management support) • Inadequate portfolio-level activities (e.g., through overlapping tasks within and among portfolios, weak decision-making, and reluctance to kill projects) • Inadequate communication management regarding information about projects and its flow across the organization • Inadequate management of project-oriented business (e.g., through low prioritization of projects, lack of project-business strategies, and frequently changing roles, responsibilities, and organizational structures)
Vähäniitty et al. (2010)	• Excessive multitasking • Firefighting • Overload • Ineffective decision-making • Missing strategic alignment • Slipping schedules • Project failures and poor profitability • Perceived need to improve project management
Krebs (2009)	• Too many projects are under way at the same time • Projects rarely get terminated, even when they should be • Not enough resources are available for the project • Portfolio is unbalanced; there is incorrect mix of risk and reward projects • There is a lack of metrics for the project • There is no vision for the project and there is lack of visionary projects • Focus goes to the small projects
Management of Portfolios (Axelos, 2011)	• Too many projects • Projects are rarely terminated • Not enough resources are available • Lack of metrics • No vision

Table 1.4   The Global Standards for Project Portfolio Management

Management of Portfolios *(MoP, 2011)*	The Standard for Portfolio Management *(PMI, 2017)* *4th Edition*
Totality of an organization's investment or segments thereof in changes required to achieve its strategic objectives	
Portfolio management practices are incorporated within two portfolio cycles and five overall principles	Portfolio management practices are within a portfolio cycle, size performance domains, and eight overall principles
Five portfolio management principles Senior management commitment Governance alignment Strategy alignment Portfolio office Energized change culture	**Eight portfolio management principles** Strive to achieve excellence in strategic execution Enhance transparency, responsibility, accountability, sustainability, and fairness Balance portfolio value versus overall risk Ensure that investments in the portfolio components are aligned with the organization's strategy Obtain and maintain the sponsorship and engagement of senior management and key stakeholders Exercise active and decisive leadership for the optimization of resource utilization Foster a culture that embraces change and risk, and Navigate complexity to enables successfully outcomes
Portfolio management cycles (portfolio definition and portfolio delivery) **Portfolio definition** Understand Categorize Prioritize Balance Plan **Portfolio delivery** Management control Benefits management Financial management Risk management Stakeholder management Organizational governance Resource management	**Portfolio life cycle** Initiation Planning Execution Optimization Monitoring and control **Six performance management domains** Portfolio strategic management Portfolio governance Portfolio capacity and capability management Portfolio stakeholder engagement Portfolio value management Portfolio risk management

The two major global standards deal with project portfolio management in somewhat similar ways. Both global standards are now principle-driven and contain life cycles and categories to be dealt with whether the categories of work are labelled portfolio delivery or performance domains. To put it bluntly, 80% of the content is somewhat similar; besides the wording, however, there are some variations when diving deeper into the standards, but, at this point, both standards are examples of global standards which can be applied when working with project portfolio management.

1.7 The Project Portfolio Management Life-Cycle Model

Varies project portfolio management life-cycle models exist. The following sections are structured around the global *Standard of Portfolio Management* fourth edition (2017) from the Project Management Institute. As illustrated in Table 1.4, the portfolio life cycle consists of five continuous stages:

- Initiation
- Planning
- Execution
- Optimization
- Monitoring and control

In addition to the portfolio life-cycle stages are the six performance management domains:

- Portfolio strategic management
- Portfolio governance
- Portfolio capacity and capability management
- Portfolio stakeholder engagement
- Portfolio value management
- Portfolio risk management

1.7.1 Life Cycle: Initiation

The initiation stage is important as it kicks off the portfolio. The main goals of this stage include:

- Validating business and operational strategy
- Identifying the portfolio components, including scope

- Defining a long-term roadmap with financial goals, performance metrics, governance, and suchlike

During this stage, the initial frameworks, governance, documentation, communication, and suchlike are put into working order. Part of the initiation stage is determining the prioritization criteria or idealization process, often defined as identification and investment/portfolio selection; which are the processes of determining which projects should populate the project portfolio. We define project portfolio selection or short investment selection as "the periodic activity involved in selecting a portfolio, from available project [and programme] proposals and projects [and programmes] currently underway, that meets the organization's stated objectives in a desirable manner without exceeding available resources or violating other constraints" (Archer and Ghasemzadeh, 1999).

Portfolio selection is important as it connects the organization's strategic goals with the selection and identification of projects, programmes, and operations. The aim is to remove factors such as power and emotion from the actual decision-making process and by doing so also eliminate potential subjectivity from the portfolio selection process. Several researchers emphasize that the portfolio selection process should be administered by a team and decisions should be based upon many different criteria that the management team can consider. The most common factors to consider are the following (list not ranked), with strategic fit regarded as the most important criteria:

- Return on investment
- Costs
- Risks
- Required resources
- Available resources
- Time frame
- Strategic fit (most important)
- Level of impact
- Constraints

Müller et al. (2008) demonstrated a positive correlation between portfolio selection that was aligned with the strategy of the organization and the attainment of desirable results of projects, such as reduced cost, enhanced quality, and customer satisfaction.

1.7.2 Essentials Techniques for Project Portfolio Selection

In literature and practice, a wide range of techniques exist for project portfolio selection. Table 1.5 is a collection of the essential techniques for project portfolio selection, grouped by the category of technique each represents and the main goal of portfolio management it provides. The various techniques are typically applied in or with the business case which is commonly used for project portfolio selection.

1.7.3 The Basics of Financial Models

> Albert Einstein should have said, "Not everything that can be counted counts, and not everything that counts can be counted".

1.7.4 Present Value (PV)

Present value is one of the first sets of calculations that the business-case analyst can use to demonstrate the value of the business case. Present value (PV) is a way of factoring the time-value of money, to calculate a project's worth. Present-value calculations are particularly useful in comparing one potential project or opportunity to another.

The formula is: Present value (PV) = FV / (1 + r)n

> **Exercise 1.2 Let us consider the present value if Future Value (FV) is US$8,000 in 4 years and an interest rate of 5%. Would that leave us with US$7.634, US$6.775, US$6.582, or US$6.575 in PV?**
>
> _____
> _____
> _____
>
> Answer: The unit of currency makes no difference in calculating present value; whether dollars or euros, the formula is still = FV / (1 + r) n. Therefore, if the interest rate is 5%, US$8,000 in 4 years will be worth US$8,000 / (1 + 0.05)4, which equals US$6.582. Note: Most basic approaches are easily calculated in Microsoft Excel or similar spreadsheet programmes available.

1.7.5 Net Present Value (NPV)

Net present value (NPV) is another way of factoring the time-value of money to calculate a project's worth. However, net present value also considers the

Table 1.5   Essential Techniques for Project Portfolio Selection Adapted by Fenech (2014)

Category of Technique	Techniques	Main Goal of Portfolio Management
Intuitive	Management judgement "gut feel"	Achieve strategic alignment of the portfolio Ensuring balance among portfolio offerings
Reactive	Reacting to external influences, contingencies, and constraints	Achieve strategic alignment of the portfolio Ensuring balance among portfolio offerings
Proactive	Strategic marketing to identify projects to develop new products, etc.	Achieve strategic alignment of the portfolio Ensuring balance among portfolio offerings
Analytical (maximize the value of the portfolio)		Maximize the value of the portfolio
Financial models	Net present value (NPV) Present value (PV) Return of investment (ROI) Intern rate of return (IRR) Discounted cash flow (DCF) Real option analysis (ROA) Payback period (PBP) Benefit–cost ratio (BCR) Profitability index (PI)	Maximize the value of the portfolio
Multi-criteria decision models	Fuzzy logic Delphi model Market potential Scoring models Bubble diagrams Analytical hierarchy process	Maximize the value of the portfolio
Optimization models	Option pricing theory	Pick the right number of offerings

project's costs in the equation. NPV calculations enable an "apples-to-apples" comparison of investment alternatives, in terms of the value of cash today, versus the interest-adjusted value of cash for various times in the future.

The formula is: Net present value (NPV) = Present value − Costs.

If Present value = US$500,000 and Costs equals = US$350,000 then NPV = US$500,000 − US$350,000 = US$150,000.

The NPV decision rules are:

◼ Business case with positive NPV should be accepted.
◼ Business case with negative NPV should be rejected.
◼ In case of mutually exclusive projects, the one with the higher NPV should be selected.

The basic approach to NPV would include a total cost of US$900,000, a total payoff per year that is used to measure net cash flow and NPV, as illustrated in Table 1.6.

Table 1.7 illustrates the slightly more advanced NPV calculation of a server consolidation project with a discount factor of 10%.

In most business cases, the expected net present value is a more reliable estimate than the traditional net present value, because it considers the uncertainty inherent in projecting future scenarios.

Expected net present value (ENPV) calculates the sum of all the possible net present values multiplied by their probabilities. This means that the expected net present value is the sum of the product of net present values under different scenarios and their relevant probabilities.

The following formula is used to calculate expected NPV: Expected NPV = (p × Scenario NPV)
Best-case scenario has a NPV of US$80,000 and a probability of 0.3.
Base-case scenario has a NPV of US$50,000 and a probability of 0.2.
Worst case scenario has a NPV of US$30,000 and a probability of 0.1.
Expected NPV = US$80,000 × 0.3 + US$50,000 x 0.2 + US$30,000 × 0.1 = 37,000.

1.7.6 Future Value (FV)

Future value (FV) is the value of an asset at a specific date.

The formula is: Future value (FV) = PV × (1 x i(n))

Table 1.6   Financial Results per Year – NPV

Year 0	Year 1	Year 2	Year 3
Total cost US$900,000	US$210,000	US$210,000	US$210,000
Total payoff pr. year	US$1,408,050	US$1,408,050	US$1,408,050
Net cash flow	US$1,198,050	US$1,198,050	US$1,198,050
NPV	-US$118,977	US$781,135	US$1,599,420

Table 1.7   Net Present Value – What It Looks Like

Year	Discount Factor (10%)	Server Consolidation		Virtualization	
		Cash flow	PV of cash flow	Cash flow	PV of Cash flow
0	1	–US$1 million	–US$1 million	–US$1 million	–US$1 million
1	0.909	–US$500,000	–US$454,500	–US$1 million	–US$909,000
2	0.826	–US$500,000	–US$413,000	–US$750,000	–US$619,000
3	0.751	–US$500,000	–US$375,500	–US$500,000	–US$375,500
4	0.683	–US$500,000	–US$341,500	-	-
5	0.621	–US$500,000	–US$310,500	-	-
Total		–US$1.5 million	–US$895,000	–US$1.25 million	–US$904,000

If Present value (PV) = US$177,700 and the effective annual interest rate (I = 3%) over a period of 4 years, then time (n= number of periods) = 4 years. This would result in a future value of US$200,000 (183, 188, 194, 200).

1.7.7 Return on Investment (ROI)

Return on investment or ROI is often used to demonstrate the per centage return that an organization makes by investing. The higher the ROI, the better it is for the company.

The return on investment (ROI) formula is: Benefits – Costs = Benefits/ Costs.

If benefits are US$230,000 and costs are US$200,000, then US$230,000 – US$200,000 = US$30,00/US$200,000 = 15% return on investment. This means that the benefits are higher than the costs, so it is not a bad business case. Still, management may have other business cases with higher ROIs, which may be more profitable to initiate.

Table 1.8   Financial Results per Year – ROI

Year 0	Year 1	Year 2	Year 3
Total cost US$900,000	US$210,000	US$210,000	US$210,000
Total payoff pr. year	US$1,408,050	US$1,408,050	US$1,408,050
Net cash flow	US$1,198,050	US$1,198,050	US$1,198,050
ROI	94%	114%	120%

Table 1.8 measures the return on investment based upon a cost of US$900,000, and a total payoff yearly, of US$1,408,050, which gives the net cash flow and return on investment.

An alternative approach (Milanov and Njegus, 2012) to the return on investment is the measurement of business value divided by effort. The concept is similar but may be used differently as well. In this case, ROI = Business value / Effort.

1.7.8 Internal Rate of Return (IRR)

Internal rate of return (IRR) is a way to express the profit earned, and the number of months it has taken to recoup the initial investment. Internal rate of return (IRR) is a way of expressing profit as an interest rate earned. This helps organizations weigh the benefits of alternative investments. When dealing with IRR, a larger number is more desirable. Let us consider US$70,000 as the initial cost of a business; US$12,000 is the net income for the first year, US$15,000 for the second year, US$18,000 for the third year, US$21,000 for the fourth year, and US$26,000 for the fifth year. The net income increases slightly year after year in this project. The investment's internal rate of return after four years is still negative at Internal Rate of return (IRR) –2%. However, at the end of project, the internal rate of return after five years is positive 9%, which makes this a good project.

Internal rate of return decision rules are:

- Business case with an IRR that is better than that of the alternative should be accepted.
- Business case with an IRR that is less than that of the alternative should be rejected.
- If there is a single business case, the concluding decision will be the same as in the case of IRR or NPV.

Table 1.9   Financial Results per Year – NPV

Year 0	Year 1	Year 2	Year 3
Total cost US$900,000	US$210,000	US$210,000	US$210,000
Total payoff pr. year	US$1,408,050	US$1,408,050	US$1,408,050
Net cash flow	US$1,198,050	US$1,198,050	US$1,198,050
IRR	–6 %	72%	96%

Table 1.10   Cash Flow for Project 1 over Five Years

Project 1	Year 0	Year 1	Year 2	Year 3	Year 4	Year 5
Initial non-recurrent cost	15.00					
Benefits		3.00	3.00	3.00	3.00	3.00
Discounted values	–15.00	2.86	2.72	2.59	2.47	2.35
Net present Value	–2.01					

Table 1.11   Cash Flow for Project 2 over Five Years

Project 2	Year 0	Year 1	Year 2	Year 3	Year 4	Year 5
Initial non-recurrent cost	10.00					
Benefits		2.50	2.50	2.50	2.50	2.50
Discounted values	–10.00	2.38	2.27	2.16	2.06	1.96
Net present Value	0.82					

Table 1.9 measures the internal rate of return based upon a cost of US$900,000 and a total payoff yearly of US$1,408,050, which gives the net cash flow and internal rate of return.

Tables 1.10 and 1.11 summarize the cash flows for the projects over their five-year life. A discount rate of 5% has been used in this example. It can be seen from the sum of all the discounted values that: Project 1 in Table 1.10 has an NPV of –US$2.01M; while Project 2 in Table 1.11 has an NPV of +US$0.82M. Project 2 is the preferred option based on a positive and higher NPV.

The project illustrated previously had the same discount rates. However, in the example in Table 1.12, three different discount rates are applied.

Internal rate of return has some drawbacks, which the modified internal rate of return (MIRR) tries to reduce. One of these flaws is that the IRR

Table 1.12 The Internal Rate of Return with Three Different Discount Rates

Year	Cash flow	Discount Rate 10%		Discount Rate 15%		Discount Rate 20%	
		Factor	Amount	Factor	Amount	Factor	Amount
0	−US$1 million	1.000	−US$1 million	1.000	−US$1 million	1.000	−US$1 million
1	−US$300,000	0.909	US$273,000	0.870	US$261,000	0.833	US$250,000
2	−US$300,000	0.826	US$248,000	0.756	US$227,000	0.694	US$208,000
3	−US$300,000	0.751	US$225,000	0.658	US$197,000	0.579	US$174,000
4	−US$300,000	0.683	US$205,000	0.572	US$172,000	0.482	US$145,000
5	−US$300,000	0.621	US$186,000	0.497	US$149,000	0.402	US$121,000
Total	−US$500,000	NPV = −US$137,000		NPV = −US$6,000		NPV = −US$102,000	

assumes that interim positive cash flows are reinvested at the same rate of return as that of the project from which they were generated. MIRR is the rate that discounts the future cash flows to an NPV that equals the initial investment, assuming returns are reinvested at the discount rate. The discount rate reflects the company's current cost of capital.

While the internal rate of return (IRR) assumes that the cash flows from a project are reinvested at the IRR, the modified IRR assumes that positive cash flows are reinvested at the firm's cost of capital, and the initial outlays are financed at the firm's financing cost. Therefore, MIRR is a more accurate reflection of the cost and profitability of a project.

If the cash flow is, −1000, −4000, 5000, and 2000, from year 0 to year 3, this would result in a negative present value of 4636, 36 and a future value of 7,600. Thus, it would result in an IRR of 25.48% and a 17.91% MIRR, which is far more realistic.

Another variation of the internal rate of return is the average rate of return (ARR). The average rate of return expresses the profits arising from a project, as a percentage of the initial capital cost. However, the definition of profits and capital costs vary. For instance, the profits may be taken to include depreciation in some scenarios. One of the most common approaches is as follows:

$$ARR = (\text{Average annual revenue/Initial capital costs}) \times 100$$

For example: a new system will cost £240,000; and is expected to generate total savings of US$45,000 over the five-year life of the project. ARR = (US$45,000 / 5) / 240,000 × 100 = 3.75%.

1.7.9 Payback Period (PP)

Payback period determines the point in time at which cumulative net cash flows exceed zero. This method involves dividing the annual returns from a proposal by the initial investment amount; and identifies the number of years it will take for an investment to "pay for itself". Under the payback period method, projects with a shorter payback period are preferred. This method is easy to use and avoids the need for complex analysis. However, by itself, the payback period is an unsatisfactory decision rule, because it takes no direct account of the timing of benefits, assumes future cash flows are fixed, and takes no account of any costs or benefits occurring after the payback date. The payback period, however, may have a supporting role in helping to illustrate particularly high returns or proposals with particularly high risks.

The formula is: Cost of project / Annual cash inflows = Payback period.

Payback period is usually expressed in years. Start by calculating Net Cash Flow for each year: Net Cash Flow Year 1 = Cash Inflow Year 1 − Cash Outflow Year 1. Then calculate the Cumulative Cash Flow = (Net Cash Flow Year 1 + Net Cash Flow Year 2 + Net Cash Flow Year 3 … etc.). Accumulate by year until Cumulative Cash Flow is a positive number: that year is the payback year. The method is illustrated in Table 1.13.

In some circumstances, it might be relevant to know how certain the business-case analyst is on the payback period, in which case, the business-case analyst adds a sensitivity analysis to it, as demonstrated in Table 1.14.

Table 1.13   Payback Period – What It Looks Like

	Server Consolidation	*Virtualization*
	Investment US$1 million	*Investment US$1 million*
Year	*Savings*	
1	US$333,333	US$250,000
2	US$333,333	US$250,000
3	US$333,333	US$250,000
4	–	US$250,000
5	–	US$250,000
Total	US$1 million	US$1.25 million
Payback period	3 years	4 years

Table 1.14   Payback Period and Sensitivity Analysis

	Server Consolidation	*Virtualization*
Payback period	3 years	4 years
Sensitivity analysis	3–4 months	5–7 months

The payback period displayed below may include a degree of uncertainty of three to seven months.

1.7.10 Discounted Cash Flow (DCF)

Discounted cash flow (DCF) converts future cash flow into present value cash flow. Discounted cash flow analysis is simple, widely used, and accepted, which works well to determine the net present value (NPV) for income or costs to be incurred over future years. It answers the question, "Will we be better off investing in this proposal, or investing in an alternative opportunity?"

The formula is: Cash flow/1+ Discount rate + Cash flow/1+ Discount rate …

The present value of US$1,000 in 10 years, with a discount rate of 6.3%, is US$1,000/ $(1 + 0.065)^{10}$ = US$532.73

The challenge with the discounted cash flow is that non-financial measurements are ignored and to some degree are too simple and inflexible.

1.7.11 Benefit–Cost Ratio (BCR)

The benefit–cost ratio is the ratio of the present value (PV) of benefits to the present value of costs. A proposal is usually worthwhile when the present value of benefits is greater than the present value of costs. Thus, this method acts like an alternative decision criterion. The benefit–cost ratio is given by the present value of benefits (cash inflows) over the analysis period divided by the Net Present Cost (NPC).

The formula is = Discounted value of incremental benefits – Discounted value of incremental costs.

As an example, let us assume, a project that costs US$6 million and accrues US$24 million in benefits has a BCR of 4.00 (US$24 million divided by US$6 million). A benefit–cost ratio of 4 means management can expect US$4.00 in benefits for every US$1 in costs. A BCR greater than 1 means the benefits outweigh the costs and the investment should be considered. If the ratio is less than 1, the costs outweigh the benefits. If the BCR is equal to 1, the benefits equal the costs.

1.7.12 Profitability Index (PI)

Profitability index (PI), also known as profit investment ratio (PIR) and value investment ratio (VIR), is the ratio of payoff to investment of a proposed project. It is a useful tool for ranking projects because it allows you to quantify the amount of value created per unit of investment.

(Wikipedia, 2014)

The formula is = Present value of future cash flows/Initial investment.

The investment is US$40,000 over a period of 5 years with a cash flow of US$18,000, US$12,000, US$10,000, US$9,000, and US$6,000. Each year the cash flow i.e., US$18,000 is used to calculate Present Value (PV) equals US$16,362 in the first year. The total present values equal US$43,679 / US$40,000 = Profitability index of 1.091.

Profitability Index decision rules are:

■ Business case with a PI that is greater than one should be accepted.
■ Business case with a PI that is less than one should be rejected.

1.7.13 Pitfalls to Look Out for in the Project Portfolio Selection Process

Portfolio selection is regarded by many researchers and practitioners as perhaps one of the most difficult processes to carry out successfully, and the common pitfalls are as follows:

■ Systematic project evaluation is often lacking.
■ Some criteria might be more important to company success than others but not included.
■ Insufficient and ineffective selection methods too many projects can pass through.
■ Reluctance to terminate projects.
■ Selection of short-term projects is overrated.
■ Absence of formalized selection methods leads to decisions that deviate from objectivity.
■ Biased decision-making.

- No strategic link between the organization and new projects.
- Scarce resources are not considered.
- Then too many projects are prioritized which leads to a resource problem.
- Low-value and low-quality projects are not rejected.
- Rarely a dynamic process.
- Lack of quality information when making decisions.
- Information shortage.
- Vital information is lacking.

1.7.14 Life Cycle: Planning

The main goal of planning is creating a portfolio management plan and coming to an agreement on all the planning activities such as performance metrics, budgeting, scope, interdependencies, prioritization, requirements, and suchlike.

1.7.15 Initial Assessment or Triage

Initial assessment or triage is the process of identifying mandatory criteria and the most likely projects or programmes for inclusion in the strategic investment portfolio so that only the best projects and programmes receive further consideration as part of the prioritization process. The initial assessment is performed, so that the organization should only undertake prioritization analysis for the best or "most likely" projects/programmes and avoid undertaking this work for mandatory investments, which must be done regardless of their strategic value. The application of initial assessment or triage is often applied through scoring rules to determine which projects or programmes to analyze. The mandatory project or programme is scored as, e.g., "Must do" project/programmes, while others could be labelled, e.g., "Discretionary" and considered as part of the prioritization process. Alternative to the scoring rules is the various essential techniques illustrated in Table 1.15.

1.7.16 Essentials Techniques for the Initial Assessment or Triage

In literature and practice, a wide range of techniques exist for an initial assessment. Table 1.15 is a collection of the essential techniques for the

Table 1.15   Essential Techniques for the Initial Assessment or Triage

Category of Technique	Techniques
Portfolio matrices	See Chapter 3 for detail
Quadrant approaches	Value to the business versus risk – see Figures 1.3 and 1.4
Banding approaches	Bubble diagram, i.e., value, ease of implementation, and size of project
Strategic alignment measures (see project portfolio selection)	Return on investment Costs Risks Required resources Available resources Time frame Strategic fit (most important) Level of impact Constraints

initial assessment or triage, grouped by the category of technique each represents.

Figures 1.3 and 1.4 both illustrate the common use of quadrant approaches with value/reward and risk.

1.7.17 Project Portfolio Prioritization

Prioritization is "the process of individual evaluation, comparative analysis, and ranking projects and programmes relative to each other and it is central to maximizing the value of the portfolio as it favours projects and

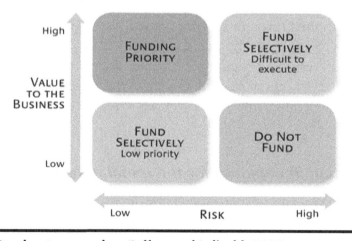

Figure 1.3   Quadrant approaches (Jeffery and Leliveld, 2004).

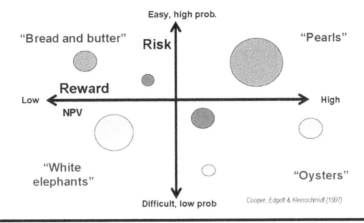

Figure 1.4 Quadrant approaches (Cooper et al., 1997).

programmes with the highest contribution". Prioritization is a standard practice which repeatedly has been found to constitute a key success factor for project portfolio management; successful businesses have implemented project prioritization processes to a high degree. In the literature, project portfolio management is a commonly cited activity. Despite the application and commonly researched topic, prioritization has traditionally been found to be a weak link in new product development and is considered the main challenge for project portfolio management.

Prioritization ranks the projects and programmes which may force comparison between projects or programmes. This works well with projects and programmes of similar nature; however, to avoid prioritizing between projects or programmes of differing natures, strategic buckets can be used to partition incomparable projects or programmes. Projects or programmes can thus be prioritized amongst each other, within the various strategic buckets. This is something that is lacking in many organizations. It is important that the prioritization is completed in an early phase of the project life cycle, but the downside is the lack of complete information.

1.7.18 Essential Techniques for Project Portfolio Prioritization

In literature and company practice, a wide range of techniques exists for prioritization. Table 1.16 is a collection of the essential techniques for project portfolio prioritization, grouped by the category of technique each represents. Chapter 3 contains the essential techniques applied in the agile portfolio, where many of them can be applied in the project portfolio approach as well.

Table 1.16 Essential Techniques for Prioritization Adapted by Fenech (2014)

Category of Technique	Techniques
Financial return approaches (see financial models)	Net present value (NPV) Present value Return of investment (ROI) Intern rate of return (IRR) Discounted cash flow (DCF) Real option analysis (ROA) Payback period (PBP) Benefit–cost ratio (BCR) Profitability index (PI)
Multi-attribute models	Pairwise (A vs. B) Simple scoring/ranking (1, 2, 3, 4, and 5)
Hybrid approaches	Combinations of the techniques
Optimization models	Weighted Shortest Job First (WSJF) – details in Chapter 3

1.7.19 Project Portfolio Sequencing

Project Portfolio sequencing is "the process of applying a sequencing logic (or algorithm) to establish the order in which mandatory requirements and prioritized investment vehicles (projects, programmes, and other work) shall be undertaken in a desirable manner without exceeding available resources or violating other constraints". For those versatile in project and programme management the process is somewhat like working with dependencies between activities. A sequencing logic must therefore include one or more of the following as illustrated in Table 1.17.

1.7.20 Project Portfolio Optimization/Risk-Balancing

Optimizing or risk-balancing "the project portfolio is the process of base-lining the risk and benefits profile of a sequenced strategic investment portfolio, applying what-if analysis to generate alternative portfolio scenarios, comparing the risk and benefits profiles of the alternative scenarios, and choosing the most optimal strategic investment portfolio based on a balance of risk versus reward over the life of the project portfolio". Optimizing or risk-balancing of the portfolio also refers to the formation of a project mix that impedes uniform portfolio content, which means evaluating projects not only on their absolute contribution but also in relation to other projects in the portfolio. Some projects may have a short-term goal other

Table 1.17 Sequencing Logic

Mandatory	Mandatory projects need to be completed for various reasons, often the "must" projects. These are often compliance, legal, and such projects. In some cases, these projects need to be completed first. This is also called "hard logic". We need to complete these projects before we can do others.
Discretionary	Discretionary projects are the preferred logic, soft logic, or best practices. It is recommended that we should do these projects after completing these projects. However, these projects and sequence are not mandatory, often "should be" projects. Here you can make changes from best practice.
Strategic	Strategic projects are those that have a high strategic fit. These projects could also be labelled Mandatory or Discretionary projects as well.
Resource	Sequencing based upon resources aims at optimizing the available resources between the proposed projects. If we are using the same and limited resources, we may complete the projects in a certain order to ensure we have the resources to complete the projects as planned.
Internal/ external	Internal and external sequencing is based upon internal and external dependencies between the projects. Some projects may be a combination of both. A project with an external dependency may not be completed before a vendor has completed their project or an internal project cannot be started before another internal business unit has completed their project.
Cost of delays	See Chapter 3 for more details

than a long-term goal. Whether the project has a short- or long-term goal could be one dimension; others could include risk, benefits, resources, and suchlike.

Achieving project portfolio optimization is one of the main goals in project portfolio management and high-performing organizations have significantly better balance while their management also actively pursues it. A balanced project portfolio allows organizations to fulfill their strategic goals while minimizing risk exposure. In the literature, it has been demonstrated that there exists a positive correlation between risk management and project portfolio success. But balancing the project portfolio is still seen by many researchers and practitioners as a challenge going forward. There are several dimensions to consider balancing a project portfolio; however, a widely accepted set of dimensions is lacking. Commonly mentioned is a balance of the following:

- High and low risk and return
- Long and short term
- Incremental and radical technological innovation
- Resource demand
- Target market
- Cash flow timing

Several of the dimensions are not mutually exclusive as, for example, radical innovation implies both a higher risk and a longer time frame, meaning that the mix of dimensions needs to be contingent on context.

1.7.21 Life Cycle: Executing, Monitoring, and Controlling

Executing, monitoring, and controlling is the ongoing process of following up on the initiatives, making sure they are performing/lead delivery, obtaining/monitoring the benefits, communications/reporting, reprioritization, and keeping an eye on the risks. Executing, monitoring, and controlling is, in the following, tied up with the performance domains of:

- Portfolio strategic management
- Portfolio governance
- Portfolio capacity and capability management
- Portfolio stakeholder engagement
- Portfolio value management
- Portfolio risk management

1.7.22 Portfolio Strategic Management

Portfolio strategic management focuses on the strategic portfolio plan and aligns the portfolio with the strategic direction. Portfolio strategic management also ensures an ongoing balance in the projects, e.g., effort vs. risk. It creates a culture of fostering the high performance of ensuring deliverables in an environment of complexity. Portfolio strategic management delivers excellence in the execution and alignment of the initiatives with strategy. In addition, portfolio strategy management ensures the ongoing development of talent management.

1.7.23 Portfolio Governance

Portfolio governance ensures roles, responsibilities, and alignment. Portfolio governance also includes the evaluation of whether a project complies with regulation, specification, or the imposed condition. The process of identifying and acting on unauthorized investment vehicles in execution, project not accorded agreed priority, projects executed out of agreed order or resource usage contradicts agreed allocations. Some of the common tools and techniques in this process are review, inspections, and suchlike.

1.7.24 Portfolio Capacity and Capability Management

Portfolio capacity and capability management is the process of assessing how well the actual performance to date, and the reforecast plan, for the project portfolio, measure up against baseline, and taking action to correct poor performance where appropriate. The common tools and techniques are variance analysis, earned value management, baseline measurements, and similar.

1.7.25 Brief Introduction to Earned Value Management

Project success is measured as the ability to complete the project according to desired specifications, within the specified budget, within the promised time schedule, and while keeping the customer and stakeholders happy. This is also true for agile projects. "If you cannot measure it, you cannot control it. If you cannot control it, you cannot manage it" (Peter Drucker). This is where earned value management becomes relevant and imperative.

Earned value management (EVM) has long been established as one of the most effective project management tools in managing scope, schedule, and cost. Its roots can be traced back to the late 1800s (Wu, 2011). Earned value management is a widely accepted best practice of industry for project management and is used across the US federal government and the commercial sector.

A common operational definition of EVM is "the use of an integrated management system that coordinates work scope, schedule, and cost goals and objectively measures progress toward these goals". Agile earned value management is a set of calculations and metrics for tracking the progress of Agile projects that evolved from traditional earned value management concepts.

Agile earned value management is defined as "a simplified set of earned value calculations adapted from traditional EVM using Scrum metrics". EVMS measures actual performance of work scope and the associated costs and the schedule versus an agreed-to baseline plan, while using disciplined means of baseline change control for documenting any changes to the agreed-to baseline plan. Earned value is an objective quantified measure of work accomplished and used in a technique to measure the project's progress by integrating scope, cost, and time. Earned value management can provide us with insights on:

- ■ Schedules
- ■ Budgets
- ■ Forecasts

EVM is the best way to determine the real status of a project, as well as indicating how much you have spent and showing how much you have achieved. Further, it tells you how much you still need to do and provides a good indication of final costs and expected completion dates. EVM builds on, and therefore enforces, good project management practice and underpins good corporate governance. Its introduction can drive the cultural and organizational change that is key to supporting these objectives.

The benefits of earned value management are:

- ■ EVM provides an objective measurement of what has been achieved on a project.
- ■ EVM enables accurate forecasting.
- ■ EVM provides project management information in a format that is easy for all stakeholders to understand and act upon.
- ■ EVM is an early warning system that allows the timely identification and analysis of progress and cost issues and corrective actions to be applied.
- ■ EVM shows stakeholders whether they are getting value for money or not.
- ■ EVM enables detailed project comparisons across programmes.
- ■ EVM can be used on a wide range of project sizes and complexity.

The disadvantages of earned value management are:

- ■ While doing Earned Value Analysis, we do not take quality into consideration. It may be possible that our project is scoring high on the earned value performance scale, but the quality of work is below par.

Quality is an important criterion in any project, but unfortunately, it is not considered in EVA.

■ In EVM, we take planned value as the baseline. We use it to do our calculations and make predictions. But there is always an element of uncertainty involved while doing any predictions. Our project may be on schedule when EVA is done, but because of unforeseeable risks, it can get delayed at later stages. So, basing our assumptions on planned value is like playing with fire.

■ The cost of implementing earned value management causes managers to avoid it. Generally, software is required.

■ In big and diverse projects, a lot of time is required to collect all the relevant data pertaining to actual costs (Table 1.18).

Let us illustrate the use and benefits of Earned Value Management with two examples: one traditional and one agile. Application and use in both cases vary to some degree. Ten modules of a software system will cost US$200,000 and the work in its entirety will take ten weeks. One module costs US$20,000 and takes one week. After one week, US$19,000 is spent while the first module is 80% complete. This gives us US$19,000 actual cost/spend versus US$20,000 of planned spend cost. Only 80% of the work has been achieved. The earned value is 80% of US$20,000, or US$16,000.

The cost performance index is calculated by EV/AC = US$16,000/US$19,000 = US$0.84 CPI. CPI is below 1, so this means we have spent too much and are behind on the budget. If CPI is above 1, we are ahead of the budget and have spent less than expected. So far, we have Actual Cost (AC) = US$19,000, Planned Value (PV) = US$20,000, and Earned Value (EV) = US$16,000. We would like to know how we are on the schedule. This is when the schedule performance index (SPI) becomes useful.

Table 1.18 Common Terms Used in EVM

Key Term	Definition
Actual costs (AC)	Actual costs
Planned value (PV)	BAC/number of sprints
Earned value (EV)	BAC x actual percent complete
Budget at complete (BAC)	EAC + AC
Cost performance index (CPI)	EV/AC − 1 is ideal
Schedule performance index (SPI)	EV/PV − 1 is ideal

EV/PV = 0.8, signifying that we are behind schedule. An SPI less than 1 indicates we are behind schedule while an SPI above 1 indicates we are ahead of the schedule. In addition, we would like to know if the final budget at completion is still US$200,000 based on US$20,000 per module × 10 modules or whether it will change. Budgeted cost at completion (BAC) is calculated by US$200,000 / US$0.84 = US$238,000. If costs change, then what about time? We know we are behind schedule, but by how much? – 80% of planned work completed in one week means 10 / 0.8 = 12.5 weeks to complete all 10 modules.

To address this question, we use agile earned value management (agile EVM), which is a simplified set of earned value calculations adapted from traditional EVM using Scrum metrics based upon story points. In this case, our BAC is US$175,000; 4 sprints are planned, and 1 sprint is complete which is 25% of the expected per cent completed. The sprint backlog includes 200 story points and 40 of these story points were completed in the first sprint. This means we have completed 20% as 40/200 = 0.2 or 20%.

The Actual Costs (AC) of the first sprint was US$65,000. Earned Value (EV) is 20% of US$175,000 = US$35,000 while the Planned Value (PV) is 25% of US$175,000 = US$43,750. Cost performance index is measured by EV/AC or US$35,000/US$65,000 = 0.53. The schedule performance index is measured by EV/PV or US$35,000/US$43,750 = 0.8. As 1 is ideal for SPI and CPI, the team is behind planned SPI by 0.8 and has used too much money as CPI is 0.53.

All in all, earned value management is an interesting metric to monitor the work in traditional and agile projects. As Allemanns states, "So in the end Agile and EV are buddies" (Allemann, 2011).

Exercise 1.3 Agile earned value management

How are these teams doing?

1. CPI 1.1 and SPI 0.8 ____
2. CPI 0.1 and SPI 0.7 ____
3. CPI 1.2 and SPI 1.2 ____
4. CPI 0.6 and SPI 1.1 ____
5. CPI 0.8 and SPI 0.8 ____

_____
_____
_____
_____

Answers: (1) fewer costs but behind on time, (2) behind on cost and time, (3) ahead of time and costs, (4) behind on costs but ahead of schedule, and (5) behind on costs and time.

1.7.26 *Portfolio Value (and Benefits) Management*

Benefits management is the active measurement of the achievement of planned benefits from the delivery and operationalization of project outputs and taking corrective action where appropriate. Jenner (2014) defines benefit management as "the identification, quantification, definition, analysis, planning, tracking, realization, and optimization of benefits". This implies benefits are "the measurable improvement from change, which is perceived as positive by one or more stakeholders, and which contributes to organizational objectives". That means benefits are measurable improvements, contribute to organizational/strategic objectives, are advantageous to stakeholders within and outside the organization, extend from identification of desired benefits through to benefit realization and application of lessons learned, are concerned with informing investment decisions and optimization of benefits realization, and seek to optimize rather than maximize benefit realization and are derived from change initiatives.

Benefits can largely be classified into the following types: Dis-benefits, emergent benefits, and intermediate and end benefits. Benefits can be financial (tangible), which are those benefits that can be quantified and valued in financial terms, e.g., cost savings, revenue generation. Alternative benefits may be non-financial (tangible), meaning those benefits that can be quantified but are difficult to value in financial terms, e.g., improved resilience. Some benefits are intangible, which are those benefits that can be identified, but cannot be easily quantified, e.g., end-user satisfaction, better access to information, improved customer service. When identifying benefits as part of the business case, we tend to use a benefits classification like "Agency and citizen benefits" which could include FTEs and costs saved in back office, increased staff time and effort freed up for reinvestment, and increased citizen service levels or a headline saying "Organizational benefits" which could include benefits such as elimination of manual paperwork, decreased data entry and tracking effort, increased intelligence for the agency, and quality of citizen service increased time to respond.

An extension of benefits management is value management which is covered in Chapter 3. Value management "is a systematic method to define what value means for organizations, and to communicate it clearly and provide methods to maximize value across portfolios, programmes, projects, and operations". Value as such is the extent to which benefits (financial and non-financial) exceed the resources required to realize them.

At the portfolio level we seek to maximize, assuring, and realizing value with the best use of resources. The projects in the portfolio are based upon a business case which promises to deliver an output. An outcome is the result of the change derived from using the project's outputs while a benefit is the measurable improvement resulting from an outcome that is perceived as an advantage by one or more stakeholders. The benefit management process focuses on the benefit tracking and expected value from the various projects.

The common tools and techniques for benefits managements are:

■ Driver-based analysis
■ Investment logic mapping
■ SWOT/PESTLE analysis
■ Benefits mapping
■ Benefits dependency network
■ Benefit pathway

1.7.27 *Project Portfolio Stakeholders Engagement*

Portfolio stakeholder engagement is the identification and analysis of the relevant stakeholders which leads to the planning and engagement of the stakeholders. Stakeholders are critical for the success of the portfolio and projects in the portfolio. This performance domain is covered in detail in Chapter 3.

1.7.28 *Project Portfolio Risk (and Issue) Management*

Portfolio risk management "is the process of reviewing risk across the portfolio with a view to identifying threats to overall portfolio performance and benefits" (PMI, 2017). It complements and uses as an input the risk management activity that is undertaken at the project level.

We conduct portfolio risk management to meet the value proposition at an agreed level of risk and by doing so create balance within the project portfolio. The more risk we take and encounter, the less value we obtain, so it is a tradeoff. The risk management process should be transparent, objective, and have integrity to increase the probability of reaching the strategic objectives within the vision.

The key concepts of risk management are included in detail in Chapter 3; however, a few topics need to be highlighted here as well. We identify, analyze, and balance the various risk factors based upon the risk appetite of our key portfolio stakeholders. This includes key concepts such as risk, threats, opportunities, attitude, appetite, thresholds, at short, medium, and long terms.

The project portfolio risk management process is started by risk management planning where all requirements are highlighted and planned for the project portfolio. Risks are then identified and categorized. Individual risks are then assessed and qualified before all risks are considered quantified. This should give a good overview of the risks within the portfolio which leads to the various risk responses and the triggers associated with them.

Issue management deals with certain negative events where the response is a workaround while risk has a likelihood and probability which deal with a risk response strategy. This could involve workarounds and other measures.

Exercise 1.4 Beat the Clock

Take five minutes and collect your thoughts, then recap the whole chapter in a one-minute speech. If you are alone, then talk aloud or take notes.

_____

_____

_____

_____

_____

Answers: No right or wrong answer.

Chapter 2

The Reality of Agile@Scale

Figure 2.1   Overview.

If you develop products that involve moving fluids through pipes, the work attributed to an English mathematician named Peter Barlow probably governs some of the design choices you make. Barlow's formula [Figure 2.2] helps us understand the relationship between the outside diameter of a pipe, its wall thickness, the internal pressure, and the tensile strength of the pipe materials. Using this formula, we can choose the pipe we use for plumbing in a home, calibrate a pump that circulates water in a swimming pool, or evaluate some key specifications for a hydroelectric plant. This formula serves an invaluable role in scaling systems that move fluids and represents an encapsulation of important knowledge that is able to withstand the test of many applications over time. There are variants that account for temperature and other variables as well. One particularly important observation about this example is that the purpose of the formula is not to make larger versions of something that has been proven in the small. Rather, the formula captures a utility function that has been found to hold up under a wide variety of conditions. If such formulas are available for scaling Agile methods,

$$P = \frac{2St}{D}$$

where

P = pressure

S = allowable stress

t = wall thickness

D = outside diameter

Figure 2.2 Barlow's formula.

we would certainly want to understand the range of applications for which they have been validated. In fact, we do see a surprising level of consistency on some noteworthy attributes. Just as Barlow's formula helps to avoid catastrophic failure in the specific domain where it is applied, we seek to illustrate scaling principles that help you to avoid failure in your domain(s).

Exercise 2.1 Where Do You Stand on Agility at Scale?

Get up and articulate what you know about agility at scale and its influences on agile portfolio management.

_____

_____

_____

_____

_____

Answers: No right or wrong answers.

The reality of agile at scale is that the agile portfolio and the initiatives included are not the same and should not be treated the same way as projects and programmes in project portfolio management. The following sections highlight some of the key differences which to some degree are due to the nature of scaling. It is important to understand the need to think of the whole solution, not just keep track of individual projects and that everything interacts in an agile portfolio, which is not likely in project portfolio management. For agile portfolio management and scaling, this can partly be explained as complexity theory and system thinking. Agile and agile portfolio management are based upon Lean thinking, production, and suchlike, where principles, techniques, and other concepts are derived from. Lean plays a major part in what and how organizations perform in the agile portfolio. Project portfolio management does not rely on lean at all! To benefit from agile, agile portfolio management applies continuous planning with adaptability which is underlined by an increased need for collaboration and interaction. In the process, the portfolio fosters increased transparency in the work and is part of the portfolio decision-making process. Agile fosters autonomy and improvisation which can create even better solutions but also increase demands on the running of the agile portfolio. The effective agile portfolio manages innovation as the culture and work environment fosters a healthy and safe environment for experimentation and creativity. These are all factors which in this chapter are labelled as the reality of scaling, as the agile portfolio management approach relies highly on scaling agile development approaches.

2.1 Understanding Complexity Theory and System Thinking

The purpose of this section is to explain the field of complexity theory for agile portfolio management and in that process provide the awareness of models from System Dynamics by Jay Forrester, Soft Systems Methodology by Peter Checkland, and Complex Adaptive Systems (CAS) by Ralph Stacey and Dave Snowden. Others might include Peter Senge and Glenda Eoyang.

System thinking has its foundation in System Dynamics, founded in 1956 by MIT professor Jay Forrester as a way of thinking to address and make sense of complicated and complex uncertain real-world problems. System thinking is a term that is gaining wider use and acceptance, but it is not widely understood. System thinking is a holistic approach with a focus on the "what" and "why" of current reality over time, across organizational functions and levels, and through various levels of structure to achieve the results we desire effectively and efficiently. System thinking combines analytical thinking and synthetic thinking. The basic idea in system thinking is to list as many different elements as you can think of, and then look for similarities between them.

In the late 1960s, Peter Checkland, based in Lancaster (UK), introduced the concept of Soft Systems Methodology (SSM). SSM is a methodology, setting out principles for the use of methods, that enables intervention in ill-structured problem situations, where maintaining relationships is at least as important as goal-seeking and answering questions, about "what" we should do as significantly as determining "how" to do it.

2.1.1 Core Concepts of Complexity Theory and System Thinking

Complex adaptive systems theory (CAS) emerged from the natural sciences and helps explain the behaviour of non-linear dynamic systems comprising many interacting parts that must adapt to a changing environment. Agile portfolio management can also handle a dynamic non-linear system. The theory of complex adaptive systems (CAS) can be used to study such systems. In CAS, self-organization emerges as agents interact through simple rules that can change and adapt. Feedback is the driving force of change. Complexity theory and complex adaptive systems like soft systems methodology (SSM) are key source sciences underlying agile process concepts (e.g., self-organization, empirical processes, decentralized decision-making). Agile practitioners demonstrate an adaptive mindset: the ability to see patterns and develop their team's ability to identify and approach effective solutioning via high-performance questions and setting up a shared vision of success, effective feedback loops, and boundaries for optimizing learning vs. telling them what to do or how to solve problems.

System thinking is the idea of taking a holistic view as we are looking at systems which are constantly changing. The system is also interdependent and interacting with other systems, which makes it all complex. Russel Ackoff states, with regard to system thinking, that "The performance of a system is not the sum of its parts, it's the product of its interactions".

System thinking has become more predominant in literature, whether it is agile in general or a performance domain in the new PMI *Project Management Body of Knowledge* (PMBOK) *Guide*, seventh edition. It helps us gain empathy with business areas and foster critical thinking with a "big picture" focus as it challenges assumptions and mental models. System thinking often reflects on the following:

- Seeking external review and advice
- Use of integrated methods, artefacts, and practices so that there is a common understanding of project work, deliverables, and outcomes

- Use of modelling and scenarios to envision how system dynamics may interact and react
- Proactive management of the integration to help ensure business results

Recognizing, evaluating, and responding to system interactions can lead to the following positive outcomes:

- Early consideration of uncertainty and risk within the project, exploration of alternatives, and consideration of unintended consequences
- Ability to adjust assumptions, and plans, throughout the project life cycle
- Provision of ongoing information and insights that inform planning and delivery
- Clear communication of plans, progress, and projections to relevant stakeholders
- Alignment of project goals and objectives to the customer organization's goals, objectives, and vision
- Ability to adjust to the changing needs of the end user, sponsor, or customer of the project deliverables
- Ability to see synergies and savings between aligned projects or initiatives
- Ability to exploit opportunities not otherwise captured or see threats posed to or by other projects or initiatives
- Clarity regarding the best project performance measurements and their influence on the behaviour of the people involved in the project
- Decisions that benefit the organization as a whole
- More comprehensive and informed identification of risks

Systems thinking helps us understand how to look "beyond the borders" to determine the effects of systems on decision-making and value realization. That is why it is important that the concept of systems thinking is understood and techniques are provided to identify external influences, problem-solving, and suchlike.

Systems thinking is a way of thinking used to address and make sense of complicated and complex uncertain real-world problems. It is a holistic approach with a focus on the "what" and "why" of current reality over time, across organizational functions and levels, and through various levels of structure to achieve the results we desire effectively and efficiently. In systems design and development, much depends on correctly determining the requirements.

Some requirements are tangible, which makes them easier to document in a model or with natural language, but some requirements, or requirement attributes, are far more intangible. However, to understand and document requirements, the product owner and the team need to make sense of the complicated problems with, and purpose of, the requirements. Systemic thinking combines analytical thinking and synthetic thinking, where system analysis is the application of system thinking. The basic idea in systemic thinking is to list as many different elements as you can think of, then look for similarities between them.

The benefits of system thinking are:

- People, purpose, process, performance, and relating systems to their environment
- Understanding complex problem situations
- Maximizing the outcomes achieved
- Helps solving complex and recurring problems
- Avoiding or minimizing the impact of unintended consequences
- Aligning teams, disciplines, specialism, and interest groups
- Managing uncertainty, risk, and opportunity
- Helps balance the needs of the organization's stakeholders
- Impacts how information is shared across the organization

The common system thinking tools and techniques are:

- Value-stream mapping
- Soft systems methodology
- Causal mapping
- Design structure matrix

Other techniques can be used in combination to clarify our thinking in the early stages of requirements engineering.

This chapter discusses the complexity models and their implications on the discipline of management. The various tools and techniques are examples to be applied, while the wrong problem-solving technique can make a problem worse.

2.1.2 The Stacey Matrix

The Stacey Matrix was developed and published by Ralph Douglas Stacey. It is designed to help understand the factors that contribute to complexity

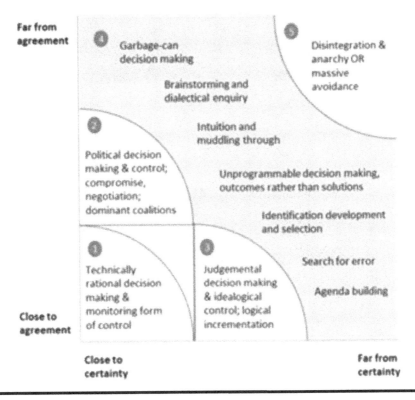

Figure 2.3   Stacey Matrix.

and choose the best management actions to address different degrees of complexity. In agile, we work in a complicated and complex world, which, in the Ralf Stacey Matrix, is in the grey/middle area illustrated in Figure 2.3, the so-called "complex decision-making realm". If certainty and agreement were close, we would choose the waterfall approach and if we were far from certainty and far from agreement, it would be chaos, and another solution would be needed. However, in this case, the agile team is in the complex decision-making realm in which we need to use system thinking. This also highlights the importance of agile initiatives in a portfolio that has far more complex initiatives than projects found in a plan-based portfolio.

2.1.3 Cynefin Framework

The Cynefin framework is a conceptual framework used to aid decision-making. Developed in 1999 by Dave Snowden when he worked for IBM Global Services, it has been described as a "sense-making device". It contains four sections, called "Complex", "Complicated", "Chaotic", and "Obvious". If initiatives are described as "Obvious", then a waterfall approach

Figure 2.4 Cynefin framework.

would be suitable, while initiatives in an agile portfolio are often labelled as "Complex "or "Complicated", which illustrates the nature of the work in the agile portfolio. If initiatives are categorized as "Chaotic" then it is recommended to leave them alone, as it would not work out well (Figure 2.4).

2.2 Adaptability vs. Predictability

The industrial age and the assembly-line mindsets have left a strong inclination to have a predictable process, a predictable output, predictable team performance, etc.; however, in the age of complex adaptive systems and knowledge work, management needs to focus on being adaptable rather than help establish predictability.

Adaptability is the ability of a system to adapt to changing market conditions and customer demands to be better fit for its purpose while predictability is the degree to which a correct prediction of a system's future can be made.

While agile methods can be extremely effective at a project level, they can impose significant complexity and a need for adaptability at the portfolio level.

Agile approaches increase the need for adaptability at the portfolio level. The iterative, dynamic nature of agile methods combined with a focus on change, improvisation, and self-organization inherent in agile initiatives, imposes change at the portfolio level.

Also, some may claim that true agility, which means adopting a posture that allows you to respond rapidly to changing market conditions and customer demands, conflicts with predictability. Martin Fowler stated that "IT organizations need to govern for value over predictability, responsiveness over cost-efficiency".

Because agile methods ask the organization to rightfully accept a certain amount of ambiguity in the delivery process, or at least acknowledge the fallacy of predictive up-front planning, each team in an agile organization must be predictable over time. This means that each team should strive to establish and maintain a stable velocity over time, such that the organization can reliably predict the impact of scope changes to the overall programme and portfolio ecosystem. If teams are not predictable over time, there is little chance of establishing a stable, predictable delivery capability.

The techniques for working with predictability versus adaptability impacts may vary, from reviewing methods, frameworks, case studies, or scenarios. The traditional approach would often focus on the fixed investment and result, while the agile portfolio relies on continuous flow and building the higher-value features first. The following illustrates one framework on continuous flow which could foster adaptability and provide some degree of predictability.

2.2.1 Continuous Flow Framework

Flow is a framework described in a book with the same name, written by Andrew Kallman along with his brother Ted Kallman (2017). Both brothers have experience working as management consultants, and the framework is based on lessons learned during their careers. The framework has gotten wide support within the software community and is believed by many to increase the chances of successful projects.

The term "flow" is described, by the authors, as a hyper-performing state in which all organizations want to be. There is an infinite number of ideas, probably one for each management consultant that exists, on how an organization should act to become better at what it does. In their book, the authors use the following words to define flow: "The state of optimal performance achieved by applying a clear, consistent, persistent and unified vision at all levels of an organization". The concept the authors describe is simple; achieving it is, however, not as simple. Vision, according to the authors, is key for any project, independent from what the project is trying to achieve. Without a clear and well-defined vision, the project will probably end up with anarchy and a lack of order. By cascading the organization's vision down the hierarchy levels, from the board of directors down to the individual teams, flow is claimed to facilitate achieving a hyper-productive state.

To achieve flow, according to the authors, a set of criteria for six parameters is vital. The six parameters are:

- Align vision (Vision)
- Right people (RP)
- Define (D1)
- Distill (D2)
- Deliver (D3)
- Drive (D4)

Below is an explanation of why the parameters are needed to achieve a hyper-performing state.

- Align vision: If the team is not led, pushed, and pulled by vision the team will be driven in multiple directions, all at once, depending on circumstances. The goals must align with the overall company goals.
- Right people: Without the right competences within the team, the possibility of reaching a hyperactive state is slim to none.
- Define: Prioritize what is going to be done and minimize the amount of noise from external parts.
- Distill: Let the group make decisions to reduce incorrect assumptions. Seek consensus in the group. Consensus does not equal unanimity.
- Deliver: Vision without execution does not provide any results. When there is an agreement on what needs to be done, execute it.
- Drive: Continue driving the project toward its goal. There might be a need to reiterate Steps 1 to 3 to achieve sustainable success.

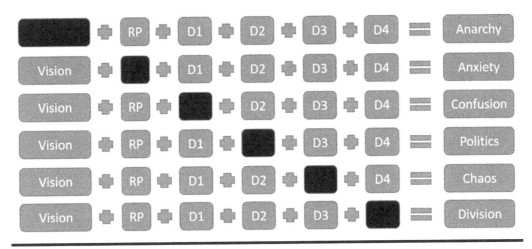

Figure 2.5   Challenges in achieving flow.

Figure 2.5 is used by Kallman and Kallman (2017) in their book to clarify what the different outcomes are when one of the six parameters is not fulfilled. When vision is missing, there is a risk of anarchy within the initiatives. When the initiatives do not have the right resources, there is a high risk of anxiety, etc. According to the authors, flow is not achievable if not all the parameters are met. The topic of shared vision management is not a new thing within business. Wang and Rafiq (2009) express the need for a shared vision to get the most out of a workforce: "Without a shared vision, the reality of a firm would be characterized by highly enthusiastic and committed individuals pulling the organization toward different directions". Christenson and Walker (2004) argue for the need for a clear project vision within the project to motivate the project members: "We argue that the key to developing an effective project vision is to make objectives and purpose clearly understood, to inspire motivation, and to ensure that the project vision is credible and challenging". Kallman and Kallman (2017) go even further regarding the role of a shared vision. They argue that creating a shared vision is top priority for management in an agile software development team:

> Vision is always the key Driver for what a project is trying to
> achieve for its product, service or result (i.e., increase revenues,
> decrease costs and/or get rid of or mitigate risk). If there is no proj-
> ect vision, your job as a leader is to define and distill agreement on
> what the vision really is (or should be), with the appropriate stake-
> holders. Understand and articulate the "why" for your team.

2.3 Lean Thinking and Lean Portfolio Management

The term Lean software development was first coined as the title for a conference organized by the ESPRIT initiative of the European Union, in Stuttgart Germany, in October 1992. Independently, in the following year, Robert "Bob" Charette suggested the concept of Lean software development as part of his work exploring better ways of managing risk in software projects. The term "Lean" was coined to describe Toyota's business during the late 1980s by a research team headed by Jim Womack, PhD, at MIT's International Motor Vehicle Program which was described in their book *The Machine That Changed the World: The Story of Lean Production*, as the English language term to describe the management approach used by Toyota. The idea that Lean might be applicable in software development was established early, only one to two years after the term was first used in association with trends in manufacturing processes and industrial engineering.

Today Lean thinking is behind the evolution of many agile processes and provides a context for discussions about customer value and process efficiency across the business.

2.3.1 Core Concepts of Lean Thinking and Lean Portfolio Management

The major theories and key thinkers of Lean thinking and Lean portfolio management are the Toyota Way, Womach, Larman and Vodde, Reinertsen, Poppendieicks, and suchlike, which are explained in the following sections.

The core idea of Lean is to maximize customer value while minimizing waste. Simply, Lean means creating more value for customers with fewer resources.

2.3.2 Lean Philosophy of Management – The Toyota Way

The Toyota Way is a set of principles and behaviours that underlie the Toyota Motor Corporation's managerial approach and production system. Toyota first summed up its philosophy, values, and manufacturing ideals in 2001, calling it "The Toyota Way 2001". It consists of principles in four sections: Long-Term Philosophy, The Right Process Will Produce the Right Results, Add Value to the Organization by Developing Your People, and Continuously Solving Root Problems Drives Organizational Learning.

2.3.2.1 Long-Term Philosophy

- Base your management decisions on a long-term philosophy, even at the expense of short-term financial goals.

2.3.2.2 The Right Process Will Produce the Right Results

- Create a continuous process flow to bring problems to the surface.
- Use "pull" systems to avoid over-production.
- Level out the workload (heijunka). (Work like the tortoise, not the hare.)
- Build a culture of stopping to fix problems, to get quality right the first time.
- Standardized tasks and processes are the foundation for continuous improvement and employee empowerment.
- Use visual control so no problems are hidden.
- Use only reliable, thoroughly tested technology that serves your people and processes.

2.3.2.3 Add Value to the Organization by Developing Your People

- Grow leaders who thoroughly understand the work, live the philosophy, and teach it to others.
- Develop exceptional people and teams who follow your company's philosophy.
- Respect your extended network of partners and suppliers by challenging them and helping them improve.

2.3.2.4 Continuously Solving Root Problems Drives Organizational Learning

- Go and see for yourself to thoroughly understand the situation (Genchi Genbutsu).
- Make decisions slowly by consensus, thoroughly considering all options; implement decisions rapidly (nemawashi).
- Become a learning organization through relentless reflection (hansei) and continuous improvement (kaizen).

2.3.3 The Five Principles of Lean Thinking by Womach

The five principles of Lean thinking are Value, Value Stream, Flow, Pull, and Perfection. The five principles of Lean thinking are defined in Table 2.1.

Table 2.1 Five Principles of Lean Thinking by Womach

Principle	Definition
Value	Value is defined by the authors as a "capability provided to customer at the right time at an appropriate price, as defined in each case by the customer". Value is the critical starting point for Lean thinking and can only be defined by the ultimate end customer.
Value stream	The value stream is defined in Lean thinking as the set of all the "specific activities required to design, order, and provide a specific product, from concept to launch, order to delivery, and raw materials into the hands of the customer". There are three types of activities in the value stream – one kind adds value, and the other two are "muda" (the Japanese word for waste): Value-added: Those activities that unambiguously create value; Type-one muda: Activities that create no value but seem to be unavoidable with current technologies or production assets; Type-two muda: Activities that create no value and are immediately avoidable.
Flow	The Lean principle of flow is defined as the "progressive achievement of tasks along the value stream so that a product proceeds from design to launch, order to delivery and raw materials into the hands of the customer with no stoppages, scrap or backflows".
Pull	The fourth Lean principle of pull is defined by the authors as a "system of cascading production and delivery instructions from downstream to upstream in which nothing is produced by the upstream supplier until the downstream customer signals a need".
Perfection	The fifth and final lean principle is perfection, defined again by the authors as the "complete".

Lean thinking applies the concepts of the three Lean principles: The Muri, Mura, and Muda, which are illustrated in Table 2.2.

There is a relation between the three principles: Mura creates Muri leading to the inability to reduce Muda. Muda, or waste, can be reduced through solving problems of imbalanced loading and overstraining of people (Smits, 2006).

2.3.4 The 14 Principles of Lean Thinking by Larman

Larman and Vodde (2008) described, in their book *Scaling Lean & Agile Development: Thinking & Organizational Tools for Large-Scale Scrum*, the

Table 2.2 The Three Lean Principles

Muri	Mura	Muda
Overburdening of people or equipment	Unevenness in workload	Waste or non-value adding activities

House of Lean Thinking and the Toyota Way, with 14 principles which are the 14 principles from the Toyota Way, i.e., grow leaders who thoroughly understand the work, live the philosophy, and teach it to others.

2.3.5 The Eight Principles of "Flow" by Reinertsen

The book *The Principles of Product Development Flow* by Donald G. Reinertsen (2009) includes the following principles:

■ Economic
■ Queueing
■ Variability
■ Batch size
■ Constraint
■ Flow control
■ Fast feedback
■ Decentralization

Several of these principles play a major role in agile portfolio management where "batch size" ensures an ongoing stream of small initiatives are completed. "Constraints" ensures the flow with the Theory of Constraints and the managing of bottlenecks, which is supported by "Flow Control" with techniques such as work-in-progress (WIP) limits.

2.3.6 The Seven Principles of Lean Software Development by Poppendiecks

The work by Poppendiecks (2003) focuses on Lean software development including the Lean principles and tools which are highlighted in Table 2.3.

The Theory of Constraints and Lean practices are very compatible. Lean is primarily oriented around principles. The Theory of Constraints emphasizes the strategic level and the ability to deliver resources even when faced with bottlenecks. Lean practices deal on the operational level with the

Table 2.3   Lean Principle – Poppendiecks

Lean Principles	Lean Tools	Comments
Eliminate waste	Tool 1: Seeing waste Tool 2: Value-stream mapping	
Amplify learning	Tool 3: Feedback Tool 4: Iterations Tool 5: Synchronization Tool 6: Set-based development	The nature of software development
Decide as late as possible	Tool 7: Options thinking Tool 8: The last responsible moment Tool 9: Making decisions	Concurrent development
Deliver as fast as possible	Tool10: Pull systems Tool11: Queuing theory Tool12: Costs of delays	
Empower the team	Tool 13: Self-determination Tool 14: Motivation Tool 15: Leadership Tool 16: Expertise	Beyond scientific management
Build integrity in	Tool 17: Perceived integrity Tool 18: Conceptual integrity Tool 19: Refactoring Tool 20: Testing	Integrity
See the whole	Tool 21: Measurements Tool 22: Contracts	System thinking

various processes and activities which may need to be reordered to remove waste.

2.3.7 Lean Tool – Value-Stream Mapping

"Whenever there is a product for a customer, there is a value stream. The challenge lies in seeing it" (Magnier, 2003).

Value-stream mapping is a pencil-and-paper tool method adopted by agile to analyze an entire chain of processes with the goal of eliminating waste. Value-stream mapping is a Lean technique to analyze the flow of material. It results in a deeper understanding of the system by mapping it out. A value stream consists of all actions, including value-added and non–value-added.

Value-stream mapping provides answers to questions such as:

■ What does the current process look like?
■ How does value flow through the process?
■ What steps in the process add value and what steps do not add value?
■ What are the waste sources in the value stream?
■ What areas of the process need the most improvement?

In agile, the team, at any level, also portfolio, uses a value-stream map to identify one or more of the following types of waste:

■ Over-production
■ Over-processing
■ Inventory
■ Motion/transportation
■ Scrap or defects
■ Waiting
■ Improper use of human intellect
■ Partially done work
■ Task switching
■ Extra features

Value-stream mapping provides optimum value to the customer through a complete value-creation process with minimum waste in:

■ Designing (concept to customer)
■ Building (order to delivery)
■ Sustaining (in-use through life cycle to service)

So, value-stream maps, adopted by agile teams, aim at creating a visual map of the process. These maps form one big picture by which we seek to improve the whole process, not just parts of it. Value-stream maps are part of the planning value and offer an excellent baseline for improvements. Some use value-stream maps to create a common language in the organization. In some cases, they may help decrease cherry-picking by forcing us to work on a one-page picture, that is, the big picture.

When working on value-stream maps, we apply five simple principles from Womach:

- Specify value from the standpoint of the end customer.
- Identify the value stream for each product family.
- Make the product flow.
- So, the customer can pull.
- As you manage toward perfection.

When creating and working with value-stream maps (VSM), the process is as follows:

1. Define and pick the product and product family.
2. Create the current-state value-stream mapping (CSVSM).
3. Create the future-state value- stream mapping (FSVSM).
4. Develop an action plan to make FSVSM the CSVSM.

In this section, we will examine this four-step process and see value-stream mapping in action.

1. **Define and pick the product and product family.**
   First, we set the stage and secure involvements. This is done by selecting a sponsor who oversees the project, secures the funding and resources, and takes part in the communication. To run the project, we employ a value-stream manager, a specialist on the process capable of running it. For support, we often form a value-stream team. With organization and resources in place, our main goal is to pick the products and processes, define goals for improvements, and set expectations with the stakeholders.

2. **Create the current-state value-stream mapping (CSVSM).**
   In Step 2, we develop a current-state value-stream map that identifies waste and helps the organization envision an improved future state. To begin this step, the group needs to define and secure scope. The group and stakeholders must then agree upon the use of symbols, as the range and possibilities are numerous. We may brainstorm to create an initial map, thereby also determining if there is any missing information. Then, we need to gather and create information or go with the flow to really understand customer value, requirements, and scheduling. With this information, we should be able to build the current-state value-stream mapping. Also, by now, we may have identified "lightning bolts" for improvements (Kaizen burst).
   Some projects use the following guidelines in this process:

- Produce according to your takt time or cycle time (your available work time/customer demand rate shift).
- Develop continuously whenever possible.
- Use supermarkets to control production where continuous production does not extend upward.
- Try to send the customer schedule to only one production process.
- Distribute the production of different products evenly over time at the pacemaker process.
- Create an initial pull.
- Develop the ability to make every part, every day.

In addition, the group should take a reality check to see if it is getting the map right and include a process of verification. Table 2.4 illustrates the current state with activities such as request, approval, etc. which provide value. Between the activities, wastes are described and measured.

3. **Create the future-state value-stream mapping (FSVSM).**
Creating a value-stream map for the current state is very much an "as-is" picture and a map of the actual and expected state, which can be good or bad. The idea of creating the future value-stream map is to draw the "to-be" map, which also can assist in working with road maps. The

Table 2.4   Current-State Process

Process	Value	Waste
Request	10 minutes	
Email supervisor		60 minutes
Approve	20 minutes	
Email tech lead		60 minutes
Technical assessment	40 minutes	
Assign developer		60 minutes
Code and test	60 minutes	
Verification		60 minutes
Verify	20 minutes	
Operations		60 minutes
Deploy	10 minutes	
SUM	160 minutes	300 minutes
Efficiency 53% (160/300)		

process and techniques for the future-state value-stream map is like the current-state map, just with more creativity and less information gathering. This process may include a critique of the current-state value-stream map and attention to various improvements.

Guidelines are needed for defining the future-state map. Lean thinking provides these guidelines to assist users in drawing this map (Rother and Shook, 1998; Marchwinski and Shook, 2003). These guidelines are summarized below:

- The production rate must be imposed by the product demand.
- Takt time is the concept that reflects such a rate.
- Establish continuous flow where possible (unique product transfer batches).
- Employ pull systems between different work centres when continuous flow is not possible.
- Only one process, called the pacemaker process, should command the production of the different parts. This process will set the pace for the entire value stream.
- Downstream from this point regarding how the items should flow in a first-in, first-out (FIFO) sequence; upstream the production, which will be triggered by pull signals.
- Pacemaker process scheduling will deal with the maximization of production, levelling on mix and volume.
- Improve the overall process efficiency.
- Projects such as work methods and cycle-time improvements, changeover time reductions, and maintenance management could be launched by the VSM team.

Table 2.5 illustrates the future state where waste has been reduced. Table 2.6 illustrates the future state where also the process is changed.

4. **Develop an action plan to make FSVSM the CSVSM.**

   In the final step, we seek to close the gap between the current-state and future-state value- stream maps. This may require some harsh decisions. Often, this step is initiated with a kick-off event and activities that focus on communication as we change management. When we have communicated clearly, we set our work plan in action, make the changes to the processes, and ensure that we measure the benefits. To measure benefits, total cycle time and process cycle efficiency may be useful metrics. Total cycle time is the amount of time it takes to complete the whole process. It can be understood by the equation: total cycle time = value-added, and non– value-added, time. Process cycle efficiency = value-added/total time and can be used to illustrate the improvements.

Table 2.5 Future State with Less Waste

Process	Value	Waste
Request	10 minutes	
Email supervisor		30 minutes
Approve	20 minutes	
Email tech lead		30 minutes
Technical assessment	40 minutes	
Assign developer		30 minutes
Code and Test	60 minutes	
Verification		60 minutes
Verify	20 minutes	
Operations		60 minutes
Deploy	10 minutes	
SUM	160 minutes	210 minutes
Efficiency 76% (160/210)		

Table 2.6 Future State with Changed Process and Reduced Waste

Process	Value	Waste
Request and approve	30 minutes	
Email supervisor/tech		90 minutes
Assessment, code, and test	50 minutes	
Verification		90 minutes
Verify and deploy	70 minutes	
SUM	150 minutes	280 minutes
Efficiency 83% (150/180)		

2.3.8 Shalloway's Lean Concepts

Al Shalloway is one of the key thinkers of Net Objectives, which was recently acquired by the Project Management Institute (PMI), so part of this content may, in 2021, be found in the certifications from disciplined agile. Shalloway's concept builds upon the Lean principles of flow, pull, perfection, and suchlike from Womach. Shalloway highlights the importance of the cost of delays which is described in Chapter 3. In addition, he focuses on the need to change the culture, which is vital in agile, the application of value streams, and Lean product management. In this case the Lean production management highlights the intake process to ensure the right number of initiatives to avoid multitasking, extra work, or people burn-out. Thinking incrementally is also a key topic with MVPs, MBIs, and MVR, which are described in detail in Chapter 3.

2.3.9 Lean Portfolio Management (LPM) Principles from SAFe

Some frameworks (see Chapter 4 for more details) consist of their own sets of principles. However, in this case, scaled agile framework (SAFe) also includes Lean portfolio management principles, which are stated below:

- Shift from tactical to strategic.
- Push decision-making down to the appropriate level.
- Align funding and capacity to outcome.
- Limit work in process and align capacity.
- Plan face-to-face with meaningful artefacts.
- Planning cadence to the appropriate level of planning.
- Focus on fast, frequent delivery of customer value.

Most of the Lean portfolio management principles are self-explanatory; however, they highlight and focus our attention on what is important, that is: strategic focus on the portfolio level; let the people who have the most knowledge of the topic make the decision; fund the portfolio not individual initiatives; apply WIP limits; foster face-to-face communication when possible; ensure proper levels of planning, where all teams are done at the same time; and, all in all, focus on customer value in everything we do.

2.3.10 The Lean Startup

The book *The Lean Startup* was written by Eric Ries in 2011 with emphasis on how constant innovation creates radically successful businesses. The content focused on vision, steer, and accelerate, where several of these concepts are vital for the agile portfolio. The vision section highlights the importance of validated learning and experiment for creating and measuring value, while steer emphasizes the importance of testing and measuring. Finally, accelerate talked about adapting and reducing waste. These are all key elements in Lean and most agile portfolio management settings.

2.4 Continuous Planning

Continuous planning is critical to adapting quickly to changing realities, customer and business stakeholder needs, and changes in the initiatives. It is important to understand how a cadence of effective agile planning cycles works and how they create the opportunity to seamlessly introduce change into the agile process. A cadence is a period of x number of sprints, let us say, a 12-week cadence consisting of 4 Scrum sprints with a 3-week duration. At the team level, a Scrum product owner may prioritize the product backlog every three weeks with a sprint duration of three weeks, however on the portfolio level, in most cases, we need a longer duration, meaning a cadence of several sprints to get work done. Also, with more teams we need to ensure a common product at the level of the cadence. This implies: the shorter the cadence the faster you need to be ready on the portfolio level. If you allow teams within the cadence to have different sprint durations, so one team does four sprints of three weeks' duration while another team has six sprints of two weeks' duration, then there will be most points for collaboration. This is also a way of introducing flexibility if teams, components, or features can do most tasks. When working agile on any level, we apply continuous planning. Continuous planning is supported by collaboration and transparency, so with continuous planning, ongoing collaboration and ways to ensure transparency which would benefit the process are possible.

2.5 From Silos to Collaboration and Increased Interaction

Increased collaboration across different fields of practice is often associated with agile methods. To gain a shared vision and understanding among stakeholders and initiatives there needs to be a willingness for collaboration and increased interaction. This topic has been a recurring pattern for several researchers (Stettina and Hörz, 2015). According to Leffingwell's framework SAFe recurring collaboration occurs across the different levels of team, programme, and portfolio. Collaboration through recurring activities, e.g., dailies, demo, and suchlike are often found at the project level, however, frequent collaboration is even more crucial at the portfolio level when pursuing an agile project portfolio management. Agile project management increases the number of interactions at the portfolio level. This is because agile's increased focus on the customer increases complexity at the portfolio level, as agile projects in a portfolio must reconcile tensions between customer needs and organizational strategy.

If teams deliver results more frequently, then they automatically need to receive feedback more often. The number of portfolio reviews (fast feedback and easy to change direction) can vary. In fast-changing environments with high subjective success criteria, getting feedback from the product's consumers is a critical success factor. Organizations operating in high-velocity markets such as these can have delivery intervals of two weeks for teams, which means that portfolio reviews in annual cycles are insufficient (Stettina and Hörz, 2015). There are different opinions among researchers regarding the influence that resource scarcity has on collaboration and interaction: some are concerned that resource scarcity inhibits collaboration due to selfish behaviour (Hodgkins and Hohmann, 2007), while others claim the opposite, that scarce resources force collaboration instead of preventing it (Sweetman and Conboy, 2018). According to Sebestyén (2017), building knowledge within an organization is an important activity to consider when pursuing an agile portfolio management approach. Knowledge building is a result of collaboration between different teams. Collaboration has a key role in development operations and entails constant organizational adaptiveness to changes in the market. Adaption requires the ability to take in feedback, internal creativity to process and analyze the information, and the ability to make decisions. Having different feedback channels is a success factor as it provides a better picture of the situation.

2.5.1 Autonomy and Improvisation

The autonomy and improvisation inherent in agile approaches have implications for a portfolio of interdependent agile projects, as greater coordination is needed between dynamic projects to ensure the emergent portfolio remains aligned to the intended portfolio. Furthermore, the commitment of agile to "people over processes" increases the interactions both within and between projects and poses challenges for management at the portfolio level.

(Fowler and Highsmith, 2001)

Increased autonomy and room for improvisation may create better solutions as we are working on something we have not done before; however, autonomy and improvisation also opens up the need to increase collaboration to develop a common product which is releasable and creates a greater range of possible outcomes, which makes the value proposal more difficult to judge.

2.6 Managing for Innovation (Culture and Work Environment)

Organizations seek to develop a culture of everyday innovation where management allows learning to happen. It must be safe to learn. At the same time, learning costs organizations time, money, and resources. This ongoing tension has caused many organizations to aspire to innovation, but not enable it. We need to create a culture and work environment with room for innovation and not manage for complacency and fear of trying. To create an environment conducive to innovation the prerequisite according to the DORA State of DevOps research programme (2020), spearheaded by Google, is Lean product management. This implies working in small batches, visibility of work in the value stream, ongoing customer feedback, and team experimentation. The DORA State of DevOps research programme (2020) identified four capabilities needed to create a culture for innovation, which are described in Table 2.7. The key capabilities are climate for learning; Westrum organizational culture; culture of psychological safety; job satisfaction and identity.

The Westrum organizational culture model is illustrated in Figure 2.6. Three types of organization are described: pathological, bureaucratic, and generative. Here it is important that the organization is generative for the most part; otherwise the culture will fail us, and innovation would suffer greatly.

Obtaining the five capabilities identified by the DORA State of DevOps research programme (2020), the organization should expect possible high performance in software delivery and organizational performance which includes managing innovation.

2.7 Transparency

Transparency of resources is considered of high importance in the pursuit of an agile portfolio management as it increases trust among

Table 2.7   Capabilities

Capabilities	Descriptions
Climate for learning	An organization with a climate for learning views learning as an investment that is needed for growth, not as a necessary evil, undertaken only when required.
Westrum organizational culture	This model of organizational culture was developed by sociologist Dr Ron Westrum. It classifies organizations as pathological, bureaucratic, or generative based on levels of cooperation, how problems are surfaced, the extent to which the organization is siloed, and how people react to failure and novelty.
Culture of psychological safety	In teams with a culture of psychological safety, team members trust each other, can resolve conflict, take calculated and moderate risks, speak up, and are more creative.
Job satisfaction	People feel supported by their employers, have the tools and resources to do their work, and feel their judgement is valued.
Identity	Employees identify with the organization they work for. They say that the organization is a good place to work. They feel that the organization cares about them. And they are willing to put in extra effort to help the organization succeed.

Pathological	Bureaucratic	Generative
Power oriented	Rule oriented	Performance oriented
Low cooperation	Modest cooperation	High cooperation
Messengers "shot"	Messengers neglected	Messengers trained
Responsibilities shirked	Narrow responsibilities	Risks are shared
Bridging discouraged	Bridging tolerated	Bridging encouraged
Failure leads to scapegoating	Failure leads to justice	Failure leads to inquiry
Novelty crushed	Novelty leads to problems	Novelty implemented

Table 1: The Westrum organizational typology model: How organizations process information (Source: Ron Westrum, "A typology of organisation culture ☑)," BMJ Quality & Safety 13, no. 2 (2004), doi:10.1136/qshc.2003.009522.)

Figure 2.6   Westrum organizational culture.

co-workers and improves decision-making (Stettina and Hörz, 2015). Furthermore, transparency can help in improving collaboration between the different roles within a portfolio. Traceability of resources as an enabler for transparency is a recurring theme in the literature (Stettina and Hörz, 2015). Previous research also advocates for one portfolio for the entire organization. However, the literature does not reject having multiple portfolios within an organization; instead it emphasizes the risk of untransparent allocation of resources that multiple portfolios engender (Stettina and Hörz, 2015). Cooper et al. (1999) concluded that the usage of high-quality–rated portfolio methods fits management well and one of these methods was proven to be the management of all projects as one portfolio.

In addition to projects, organizations tend to start other initiatives that consume from the same pool of resources as the projects. One example of such an initiative can be the maintenance of projects. It is therefore of high importance to group other initiatives within the portfolio to prevent invisible projects draining resources originally assigned to the portfolio. Not doing so has been shown to decrease transparency and cause great frustration among workers within an organization (Stettina and Hörz, 2015). It is argued that project visibility can have a great influence on the effectiveness of a portfolio. A project having high visibility refers to its stakeholders being aware of its existence, status, and problems. High visibility can lead to better support from stakeholders, increased effort and commitment of project teams, and effective resource-sharing on both project and portfolio levels. Furthermore, visible information about projects can also facilitate portfolio decisions; thus, effectiveness is easier to achieve. Methods of making decisions can be secretive; however, ultimate decisions, and the reasons behind them, must be transparent. This kind of transparency reflects the integrity in decision-making and encourages a unified and moral organization. At the portfolio level, most frameworks apply a range of artefacts, meetings, and a set of information radiators to foster transparency.

2.7.1 Final Thoughts

While agile methods can be extremely effective at a project level, they can impose significant complexity and a need for adaptiveness at the portfolio level.

Firstly, agile initiatives result in a high degree of complexity at the portfolio level. This is because agile increases focus on the customer and increases complexity at the portfolio level, as agile initiatives in a portfolio must reconcile tensions between customer needs and organizational strategy.

In addition, the autonomy and improvisation inherent in agile methods have implications for a portfolio of interdependent agile initiatives as greater coordination is needed between dynamic projects to ensure the emergent portfolio remains aligned to the intended portfolio.

Furthermore, the commitment of agile to "people over processes" (Fowler and Highsmith, 2001) increases the interactions both within and between initiatives and poses challenges for management at the portfolio level.

Exercise 2.2 Stand, Stretch, and Speak

It is time to recap and articulate what you have learned in this chapter, so get up, stretch after a long time, and then articulate what you have learned from this chapter.

_____
_____
_____
_____
_____

Answers: No right or wrong answers.

Chapter 3

Agile Portfolio Management (APM)

Figure 3.1   Overview.

Agile portfolio management is a powerful tool when the amount of development and teams reaches a certain level. Sometimes the terms large-scale, scaled, two or more teams, scaling agile and suchlike are used to describe the delivery model. The situation is commonly where the organization has a fair number of teams conducting software development which needs to be focused and coordinated. Agile portfolio management is the glue between agile software development and company strategy. Agile portfolio management employs an agile mindset to provide real business value and continuous improvements. It is business value focused on shorter releases and the ability to reprioritize when needed, and is highly transparent. Agile portfolio management activities are like project portfolio management but just quite different. Agile portfolio management still defines a clear vision, objectives, and measurable goals where business value is aligned with our strategy. The organization needs to ensure the right amount of portfolio backlog items are included where risk and dependencies have been assessed, and backlog items are prioritized and supported by stable team-capacity planning. The fundamental principles and techniques of agile portfolio management are similar to what you know from agile software development; it is all about strategic themes, value streams, portfolio backlog, lightweight business case, epics, portfolio Kanban, funnel, roadmap, epic value statements and suchlike.

This chapter includes an introduction to agile portfolio management, in the following sections:

- 3.1 Agile Principles
- 3.2 Explaining Roles and Responsibilities
- 3.3 Agile Level of Governance
- 3.4 The Portfolio Kanban aka Agile Portfolio Planning Kanban Wall
- 3.5 Ongoing Agile Portfolio Ceremonies
- 3.6 Portfolio Artefacts
- 3.7 Agile Requirements Levels (Scope Decomposition)
- 3.8 Agile Portfolio Budgeting and Resources
- 3.9 Identify the Portfolio Value in an Initiative
- 3.10 Portfolio-Wide Stakeholder Analysis

The second part of this chapter contains all the activities you have previously encountered mainly within portfolio selection and portfolio monitoring and controlling, but here in the agile way.

Portfolio selection:

- 3.11 Align All Work to the Strategy
- 3.12 Estimation of Initiatives
- 3.13 Portfolio Prioritization – Sorting/Ranking the Portfolio
- 3.14 Bottlenecks and Cost of Delays
- 3.15 Qualify Ideas for Portfolio Inclusion – The Agile Business Case
- 3.16 Visualize and Present the Portfolio Values
- 3.17 Managing Portfolio Risks
- 3.18 Portfolio Metrics Worth Tracking – Measuring Progress and Value
- 3.19 The Agile Project Management Office (PMO)
- 3.20 Exploring EDGE
- 3.21 Transformational Leadership for a Successful Portfolio

Organizations apply agile portfolio management to gain value. Value consists of various components; however, the common benefits of agile portfolio management are the following:

- Sustainably more productive
- Happier people
- Improved prioritization across projects, programme, and portfolios
- Greater degree of control and predictability across feature releases
- Greater control over funding and approval of projects
- Increased focus on value realization
- Increased customer feedback opportunities
- Improved collaboration across teams/departments/portfolios
- Greater visibility on project progress across the portfolio
- Better ability to manage dependencies across the teams
- Ability to increase resource capability and flexibility across the portfolio
- Increased risk mitigation activities

These common benefits are supported by the usual benefits of agile portfolio management (Laanti and Kangas, 2015):

- Epics. Avoid a long queue of development items that will get outdated. Specify the new epics just-in-time when needed. Focus on value derived from each epic.
- Prioritization. Clear visibility and communication of what needs to be implemented. Generically, the fractal backlog structure helps development teams to identify what is the larger entity that the stories under development will comprise of. A change of priorities in the portfolio backlog enables the company to quickly change its strategic direction.
- Epic owner. Each epic has an epic owner who is responsible for making all the decisions regarding the contents of that epic. An epic owner remains the same from the idea until the epic is ready, and participates in all negotiations and meetings considering the epic, this process resulting in a lot of tacit information.
- Enterprise architect. Architecture is a business decision. What architecture solutions are used impacts the return on investment, i.e., the payback of each investment decision made. Thus, enterprise architects analyze and make decisions regarding the possible future architecture solutions, e.g., what cloud solution, database, or framework a company should use.

- Programme portfolio management. Programme portfolio management is a group of senior managers, strategy planners, and directors that make portfolio decisions and prioritize the portfolio backlog.
- Strategic themes. Strategic themes express the intent to which direction the enterprise would like to develop its portfolio, i.e., what kind of new strategies it will implement in the future. Epics are derived from strategic themes.
- Portfolio metrics. Portfolio metrics measure the enterprise's performance on the highest level. They can include measures like employee engagement and market share/development.

Agile portfolio management may sound like a beautiful rose, but it is not without thorns. Some may argue it is quiet when it is going well, noisy when it is not. Chapter 7 includes a wide range of challenges and pitfalls researchers have identified in the literature and in organizations when implementing agile portfolio management. Project portfolio management has been maturing for more than 70 years and it is still not easy, while agile portfolio management has been employed for less than 10 years and already organizations have witnessed a beautiful flower garden in the making, if we are staying with gardening terminology.

Agile portfolio management is not a replacement for project portfolio management. Mostly, larger organizations do have extensive agile software development where agile portfolio management would work well; however, most organizations still need a portfolio of portfolios or multiple portfolios. Think of a portfolio as a container. Some projects or programmes fit the project portfolio management-based container while others, the agile software development initiatives, have a better fit with the agile portfolio management container.

Reading this chapter may cause some degree of information overload as it is a lot of information to grasp and in the process, you may consider what to do in your organization. Chapter 4 contains a description of the various frameworks on the market where the information of this chapter may be implemented and applied in various ways as more generic content. A framework is just a one-size-fit-all approach; this is where Chapter 8 on tailoring might be relevant as frameworks need to be adapted to the organization to provide the highest value. Some organizations are a mix of project portfolio management and agile portfolio management; Chapters 5 and 6 might be of help to understand how everything works and perhaps what to do.

If you are in an organization which is going to apply agile portfolio management but not sure whether a framework is the best approach, research by Horlach et al. (2019) and others identifies the agile portfolio management design goals and principles your organization should look for:

■ Customer solution-driven portfolio management
■ Multi-level cross-functional portfolio governance body
■ Aligned autonomous portfolio decision-making
■ Synchronized short portfolio cycles
■ Alignment of portfolio management with adjoining strategic management processes
■ Extension toward innovation management capabilities integration

Agile portfolio management is suggestive, but it is not always necessary. Unfortunately, agile portfolio management can be overused. So read this chapter with care and see whether it makes sense in your organization; if not, do something else.

Exercise 3.1 Think It, Ink It

It is time to read about agile portfolio management. What do you already know? Think about it, then write it down.

_____

_____

_____

_____

_____

Answers: No right or wrong answers.

3.1 Agile Principles

On December 2, 2001, at The Lodge (Aspen Room) at Snowbird ski resort in the Wasatch mountains of Utah (US), 17 advocates (14 took part in the meeting; not present were Ward Cunningham, Kent Back, and Dave Thomas) of lightweight development processes met to talk at the "Lightweight methods conference", ski, relax, and try to find common ground, and, of course, to eat. The intention was to write the agile manifesto to avoid codification of practice but what emerged was the Manifesto for Agile Software Development with emphasis on technical practices, strong teams, and

Table 3.1 Agile Principles High-Level Overview

	Strategic Planning		Initiative/Operations		
Portfolio Life-Cycle Stages	Initiation	Planning	Executing	Optimization	Monitoring and controlling
Portfolio Kanban	Funnel	Review/ analyzing	Portfolio backlog	Implementation	Done
Projectized					
Recurring	3.1 Agile Principles				

mindfulness. Representatives from Extreme Programming (Martin Fowler and Ron Jeffries), SCRUM (Jeff Sutherland, Ken Schwaber, and Mike Beedle), DSDM, Adaptive Software Development (Jim Highsmith), Crystal (Alistair Cockburn), Feature-Driven Development, Pragmatic Programming (Andy Hunt), and others (Bob Martin, James Grenning, Jon Kern, and etc.) sympathetic to the need for an alternative to documentation-driven, heavyweight software development processes convened. These people represent the agile movement which is not anti-methodology, as:

- We want to restore credibility to the word "methodology".
- We want to restore a balance.
- We embrace modelling, but not to file some diagram in a dusty corporate repository.
- We embrace documentation, but not hundreds of pages of never-maintained and rarely used tomes.
- We plan but recognize the limits of planning in a turbulent environment.

The Manifesto for Agile Software Development was developed with the purpose of uncovering better ways of developing software by doing it and helping others to do it. Later, Kern (Lockard, 2019) was quoted as saying, "Four measly bullets and all this s **t happened".

3.1.1 Core Concepts of Agile Principles

Before going into details of the agile manifesto, the 12 principles of agile software, and the declaration of interdependence for modern management, it is important to highlight that agile portfolio management is not going to be agile if it violates the values and principles in the agile manifesto, the 12 principles of agile software, and the declaration of interdependence for modern management. This is fundamental to agile; it is relevant for agile history and is still very relevant today.

The second point to highlight is concepts such as "doing Agile versus being Agile" by Highsmith (2002) which stress the importance of *being* agile rather than just *doing* agile, meaning the benefits from really understanding and applying the agile values and principles are so much greater than from just applying the ceremonies and artefacts. This point is often downplayed in agile portfolio management; however, it is equally as important here as it is on the team level.

3.1.2 Agile Manifesto Values and Principles

The Manifesto for Agile Software Development contains fours statements with the following syntax:

We value: <left> over <right>. That is, while there is value in the items on the right, we value the items on the left more. We are uncovering better ways of developing software by doing it and helping others to do it. Through this work, we have come to value:

- Individuals and interactions over processes and tools
- Working software over comprehensive documentation
- Customer collaboration over contract negotiation
- Responding to change over following a plan

3.1.3 Individuals and Interactions over Processes and Tools

The value and principle of "Individuals and interactions over processes and tools" has a strong emphasis on communication, management, and commitment. Project management and communication have, for many years, been intricately connected as organizations have witnessed how projects have failed due to lack of communication, while other projects with good communication practices have performed far better than average. In agile, communication is a vital and integral part of various life cycles. These cycles can range from every few minutes with pair programming, every few hours with continuous integration, every day with a daily standup meeting, to every iteration with a review and retrospective. For the team to achieve their full potential, agile management must provide a supportive environment where honesty, conflict resolution, and self-organization thrive. Agile methodologies facilitate commitment and self-organization by encouraging team members to pull items from a prioritized work list, manage their own work, and focus on improving their work practices.

"To create high-performing teams, Agile methodologies value individuals and interactions over processes and tools. Practically speaking, all of the Agile methodologies seek to increase communication and collaboration through frequent inspect-and-adapt cycles" (Sutherland et al., 2012).

3.1.4 *Working Software over Comprehensive Documentation*

The principle of "Working software over comprehensive documentation" is perhaps the most important value that agile offers in the process of delivering small chunks of working software at set intervals. The phrase "working software" may have different meanings from team to team, as does the "definition of done" based on the working software. However, the use of working software is a great way for the team to demonstrate high value and high performance to stakeholders. It can foster increased communication and interactions, thereby supporting other values.

In terms of documentation, we do not value comprehensive documentation, but just enough documentation to get by. Kent Beck (2007) seems to suggest that well-written code is its own documentation. Hoda et al. (2010) suggest a documentation pattern or framework that will ensure just enough documentation.

Table 3.2 demonstrates the patterns or types of documentation, the problems, and the solutions. Agile patterns suggest that instead of using traditional documentation to measure and show success, it can be documented as simply as documenting positive customer feedback. The message is loud and clear – it is "just enough", and far from comprehensive.

3.1.5 *Customer Collaboration over Contract Negotiation*

"Over the past two decades, project success rates have more than doubled worldwide. These improvements occurred because of smaller projects and more frequent deliveries, which allowed customers to provide feedback on working software at regular intervals" (Sutherland et al., 2012).

Table 3.2   Documentation

Pattern	Problem	Solution
Fake documentation	How do you coordinate the timing of documentation produced across agile and non-agile projects?	Time the production of a minimal amount of traditional documentation to coordinate with non-agile teams
Time stamp	How do you clarify who initiated a change request?	Documents change decisions with time stamps on wiki
e-backup	How do you avoid losing all your story cards and task post-its?	Make electronic back-up of paper artefacts
Project dictionary	How do you translate business requirements into technical tasks?	Engage your customers to document business terms, their meaning and context of use into a project dictionary
Advantage agile	How do you demonstrate the agile advantage over successful non-agile projects measured using traditional metrics?	Document positive customer feedback

Agile methodologies foster collaboration by having a customer advocate work together with the development team. Agile methods, such as Scrum and XP, turn to product owners and customers to create roles and foster an environment, where verbal customer collaboration adds value. This value stands in strong opposition to the written contract negotiation over software requirements or legal practicalities. In agile, we seek verbal customer collaboration as soon as possible to receive feedback. However, this does not mean we have not had contract negotiations.

3.1.6 Responding to Changeover Following a Plan

To create products that will please customers and provide business value, teams must respond to change. Industry data shows that over "60 percent of product or project requirements change during the development of software" (Sutherland et al., 2012). One may argue that customers rarely know what they want (requirement churn) until they see the working software. If customers do not see the working software until the end of a project, it is too late to incorporate their feedback.

Exercise 3.2 Manifesto That Makes You Go "Hmm …"

You may recall the song "Things that make you go hmm" from C&C Music Factory; however, read the following eight statements inspired by Cockburn and Highsmith (2002) and let us see if they make you go "hmm".

1. Can we have a successful agile portfolio by delivering individuals and interactions with less emphasis on processes and tools?
2. Can we have a successful agile portfolio by delivering processes and tools with less emphasis on individuals and interactions?
3. Can we have a successful agile portfolio by delivering working software with less emphasis on comprehensive documentation?
4. Can we have a successful agile portfolio by delivering comprehensive documentation with less emphasis on working software?
5. Can we have a successful agile portfolio by delivering customer collaboration with less emphasis on contract negotiation?
6. Can we have a successful agile portfolio by delivering contract negotiation with less emphasis on customer collaboration?
7. Can we have a successful agile portfolio by delivering responding to change with less emphasis on following a plan?
8. Can we have a successful agile portfolio by delivering following a plan with less emphasis on responding to change?

_____
_____
_____
_____
_____

Answers: No right or wrong answers.

3.1.7 The Twelve Principles of Agile Software

According to Kent Beck (2000), the Manifesto for Agile Software Development is based on 12 principles of agile software. These values are not just something the creators of the Manifesto for Agile Software Development intended to give lip service to and then forget. They are working values. Each individual agile methodology approaches these values in a slightly different manner, but all these methodologies have specific processes and practices that foster one or more of the following principles:

1. Our highest priority is to satisfy the customer through early and continuous delivery of valuable software.

2. Welcome changing requirements, even late in development. Agile processes harness change for the customer's competitive advantage.
3. We deliver working software frequently, from a couple of weeks to a couple of months, with a preference for the shorter timescale.
4. Businesspeople and developers must work together daily throughout the project.
5. We build projects around motivated individuals. We give them the environment and support they need and trust them to get the job done.
6. The most efficient and effective method of conveying information to and within a development team is face-to-face conversation.
7. Working software is the primary measure of progress.
8. Agile processes promote sustainable development. The sponsors, developers, and users should be able to maintain a constant pace indefinitely.
9. Continuous attention to technical excellence and good design enhances agility.
10. Simplicity – the art of maximizing the amount of work not done – is essential.
11. The best architectures, requirements, and designs emerge from self-organizing teams.
12. At regular intervals, the team reflects on how to become more effective, then tunes and adjusts its behaviour accordingly.

To understand the underlying values and practical applications of the 12 principles of agile software, review the summary in Table 3.3.

It was difficult for the 17 people back in Utah to agree upon a detailed description of the values. This is because different backgrounds and philosophies come into play. But, when all was said and done, it was their hope that the Manifesto for Agile Software Development and supporting values would give you enough information to build your own agile work habits on any level. The Manifesto for Agile Software Development and the 12 principles of agile software were written almost 20 years ago. Some years ago, Laurie Williams (2012) conducted two surveys at North Carolina State University to weigh the community's view of the principles and use of the associated practices. The findings were published in an ACM article (2012), "What Agile Teams Think of Agile Principles". It turned out that 11 of the 12 principles had a mean score of 4.1 out of 5 or higher, indicating a high level of support for principles that had been spelled out ten years earlier.

Table 3.3   Twelve Principles of Agile Software

Name	Value	Principle	Practices
Our highest priority is to satisfy the customer through early and continuous delivery of valuable software.	Commitment Feedback	Satisfy the customer	Portfolio backlog Product backlog Whole team Incremental deployment Small releases Frequency delivery
Deliver working software frequently, from a couple of weeks to a couple of months, with a preference for the shorter timescale.	Focus Commitment	Frequent delivery	Portfolio reviews Incremental deployment Small releases Sprint review Definition of done Acceptance tests
Working software is the primary measure of progress.	Commitment Feedback	Working software	Portfolio Kanban Incremental deployment Small releases Definition of done Acceptance tests
Welcome changing requirements, even late in development. Agile processes harness change for the customer's competitive advantage.	Openness Commitment Focus	Embrace change	Portfolio planning Sprint planning Planning game Product backlog Customer involvement
Businesspeople and developers must work together daily throughout the project.	Focus Commitment	Cross-functional collaboration	Real customer involvement Whole team Osmotic communication Daily Scrum
Build projects around motivated individuals. Give them the environment and support they need and trust them to get the job done.	Commitment Courage	Support and trust	Servant leadership Motivation

(Continued)

Table 3.3 (Continued)   Twelve Principles of Agile Software

Name	Value	Principle	Practices
The most efficient and effective method of conveying information to and within a development team is face-to-face conversation.	Communication Openness	Face-to-Face conversation	Osmotic communication Servant leadership
The best architectures, requirements, and designs emerge from self-organizing teams.	Simplicity Feedback Courage	Self-organization	Test-driven development Refactoring Osmotic communication Servant leadership
Continuous attention to technical excellence and good design enhances agility.	Courage Simplicity Focus	Technical Excellence	Testing Portfolio retrospective Sprint retrospective, pair programming Test-driven development Refactoring
Agile processes promote sustainable development. The sponsors, developers, and users should be able to maintain a constant pace indefinitely.	Commitment Communication	Sustainable pace	Real customer involvement Motivation
Simplicity – the art of maximizing the amount of work not done – is essential.	Focus Simplicity	Keep it simple	Portfolio backlog Product backlog Refactoring Seeing waste
At regular intervals, the team reflects on how to become more effective, then tunes and adjusts its behaviour accordingly.	Commitment	Inspect and adapt	Portfolio retrospective Sprint retrospective Root-cause Analysis Seeing waste Value-stream mapping

The authors of the Manifesto for Agile Software Development and the original 12 principles defined the essence of the agile trend that has transformed the software industry over more than a decade. That is, "they nailed it" (Williams, 2012).

3.1.8 Declaration of Interdependence for Modern Management

In 2005, a group headed by Alistair Cockburn and Jim Highsmith wrote an addendum of principles, the "Declaration of Interdependence for Modern Management" to guide software project management according to agile development methods. The group, not wanting to coin a new buzzword, instead worked out six rules of operation.

"The sentences were formed as two clauses: We accomplish X – by doing Y. That is, Y is what you can see us do, and the reason we all care about that is because we're trying to set up X" (Cockburn, 2012).

The Declaration of Interdependence for Modern Management is as follows:

We …

- Increase Return on Investment by – making continuous flow of value our focus.
- Deliver reliable results by – engaging customers in frequent interactions and shared ownership.
- Expect uncertainty and manage it through – iterations, anticipation, and adaptation.
- Unleash creativity and innovation by – recognizing that individuals are the ultimate source of value and creating an environment where they can make a difference.
- Boost performance through – group accountability for results and shared responsibility for team effectiveness.
- Improve effectiveness and reliability through situational-specific strategies, processes and practices.

(Written, 2005 by David Anderson, Sanjiv Augustine, Christopher Avery, Alistair Cockburn, Mike Cohn, Doug DeCarlo, Donna Fitzgerald, Jim Highsmith, Ole Jepsen, Lowell Lindstrøm, Todd Little, Kent McDonald, Pollyanna Pixton, Preston Smith, and Robert Wysocki)

Table 3.4   The Declaration of Interdependence for Modern Management

Accomplish This	*By/Through This*	*And*
Increased ROI	Focusing on "flow of value" (e.g., not "tracking effort").	Continuous (one-piece) flow, preferably
Reliable results	Engaging customers in frequent interactions	Shared ownership
Unleash creativity and innovation	Recognizing individual human beings as the ultimate source of value	Creation of an environment where individual people can make a difference
Manage uncertainty	Iterations, anticipation, and adaptation	Anticipation and adaptation (i.e., think ahead, plan, iterate, deliver, reflect, adapt)
Improve effectiveness and reliability	Situational-specific strategies, processes, and practices. (i.e., no one answers, folks just get used to it)	
Boost performance	Group accountability for results (i.e., the whole group is singly accountable, no in-team blame)	Shared responsibility for team effectiveness

The Declaration of Interdependence for Modern Management is summarized in Table 3.4, based upon an adaptation from Cockburn (2012) to demonstrate what is accomplished and how it is accomplished.

"One of the issues with the declaration of interdependence is that it may sound platitudes" (Cockburn, 2007).

As it only identifies causes and effects, no bad guys. The application of the Declaration of Interdependence is to improve agile software development as a default mode of management and is appropriate for agile at any level.

3.2 Explaining Roles and Responsibilities

Adapting an agile portfolio approach requires the right set of roles and responsibilities to ensure work gets done; however, too few roles may not include the critical mass to get work properly done while an extensive use of roles would cause waste as time is spent coordinating, or some roles are

Table 3.5 Explaining Roles and Responsibilities High-Level Overview

	Strategic Planning		Initiative/Operations		
Portfolio Life-Cycle Stages	Initiation	Planning	Executing	Optimization	Monitoring and controlling
Portfolio Kanban	Funnel	Review/analyzing	Portfolio backlog	Implementation	Done
Projectized					
Recurring	3.2 Explaining Roles and Responsibilities				

just not pulling their weight. We want to have more people doing the actual work than talking about doing the actual work, which should be a real concern if applying some of the frameworks.

Each framework described in Chapter 4 has its own unique set of roles and responsibilities which can be applied and adapted; however, examining them illustrates the common roles most agile portfolios are applying to some degree.

At the team level, most seem to apply the common Scrum roles with a team, Scrum master and product owner where the agile/Scrum team is responsible for delivering the product, the Scrum master facilitates the process and removes the impediments, while the product owner is the voice of the customer, prioritizes the work, and makes the product decisions. Variations are the business owner in enterprise Scrum which is a variant of the product owner and the use of chief product owner and chief Scrum master in some Scrum implementations as coordinators and teams leads for several of their own kind. An interesting variant is the nexus integration team which handles dependencies and such across the teams while many frameworks use meetings such as scrum of scrum to handle these.

The roles of product owner and Scrum master are also found on the programme level. The product owner may involve into product management, programme product owner or area product owner as seen in LeSS and RAGE. The responsibilities remain the same, but involve managing the next level. In SAFe the Scrum master changes to the release train engineer to put emphasis on the release trains. At this level, some frameworks use programme management to manage the team level.

The agile portfolio level has roles to ensure the prioritization and continual involvement of epics and business cases. This role has varied names in the various frameworks such as portfolio management, portfolio product

Table 3.6   Sample RACI Chart

Activity/Person	*Portfolio Product Owner*	*Portfolio Scrum Master*	*Portfolio Executive*
Portfolio backlog refinement	A	I	R
Conducting portfolio retrospective	C	A	R
Portfolio planning	A	C	R

owner, epic owners, or portfolio owner (RAGE). In addition, at the portfolio level we find roles to facilitate the process and flow like a portfolio Scrum master and suchlike.

Besides the more common roles and responsibilities, most frameworks include a set of additional or supporting roles ranging from enterprise architect, testing, environments, DevOps, and suchlike, which also are needed to make the agile portfolio run.

Roles and responsibilities can be complex during many agile transformations and in major organizations in general. In these instances, the responsibility assignment matrix may prove to be a useful tool to ensure all roles and responsibilities are covered and how the activities are divided between the various roles. Table 3.6 illustrates a sample RACI chart for an agile portfolio. The terminology for a RACI chart is the following: R = responsible, A = accountable, C = consulted, and I = informed. Only one role can be responsible, while the others can be shared and multiplied.

It is evident that the agile portfolio encompasses a wide variety of roles in organizations and the focus is on value across the whole portfolio, not within a single initiative. Some organizations combine the roles and responsibilities above with other frameworks such as Spotify, see Chapter 4 or thoughts from Laloux and Wilber (2014) on reinventing organizations or Holacracy (Bernstein et al., 2016).

3.3 Agile Levels of Governance

Agile level of governance consists of five or six levels of planning. Traditionally we talk about the multiple levels of agile planning, which are five; however, the research highlighted by Vahaniity et al. (2010) includes six levels, as illustrated in Table 3.8. Whether it is five levels or six is not important. The daily, iteration/sprint and the release/project level are what we call the team level. This is where work gets done as we know it from Scrum,

Table 3.7   Agile Levels of Governance High-Level Overview

Portfolio Life-Cycle Stages	Strategic Planning		Initiative/Operations		
	Initiation	Planning	Executing	Optimization	Monitoring and controlling
Portfolio Kanban	Funnel	Review/ analyzing	Portfolio backlog	Implementation	Done
Projectized					
Recurring	3.3 Agile Levels of Governance				

Table 3.8   Level of Governance

Portfolio Management as	Product portfolio management	**Cycles of Control**
Business-level investment setting		Business management
High-level goal setting		Product management
Resourcing decisions across a portfolio of planned and ongoing projects	Development portfolio management	Project portfolio management
Mechanism for resolving mid-iteration emergencies		Project management Iteration management
Time management for an individual developer		Daily work

Kanban, and similar frameworks. The remaining two or three levels are the portfolio level, which includes product management, and the strategy level, which is closely related. Sometimes we introduce a programme management level between these levels to manage the team level.

The adaptive level of governance is where our focus is when working with an agile portfolio. Governance is also a matter of structuration versus agility, which is covered later in this chapter. This level of governance helps us to have the holistic overview which supports continuous planning and concepts such as lean budgeting.

An important part of the level of governance is release planning which in many agile organizations is practised as continuous delivery, to align with business patterns such as marketing or customer training efforts. Every release is incrementally planned and then focused on a goal based on business value and an appropriate level of detail based on the initial clarity of the scope.

Figure 3.2   Portfolio governance.

Another view on the idea of portfolio governance is illustrated in Figure 3.2. The portfolio backlog contains a wide range of initiatives which are prioritized based upon value and other criteria. The portfolio governance, whether it is a backlog, Kanban, funnel, or suchlike, will make the decision to move the initiative forward toward implementation, transform it, or remove it from the board.

3.3.1 *Cycles of Control*

Surprisingly, the notion of control in organizations "embracing agile" has almost exclusively been explored on the level of the individual project or team. When observing control in organizations, Mahadevan et al. (2015) define control by means of "mechanisms" permitting an organization to proceed toward its goals. Traditionally, structured Stage-Gate or waterfall practices aid control, while hierarchy and structure are central; whereas, in contrast, agile information system development (ISD), approaches stimulate autonomous control in development teams, customer involvement, and flexible "facilitative control practices". Control, in an agile project management context, is an imperative contingency affecting the capability of software teams to react to altering user requirements. According to Maruping et al. (2009) under circumstances "of high requirements change", the use of agile methodology and control modes that stimulate autonomous teams are essential and effective in realizing improved project quality. As agile is said to stimulate innovation through working software and reduced documentation, the focus of control may shift in nature and, therefore, control mechanisms must adjust accordingly. This would imply that business outcome controls are emphasized as opposed to process controls in agile organizations. The second implication underlines transparent and trusted communication through meetings, demos, and, occasionally, elements such as live dashboards. It can be argued that the presence of these elements is essential at all levels of organizations, especially in firms implementing agile methods.

3.4 The Portfolio Kanban aka Agile Portfolio Planning Kanban Wall

The Kanban method is a change management method, not a framework. Kanban employs a set of management practices for software derived from Toyota Production Systems (TPS) and Goldratt's Theory of Contracts (ToC). Kanban is a Japanese word and means visual record or card. In Lean technique, it is used for signal mechanics. Kanban describes a process for driving change in an organization, a process that has sufficient detail as to be repeatable. The context for which the process could be applied started out specifically as software maintenance, then expanded as general software development, and has grown to cover IT operations, IT services, and other areas of knowledge work. There is a certain belief and hope that Kanban will develop as a general-purpose change management approach for knowledge worker industries. Rather than focusing on being agile, which may (and should) lead to being successful, Kanban focuses on becoming successful, which may lead to being agile at any level.

"Information radiator" is the generic term for any of several handwritten, drawn, printed, or electronic displays that a team places in a highly visible location, so that all team members, as well as passersby, can see them. It conveys the latest information immediately: for example, the count of automated tests, velocity, incident reports, progress radiators, work breakdown structure, continuous integration status, and so on.

The phrase "information radiator" originates from the Toyota Production System (TPS) in the 1980s, where it was known as "visual controls". In 2000, Kent Beck used the term "Big Visible Chart" in *Extreme Programming Explained* (2000) and in 2004 it became part of the book *Crystal Clear* by Alistair Cockburn (2004). Information radiators are tools for conveying two

Table 3.9 The Portfolio Kanban High-level Overview

	Strategic Planning		*Initiative/Operations*		
Portfolio Life-Cycle Stages	Initiation	Planning	Executing	Optimization	Monitoring and controlling
Portfolio Kanban	Funnel	Review/ analyzing	Portfolio backlog	Implementation	Done
Projectized					
Recurring	3.4 The Portfolio Kanban				

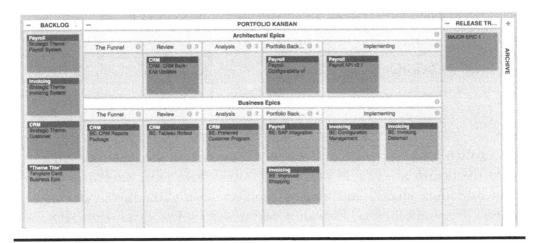

Figure 3.3   Portfolio Kanban from Leankit (2019).

messages: one, the team has nothing to hide from others; and two, the team has nothing to hide from itself. A portfolio Kanban is an example of an information radiator and the easiest and most visual portfolio management tool. Figure 3.3 is an example of the typical portfolio Kanban.

3.4.1 Core Concepts of the Portfolio Kanban

David Anderson (2010) defined three foundational Kanban principles:

- Start with what you do now.
- Agree to pursue incremental, evolutionary change.
- Respect the current process, roles, responsibilities, and titles.

The fundamental Kanban principles are important for the agile portfolio as it highlights simplicity: start simple and make it work; expand with continual improvements and do not stop making improvements. This stresses the need for portfolio retrospectives and similar meetings at the portfolio level, so continually improvements are identified.

Kanban core properties:

- Visualize workflow (with a Kanban board 看板).
- Limit work-in-progress (with Kanban かんばん).
- Measure and manage flow.
- Make process policies explicit.
- Use models to recognize improvement and opportunities (implement feedback loops).

Table 3.10 Information Radiator/Simple Kanban Board

To Do	In Progress	Done
As a user …	As a user …	As a user …
As a user …	As a user …	As a user …
	As a user …	

The Kanban core properties are very much applied in the agile portfolio where the boards are vital to visualize the workflow; most Kanban boards apply work-in-progress limits to avoid bottlenecks and the theory of constraints. The portfolio level measures and manages flow by ensuring initiatives or epics are reduced to the relevant batch size – think Reinertsen. The portfolio process should include explicit processes, as illustrated in the fundamental principles of ongoing processes for continual improvements, CSI, PDCA, and similar mechanisms. Table 3.10 illustrates the basic Kanban board which on the portfolio layer is expanded to something more like Figure 3.3.

Cockburn (2004) defines a good information radiator/portfolio Kanban board:

■ Is large and easily visible to the casual, interested observer
■ Is understood immediately
■ Changes periodically, so that it is worth visiting
■ Is easily kept up to date

This implies that the information radiators/portfolio Kanban board are:

■ Simple
■ Predictive to avoid problems
■ Reflective and show changes
■ Updated
■ Few in numbers but highly visible

Information radiators are typically used to show status information (Cockburn, 2004) where it is important to apply the proper portfolio metrics which are covered later in this chapter.

Today, looking for information on delivery is wasteful as it requires extra work; time is wasted on reacting, people must wait, customers are not willing to pay for status reports, and the value of the information tends to decrease. An underlying value in XP and Scrum is required to build an effective information radiator.

The Kanban board or portfolio Kanban is an excellent example of the highly visible information radiator with agile metrics that are commonly applied throughout the portfolio. Some Kanban boards are simple and contain information on what to do, what is in process, and what has been done.

From a high-level perspective, portfolio Kanban and task boards have been inspired by William Edwards Deming with his quality theories on the Plan-Do-Check-Act cycle. The "Plan" phase establishes objectives and defines methods to reach them. The "Do" phase implements what you have planned while the "Check" phase measures and compares current results against expected results. The "Act" phase takes actions to improve what you have implemented.

The core properties making process policies explicit refer to the use of Kanban boards to demonstrate progress and communication.

The application of Kanban portfolio retrospectives is illustrated as:

■ We have more choice on when and how to reflect and improve.
■ Regularly scheduled retrospective as with Scrum.
■ After an epic has been delivered.
■ When we must "Stop the line".
■ Weekly mini retrospectives.

The portfolio Kanban, aka the agile portfolio planning Kanban wall, is a much applied and powerful tool which even with a lack of empirical evidence, seems to provide most of the following benefits:

■ Summarizes and monitors performance
■ Makes performance visible
■ Proactively identifies problems
■ Drives improvements
■ Gauges progress against goals
■ Makes better decisions
■ More effective collaboration
■ Concise overview (visibility, transparency, communication, better control)
■ Helps management make the right decisions
■ Provides balance among portfolio offerings

3.4.2 Set Up Your Portfolio Tracking Kanban Board/Walls

Setting up the organization's first Kanban board or wall can be a daunting task. The first rule is to keep it simple, so do not add information that you do not use today unless there is a good reason or there is a strong stakeholder supporting the need. The second rule is that everything we do should provide us with value. Value is supported by good flow and a minimum amount of waste. Ensure all information on the Kanban board really provides some much-needed insights and ensure it can be updated effectively. If not, you are just creating waste. The third rule is that the Kanban board tracks the work of the teams in the portfolio, so the information on the Kanban board would provide them with value; otherwise reconsider whether it should be included. The fourth rule is to start small and then see how it goes. Do not build a too-big or extensive Kanban board for a start. Keep it simple and then expand upon the Kanban board as part of your continuous improvement process. The fifth rule is having an ongoing process for continual improvements which should include the Kankan boards.

3.5 Ongoing Agile Portfolio Ceremonies

Ongoing agile portfolio ceremonies are the meetings, activities, and suchlike which make the agile portfolio work and blossom. A wide range of the ceremonies are as at the team level, except adapted to the task needed to be conducted at the agile portfolio level.

Let us illustrate the ongoing portfolio ceremonies/meetings first as being, as some might say, more traditional, by taking, at the outset, disciplined agile delivery portfolio activities, before illustrating the ceremonies from a Scrum-related perspective, which is much more like the team level.

Table 3.11 Ongoing Agile Portfolio Ceremonies High-Level Overview

	Strategic Planning		*Initiative/Operations*		
Portfolio Life-Cycle Stages	*Initiation*	*Planning*	*Executing*	*Optimization*	*Monitoring and controlling*
Portfolio Kanban	Funnel	Review/ analyzing	Portfolio backlog	Implementation	Done
Projectized					
Recurring	**3.5 Ongoing Agile Portfolio Ceremonies**				

In disciplined agile delivery, we have a meeting for identifying potential value including envisioning the future, obtaining customer feedback, and suchlike. The identified potential values need to be explored using experiments, focus groups, ROI, and finalized in the business case. The potential endeavours are then prioritized by business value, risk, WSJF, due date, dependency, and suchlike. In addition, we need to manage the portfolio budget to start the portfolio. The endeavours or epics/business cases are then initiated, and the portfolio is managed, assessed, and governed while delivering the planned IT capabilities.

The ongoing agile portfolio ceremonies in a Scrum approach would include portfolio planning or portfolio planning meeting (RAGE) which is the portfolio variant of the sprint planning. This is where work is planned for the next period forward. The portfolio would start and, at some point, a portfolio review (like sprint review) would be conducted to ensure deliverables are as expected. While the portfolio is running a portfolio grooming meeting (RAGE) or portfolio backlog, refinement grooming is done continually where new epics, business cases, and initiatives are included, some are removed while others are elaborated upon to ensure the portfolio backlog is in the right state for the forthcoming work. Running an agile portfolio includes the portfolio retrospective (like sprint retrospective) where work at the portfolio level is considered, adapted, and improved. Table 3.12 contains a list of the three SAFe events and the four RAGE ceremonies, then is compared also with DAD and scaled Scrum. Frameworks may see various names for events, rituals, or ceremonies; however, many of these "meetings" are to some degree similar in purpose.

3.6 Portfolio Artefacts

Portfolio artefacts are all the various kinds of documents, logs, or deliverables that are applied. There may be many artefacts that are not described here, either because they are somewhat generic, such as updates, because they are industry specific, or because the output is a result of a specific method that was used to create it.

The content in this section is not meant to describe how to develop or create a portfolio artefact but to discuss and highlight the common applied portfolio artefacts which are needed to implement an agile portfolio. As illustrated later in this section, various frameworks include their own kind of artefacts, so it is a bit of a mess which we try to untangle.

Table 3.12 Portfolio Ceremonies

Ceremonies	Explanation	SAFe	DAD	Scaled Scrum	RAGE
Portfolio sync	The Portfolio sync provides visibility into how well the portfolio is progressing toward meeting its strategic objectives and may include reviewing value-stream and programme execution and governance of other portfolio investments	Yes	YES	YES	YES
Participatory budgeting	This event enables LPM to collaborate with business owners and other relevant stakeholders to right-size the investments in value streams and helps manage the approval process of epics in the portfolio Kanban	YES	NO	NO	NO
Strategic portfolio review	This event enables LPM to create alignment and investment guidance to inform rapid, high quality, decentralized decisions; adapt to meet changing needs; and provide governance necessary to effectively respond to new and changing opportunities	YES	YES	YES	YES
Portfolio grooming	Improve business cases and estimates	YES	YES	YES	YES
Portfolio planning	Select business cases to be added to the portfolio backlog	YES	YES	YES	YES
Portfolio review	Decisions on what to do with the initiatives (See Figure 3.2) Commit (fund it), kill (remove it), or transform (cut scope, change focus)	YES	YES	YES	YES
Retrospective	Decisions on how to improve the portfolio process	YES	YES	YES	YES

One kind of agile portfolio artefact is logs, where the portfolio backlog may be the most common and important one. This is where all the work that needs to be done is included. However, many other logs exist.

The portfolio level also includes a range of strategy artefacts ranging from the business case, vision statement, or business canvas to the project charter.

Table 3.13   Portfolio Artefacts High-Level Overview

	Strategic Planning		*Initiative/Operations*		
Portfolio Life-Cycle Stages	*Initiation*	*Planning*	*Executing*	*Optimization*	*Monitoring and controlling*
Portfolio Kanban	Funnel	Review/ analyzing	Portfolio backlog	Implementation	Done
Projectized					
Recurring	**3.6 Portfolio Artefacts**				

Plans are another type of portfolio artefact where the road maps are commonly applied. Similar are hierarchy charts which could include the user story map and such.

At the portfolio level we rely heavily on visual data and information where portfolio metrics (see Section 3.18) are one type. These could include affinity diagrams, burnup/down, portfolio metrics, and suchlike. Part of visual data and information could be additional reports and information on topics such as epics.

Table 3.14 illustrates which artefacts are applied in which frameworks. Some portfolio artefacts are universally applied while others are more specific to the framework.

Another aspect of the use of portfolio artefacts is the close relationship between portfolio artefacts, portfolio roles, and portfolio ceremonies. An example of this relationship is the portfolio grooming meeting where the product-owner–type role continuously updates and adapts the portfolio backlog, so it is ready for additional work. The impediments log is a common Scrum-master–type artefact while portfolio metrics may be applied by most roles and at various portfolio ceremonies or while running the portfolio.

3.7 Agile Requirements Levels (Scope Decomposition)

Initiatives are derived from the vision and may be decomposed into epics, which is the smallest level of requirement on the portfolio level. Initiatives and epics represent product and functionality which may be illustrated as MVP, MMP, and suchlike to highlight the various stages of the development. As initiatives and epics move across the portfolio Kanban the done criteria describe the expectations. Lastly, minimum acceptance criteria is a tool to enforce acceptance criteria throughout the portfolio.

Table 3.14 Portfolio Artefacts

Artefacts	SAFe	DAD	Scaled Scrum	RAGE
Portfolio metrics	X	X	X	?
Portfolio Kanban	X	?	X	?
Portfolio roadmap or solution Investments by horizon	X	?	(X)	?
Portfolio vision and/or strategic themes	X	?	X	?
Business case	X	X	(X)	X
Agile charter	?	?	(X)	X
Portfolio backlog	X	?	X	X
Cost of delay profiles	X	?	X	?
Portfolio budget/participatory budgeting	X	X	(X)	(X)
Impediments log	?	?	X	?
Decision matrix	?	?	?	X
Portfolio canvas	X	?	?	?
Guardrails	X	(X)	(X)	?
Epics (e.g., Business/enablers)	X	X	X	X

Table 3.15 Agile Requirements Levels High-Level Overview

	Strategic Planning		Initiative/Operations		
Portfolio Life-Cycle Stages	Initiation	Planning	Executing	Optimization	Monitoring and controlling
Portfolio Kanban	Funnel	Review/ analyzing	Portfolio backlog	Implementation	Done
Projectized					
Recurring	**3.7 Agile Requirements Levels**				

3.7.1 Track the Flows of Initiatives and Epics

The highest level of requirement or project in the agile portfolio is an initiative. An initiative is like a project in the traditional project portfolio management approach which is derived from the vision. Various frameworks may use different wordings, and a common definition of requirement levels does not exist. The initiative may contain various themes or headlines for topics to be including, as recognized from the road-map approach. The initiative may be broken down into epics. Some define epics as large user story; however, it is clear it is a high-level requirement or functionality. Epics is the smallest level of requirements at the portfolio level. When teams work on the initiatives and/or epics thy will be broken down into user story/features/tasks as product increments. An initiative may be decomposed into x amounts of epics where x amounts of teams may work on one or more of these epics to share the workload, maximize the competence, and suchlike. Design a portfolio-level visualization system to track the flow of MMPs across multiple investments simultaneously.

Minimal viable product (MVP) is the minimum pared-down version of the product that can be released and still provide enough value that people are willing to use it. MVP can be used to test a hypothesis. The MVP is used to create the minimal marketable feature. In the hierarchy of vision to epic to user story/feature, the minimally marketable feature (MMF) represents the smallest slice of product functionality that still allows the organization to meet its market objectives with the product. This is a fully functional, single feature that could be deployed on its own. The MMF is part of the minimal marketable release. Minimal marketable release (MMR) is a fully functional release of a product that represents the smallest possible feature set that addresses the current needs of your customers. The MME is a minimal marketable product. Minimal marketable product (MMP) is the first release of a minimal marketable release and used to shorten initial time-to-market. This is illustrated in Figure 3.4.

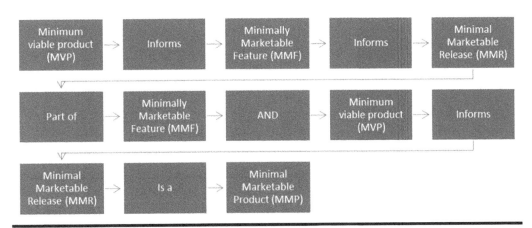

Figure 3.4   Flow of MMP adapted from Ambler and Lines (2012).

3.7.2 How to Know When Initiatives Are "Done"?

The agile concept of the definition of "done" rises above the human tendency to leave things in an almost finished state. It also stresses the importance of agreements on the quality requirements for the work when something is "done". However, "done" is not always shippable code, depending on the way of working.

The definition of "done":

- It provides a checklist which usefully guides activities such as discussion, estimation, design.
- It re-enforces that the agile principle of working software is a primary measure.
- "Done" is an agreement and may be ready for shipping or just ready for testing; it is a portfolio decision.
- "Done" for some portfolios may include fully designed, coded, and tested, while for others it is just coding.
- Removes ambiguity.
- Fosters communication and collaboration in the team as the team and the customers need to discuss what "done" looks like.
- Limits the cost of rework once a feature has been accepted as "done".
- Limits the risk of misunderstanding and conflict between the development team and the customer or product owner in the context of an explicit contract.
- Some teams use the "done" criteria as a stage model.
- When a feature or user story is "done", then the task/Kanban board is updated by the team.
- The definition of "done" exists at various levels; release (potentially shippable state), iteration/sprint (collection of features developed within a sprint), or feature (story or product backlog item).

It is simple, easy-to-use and includes a range of benefits. It is a fundamental of agile project management. Just ensure an explicit definition and agree to the accepted criteria for "done" during portfolio planning.

An addition concept is the definition of ready (DoR) which is a kind of the "DoD for the product owner or product management". When an initiatives or epic is considered "ready" it means it is ready to be part of the next step of the planning. It may not be ready if customer needs are not clarified or requirements are not yet clear.

3.7.3 Acceptance Criteria at the Portfolio Levels

When epics are decomposed into user stories or features on the team level each user story will have unique acceptance criteria. However, on the portfolio level some frameworks apply minimum acceptance criteria that have to be enforced on a range of initiatives or epics. By doing so, all user stories or features will include the minimum acceptance criteria as part of their acceptance criteria on the team level, which is a tool to enforce policies, quality requirements, and suchlike throughout the portfolio.

3.8 Agile Portfolio Budgeting and Resources

Traditional portfolio management tends to apply annual budgeting or ad-hoc budgeting which means each project or programme in the portfolio is individual funded. The portfolio budget is then the sum of all the projects and programmes budgets. This also means that resources are reserved and allocated to a project based upon "once-and-for-all" decisions made annually for the portfolio. If a project or programme exceeds budgets it is reported at fixed points, e.g., quarterly and leads to disaster recovery. The risk assessments and contingency for all projects and programmes are based on the known state at the start of the financial year.

The traditional budgeting approach leads to unwanted issues and behaviours as each project or programme has its own budget which is inflexible. We may call this "my budget" syndrome. With this approach we have seen potentially valued initiatives being dismissed too early, or the organization lacks the ability to introduce new valuable initiatives, which hinders progress and innovation as not all initiatives are made up at the end of the previous year. This approach also causes a behaviour where projects and programmes

Table 3.16   Agile Requirements Levels High-Level Overview

	Strategic Planning		*Initiative/Operations*		
Portfolio Life-Cycle Stages	*Initiation*	*Planning*	*Executing*	*Optimization*	*Monitoring and controlling*
Portfolio Kanban	Funnel	Review/ analyzing	Portfolio backlog	Implementation	Done
Projectized					
Recurring	**3.8 Agile Portfolio Budgeting and Resources**				

are reluctant to give up initiatives in the plans or stop current initiatives as funds have been granted. This approach also tends to be obsessed with cost over value/benefits as cost/capacity is the limited factor for putting more into the portfolio. The annual traditional budgeting is yearly, meaning that initiatives are fitted into a fixed and often inappropriate timeframe because of budgets, which results in less successful projects or programmes due to unrealistic timeframes.

Going even further, some may argue that the traditional budgeting approach is broken as it is not flexible, too much time is used managing it, the quality of data which we base our decisions upon are poor, and the management of resources is costly at best. We need to do it differently for the agile portfolio and each framework (see Chapter 4) has, to some degree, their own ways of dealing with this problem. Here are some of the common approaches that can be applied within most organizations and frameworks.

In disciplined agile delivery (DAD), the concept of "stable team budgeting" was proposed, meaning that we fund x number of stable teams, either feature or component teams. By doing so, costs and resources would remain fixed as stated in the project triangle and focus for the portfolio would be on managing the scope which provides the highest value to the organization.

Another concept from disciplined agile delivery (or DAD) is "rolling wave budgeting", meaning that we do high-level budgeting for the whole year but detailed budgeting for each quarter and similar period. This means x number of teams would be funded for the next quarter, then we make decisions for the next quarter. We may know that we have funding for x number of teams but not which one or whether all funding should be used on the teams.

The existing approach contains truly little competition between the projects or programmes when funding is completed. Some may do well while others poorly, but the funding would remain stable. We want to approve business cases and suchlike as probationary, meaning funding is conditional. If projects do not deliver, then funding may be taken away. This also implies that each existing and ongoing business case continually needs to compete with new and existing business cases. If an excellent business case comes up, then another business case or two may have their funding stopped. Working like this requires initiatives to be able to deliver MVP or suchlike going forward, so they still have to provide value even if stopped earlier than expected.

One major challenge is how to align demand to capacity due to competing priorities, which means frequent tradeoff decisions need to be taken. The fear is of high multitasking, which would increase the cost of what being delivered. In the agile portfolio we can add more teams or reduce competing goals.

In scaled agile framework, or SAFe, they have a concept called "Lean budgets". Lean budgets strive to move away from traditional annual budgets using participatory budgeting, fund value streams, and guide investment by horizon. This should increase throughput, morale, and control of the empowered agile portfolio. Participatory budgeting is about having the right people involved in making the decisions about what to do. SAFe is based upon value streams so funding them is like the concept of stable teams, so it is merely a matter of what to do. The last concept is guide investment by horizon which is based upon McKinsey's three horizons of growth model. The first horizon is the near future, where focus is on maintaining and defending what we have and need. The second horizon focuses on developing more value in the future, while the third horizon has the longest timeframe and the most value as new ideas are explored. The model is illustrated in Figure 3.5.

It is important to understand that agile methods can no longer be supported by traditional budgeting approaches as the traditional manner of defining a budget for a fixed set of initiatives per year must become more dynamic to facilitate this new way of working. Rather than monitoring through process controls and traditional budget controls, for agile methods it is more appropriate for portfolio managers to focus on business and customer value.

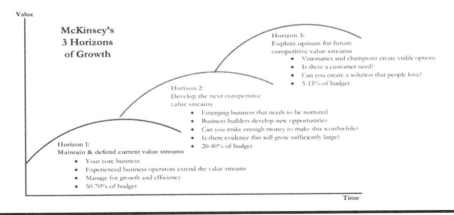

Figure 3.5   McKinsey's 3 Horizons of Growth.

Exercise 3.3 Build in Body Breaks

Time for a short break, but quickly recap what you just have learned before taking a well-deserved break.

_____

_____

_____

_____

_____

Answers: No right or wrong answers.

3.9 Identify the Portfolio Value in an Initiative

Agile is all about value delivery, but unfortunately, many people do not know how to identify and measure value. Value management at the portfolio level has been proposed as an appropriate way to enhance the benefits from initiatives, particularly when involving multiple stakeholders. The literature highlights the need for guidance on understanding and measuring value. The need to widen the definitions of portfolio value is being proposed and more comprehensive definitions of portfolio value are starting to be applied in empirical research. With the recognition of the multiple dimensions of strategic value expected from the agile portfolio, there is a need to delve deeper and continue to find better ways to comprehensively identify and measure portfolio values. By focusing only on the financial value of the portfolio, organizations may not be allocating and developing their resources with a long-term vision and may be missing out on strategic opportunities.

Table 3.17   Identify the Portfolio Value in an Initiative High-Level Overview

	Strategic Planning		Initiative/Operations		
Portfolio Life-Cycle Stages	Initiation	Planning	Executing	Optimization	Monitoring and controlling
Portfolio Kanban	Funnel	Review/ analyzing	Portfolio backlog	Implementation	Done
Projectized	3.9 Identify the Portfolio Value in an Initiative				
Recurring					

Many organizations lose sight of value in their initiatives. While there are a variety of roles which are in theory tasked with ensuring value is delivered, often the responsibility ends up being diluted and not focused on. This is where the concept of value management as a distinct discipline that applies at many levels crosses many initiatives, and may be embodied in many roles. Value management occurs at multiple levels. ICAgile uses the terms "business stewardship" to refer to work done at the level of a single initiative/project/team and "value management" to apply to a wider portfolio-level focus.

It is important to relate value management to the agile manifesto (see Section 3.1): "Agile is a Mindset, outlined by a set of values in the Agile Manifesto". We seek to understand how the agile manifesto influences the way we undertake value management at the portfolio level. The application of value management is in the frameworks (see Chapter 4) conducted with various agile flavours.

Value management at the portfolio level is important as value management drives decision-making. Where there are more initiatives to be funded than funds available, and where there are choices to be made about the sequence of initiatives, portfolio management is used to decide between the initiatives. This implies an understanding of the common tradeoff decisions which need to be made at the portfolio level.

Value management is about outcomes, not just benefits, which is covered later in this chapter. Also, it is important to consider that value is time, cost, or delay, and understanding urgency, which is also covered in this chapter.

Value management consist of six step which are illustrated below. The first three steps are elaborated upon in this chapter while delivering the portfolio value, confirming, and tracking are in Section 3.18.

- Identifying and assessing the portfolio value
- Ensuring portfolio value alignment with strategy
- Planning the portfolio value
- Delivering the portfolio value
- Confirming the portfolio value
- Tracking and reporting on the portfolio value

3.9.1 Identifying and Assessing the Portfolio Value

The aspects of value consist, according to Jim Highsmith, of product, quality, and constraints. The value of the product is the mind and experience of the customer and the flow of value. The common approach to identifying and assessing the product value is using financial metrics commonly found in the business case which are described in Section 3.15.

Understanding quality in relation to value is understanding that the fastest path to value is to focus on quality; and on the hazards and long-term risks of incurring technical (quality) debt. This puts emphasis on the importance of everyone "owning" quality and the high risk of poor quality and incurring technical debt.

The third aspect of value is constraining, and the use of constraints, which are time, cost, quality, scope, risk, and suchlike. The constraints influence one another, so it is of great value if time can be reduced in the development as it may impact the needed costs and suchlike.

First, we stated that value consists of product, quality, and constraints. However, we also need to understand how value is perceived and measured from the customer's perspective and ensures that the customers does not fall into the trap of being an order taker but leverages high-performance questions and interview techniques to ensure a clear and consistent measure of value; and common language and currency of value enables and empowers all team members to make value-informed decisions and understand how they each can create optimal value.

3.9.2 Ensuring Portfolio Value Alignment with Strategy

We need to identify and assess value to plan it, keep track of it, and obtain it. The value alignment needs to fit with the strategy (see later in this chapter for more details).

The agile portfolio is focused on delivering, managing, and measuring continuous customer value with tight business strategy alignment and optimal investment intensity. This implies the importance of aligning organizational structure and initiatives outcomes with strategy, customer, and business value and how to measure and manage value against constraints. The following steps can be applied:

- Identify/confirm strategic drivers
- Align objectives with drivers
- Identify what we can measure
- Gather facts (as-is)
- Define target measures (to-be)
- Measure value

3.9.3 Planning the Portfolio Value

Planning the portfolio value is all about ensuring the value identified, assessed, and aligned with the strategy is delivered in the right order with the highest-ranked initiatives first. Planning can take place in the portfolio backlog as backlog refinement, applying ranking, prioritization, and such-like. Backlog management can be supported by various techniques to support the various portfolio decisions.

These are some of the common techniques:

■ Purpose alignment model
■ KANO analysis
■ Chartering
■ Value-stream mapping
■ Customer-valued prioritization
■ Relative prioritization
■ Product roadmap
■ Risk-adjusted backlog

Let me illustrate how this could work out. We have a bunch of epics which we rank based upon business value as illustrated in Table 3.18. In addition, we estimate them using the Fibonacci scale and measure costs. To measure costs, one way is to figure out the costs of the team, then based upon velocity calculate cost for each story point. This team has 5 team members, each having an hourly rate of US$100. The sprint is 2 weeks. One week is

Table 3.18   Planning the Value

Business Value	Epic	Cost	Estimate	Kano
5	Epic 1.2	1,600 US$	8	Delighters
5	Epic 1.3	1,600 US$	8	Delighters
3	Epic 1.4	1,000 US$	5	Satisfiers
5	Epic 2.1	600 US$	3	Satisfiers
1	Epic 2.2	1,000 US$	5	Satisfiers
2	Epic 2.3	400 US$	2	Delighters
5	Epic 3,1	200 US$	1	Dissatisfiers
1	Epic 3.2	400 US$	2	Dissatisfiers

40 hours. The team has a velocity of 40. The cost is 5 team members x 40 hours x 2 weeks x US$100 = US$8,000. US$ 8,000/40 story points = US$200. In addition, the Kano model has been added.

3.10 Portfolio-Wide Stakeholder Analysis

At the portfolio level stakeholders extend beyond those identified for any single initiative. Stakeholders in the portfolio need to be identified and their interests protected. In this chapter we will cover how to build an understanding of the stakeholders across the value stream; to articulate who the stakeholders and how their needs are identified. This includes techniques to evaluate organization-wide stakeholders.

3.10.1 Core Concepts of Portfolio Stakeholder Analysis

Stakeholder management is the process of identify and analyzing stakeholders, which is conducted by the product owner and conveyed to the team to ensure the solution fits the stakeholders.

3.10.2 Identify Stakeholders

Stakeholder analyses no doubt have always been important. Pulitzer Prize–winning historian Barbara Tuchman illustrates this in her sobering history *The March of Folly: From Troy to Vietnam*, which recounts a series of disastrous misadventures that followed in the footsteps of ignoring the interests of, and information held by, key stakeholders.

We need to identify stakeholders to ensure that the appropriate parties are represented, informed, and involved. Stakeholders are one of the

Table 3.19   Portfolio-Wide Stakeholder Analysis High-Level Overview

	Strategic Planning		Initiative/Operations		
Portfolio Life-Cycle Stages	Initiation	Planning	Executing	Optimization	Monitoring and controlling
Portfolio Kanban	Funnel	Review/ analyzing	Portfolio backlog	Implementation	Done
Projectized					
Recurring	**3.10 Portfolio-Wide Stakeholder Analysis**				

key sources for requirements and for this you need to know the number of stakeholders that you are eliciting information from. By knowing the number, you can determine which elicitation techniques work best.

Stakeholders are vital for project success. Some may recall the butterfly effect, where a butterfly may spread it wings in China and cause a flood in Europe. Stakeholders, identified and analyzed or not, have a similar ability to influence the project.

Stakeholders are not donkeys; however, let us start with the tale of two donkeys. The two donkeys as illustrated in Figure 3.6 were bound by a rope and unable to reach their food. When both donkeys moved in opposite directions, neither of the donkeys were able to reach their food. At some stage one of the donkeys moved toward the other donkey and they were able to eat half of the food before moving together to the second part of the food.

This story highlights the importance of stakeholders and the need to know how they move and what kind of food triggers them. If stakeholders move in opposite directions with conflicting requirements, then the products cannot be scoped. If the stakeholders can agree on the goals and scope and move in the same direction the road ahead can clearly be described by the product owner to the team.

Surveys of more than 8,000 projects show that most project failures involve stakeholder problems (Johnson and Johnson, 1999). Stakeholder management is the process of identifying the right stakeholders and ensuring the stakeholders' engagement in the project or activities.

PMI (2017) defines a stakeholder as "An individual, group, or organization who may affect, be affected by, or perceive itself to be affected by a decision, activity, or outcome of a project".

An alternative definition by Freeman et al. (2007) is that "A stakeholder in an organization is (by definition) any group or individual who can affect or is affected by the achievement of the organization's objectives". The fundamental problem of stakeholder management is a failure to see that the needs of each stakeholder group, including shareholders, are different and that different means best meet these needs (Figure 3.7).

Figure 3.6   Two donkeys.

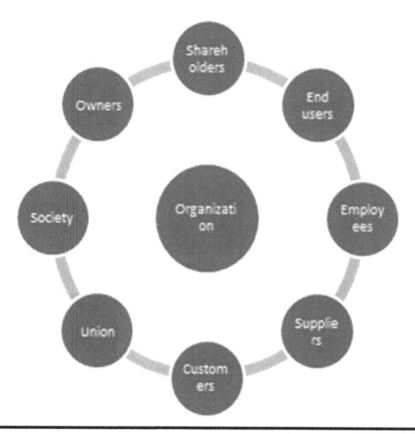

Figure 3.7   Stakeholders.

The fundamental problem of stakeholder management is a failure to see that the needs of each stakeholder group, including shareholders, are different; and that for the best results, all these different needs must be met accordingly. In simple terms, this means that a stakeholder is a person or an organization that has a direct or indirect influence on the requirements of the system, and is essential in requirements management, as well as being the most important source of requirements. The stakeholders are those who are affected by the success or failure of the solution. They are the users or customers that may approve the solution and have an interest in it.

That said, it simply means that a stakeholder is a person or an organization that has a direct or indirect influence on the requirements of the system and is essential in requirements engineering and the most important source of requirements. The stakeholders are those who are affected by the success or failure of the solution. They are the users, the customers, may sign off on the solution, and have an interest in the solution.

Several tools and techniques for identifying stakeholders involve documentation analysis or organization charts which PMI defines as organization process assets. "Plan, processes, policies, procedures, and knowledge bases that are specific to and used by the performing organization".

Some stakeholders would most likely be identified as external stakeholders who may have influence or control over the enterprise environment factors which are "Conditions, not under the immediate control of the team, that influence, constrain, or direct the project, programme, or portfolio". Table 3.20 contains a list of some of the commonly used techniques to identify the right stakeholders.

Table 3.20   Techniques for Identifying Stakeholders

Technique	Description
Brainstorming	Brainstorming is a group or individual creativity technique by which efforts are made to find stakeholders by gathering a list of possible stakeholders spontaneously contributed by its member(s)
Brainwriting	A written form of brainstorming where each participant writes one stakeholder on a piece of paper before passing it on
Interviews	One-on-one interview, i.e., ask your sponsor
SWOT analysis	Strengths, weakness, opportunities, and threats
PEST/PESTLE	Political, economic, social, and technological analysis, legal and environment
Pre-mortem	The team imagines that a project or organization has failed or succeed, and then works backward to determine what stakeholders could lead to the success or failure of the project or organization
Change of perspective – Edward de Bono's *Six Thinking Hats*	Sequence of methods for the identification of stakeholders Clarification of the situation Putting on the white hat to collect facts and figures relevant to the topic (flipchart, post-it on pin wall) Putting on the black hat, e.g., to identify stakeholders
Analogy	Comparison with similar projects Documentation analysis and prior product owner experience
Organization chart	Examine the organization chart for relevant stakeholders
Onion model	See Figure 3.8
Analyzing the context of the project	This will be covered in next chapter

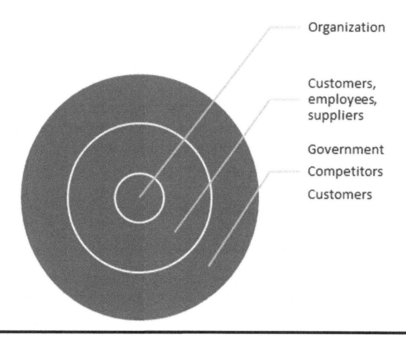

Organization

Customers,
employees,
suppliers

Government

Competitors

Customers

Figure 3.8   Onion model.

The onion model (Figure 3.8) comes from the two-tier Freeman et al. (2007) model, which is a common way to show the findings in terms of primary and secondary stakeholders of the project.

3.10.3 Analyze Portfolio Stakeholders

Stakeholders are identified as a source for requirement. Next is the stakeholder analysis which is defined as "A technique of systematically gathering and analyzing quantitative and qualitative information to determine whose interests should be taken into account throughout the project".

Stakeholder analysis takes place during the identifications of the stakeholder process; however, this section will emphasize obtaining information on the stakeholders to determine stakeholders' values regarding the product using elicitation techniques to provide a baseline for prioritizing requirements.

The next step of stakeholder management would include a quality assessment of clauses of the different stakeholders. In this case, the methods for mapping are Mitchell et al.'s (1997) framework, which divides the stakeholders in respects of power, legitimacy, and urgency as illustrated in Figure 3.9. The numbers illustrate whether or not the stakeholders hold power and/or legitimacy and/or urgency. The only types of stakeholders holding them

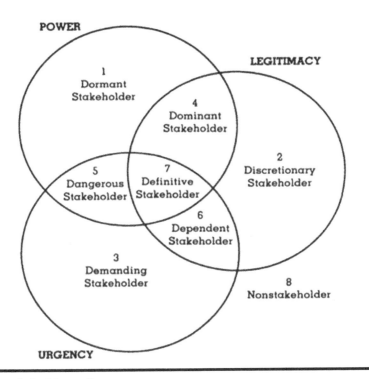

Figure 3.9   Stakeholder salience.

Table 3.21   How Stakeholders Interact

Relationship Type	Allied	Cooperative	Neutral	Competitive	Threatening
Relationship	Cooperative Strategic				
Trust		Knowledge-based trust			
Communication			Direct content		
Learning				Single loop	
Power	Exceptionally low				Extremely high

all are represented by the number seven. In terms of additional knowledge of the stakeholder's relationships, do they have something at risk, or moral claims that may be of value? This approached is defined as "stakeholder salience".

The stakeholder analysis also needs to take into consideration how stakeholders interact. Table 3.21 illustrates this with five types of relationship and five variables such as trust and power, which should be tailored to your situation.

However, a range of techniques for analyzing stakeholders should be known and employed by the professional product owner. Table 3.22 highlights the major techniques that are used to analyze stakeholders. The techniques are, to some degree, illustrated in the following part.

The power-and-interest grid is a common technique, as it can be used to manage the stakeholders actively to keep them satisfied and, in general, keep them onside, informed, and even to ignore some with little power and interest. Table 3.23 illustrates this mode.

Table 3.22   Major Techniques That Are Used to Analyze Stakeholders

Technique	Description
Power/interest grid	See below
Extended power/interest GRID	See below
Stakeholder influence diagram	A variation of the onion model
Network model	Use the onion model with arrows
Onion models/diagram	Use the onion model with arrows
CATWOE	Customer, actor, transformation, world view, owner, environment
VOCATE	Viewpoint, owner, customer, actor, transformation, and environment
PARADE	Perspective, activity, recipient, actor, decision-maker, and Environment
Responsibility Assignment Matrix (RAM)	A grid that shows the project resources assigned to each work package.
Outline your stakeholders' personalities.	MBTI, Belbin, DISC, Strength based leadership
Learning style	Are they visual people? Auditory people? Kinesthetic people? Everyone has a primary learning and interaction style. Knowing your stakeholders' preferred style puts you in a better position to tailor your message to your audience.
RACI	A common type of responsibility assignment matrix that uses responsible, accountable, consult, and informs statuses to define the involvement of stakeholders in project activities.

Table 3.23 Power/Interest Grid

Level of Power	High power/low interest	High power/high interest
	Low power/low interest	Low power/low interest
	Level of Interest	

Table 3.24 Extended Power/Interest Grid

Power/ Influence	*High*	*High power/low interest*		*High power/high interest*
	Medium	*Medium power/low–high interest*		
	Low	*Low power/low interest*		*Low power/medium– high Interest*
		Low	Medium	High
		Level of Interest		

If the stakeholder analysis process is more extensive or complex, it may be useful to use the extended power-and-interest grid, which has a higher degree of detail, to analyze it (illustrated in Table 3.24).

The onion model or onion diagram is also a common methodology for analyzing stakeholders. The concept is to identify the stakeholders, and the impact for the stakeholders. The closer you get to the centre, the higher is the impact for the stakeholders. The stakeholder influence diagram is a variant of the onion models. Figure 3.10 illustrates this.

So far, stakeholder analysis has focused on getting more insights into the stakeholder; however, an important part of this process is also the focus of roles and responsibilities. With the stakeholders, we need to know who is doing what. The techniques to use are the RACI and responsibility assignment matrix, both of which link resources to work that needs to be done. A less common variant of the RAM and RACI is the RASCI model which includes responsible, accountable, supportive, consulted, and informed. Table 3.25 illustrates the RASCI.

In total, the work of the product owner in identifying and assessing stakeholders with the team would most likely include most of the tasks listed and the results would be categorized in a matrix for stakeholder managements.

- Brainstorm who are the key stakeholders and why.
- List potential stakeholders or form pairs of clusters of stakeholders.
- Differentiate and group stakeholders.
- Determine stakeholder influence and importance.

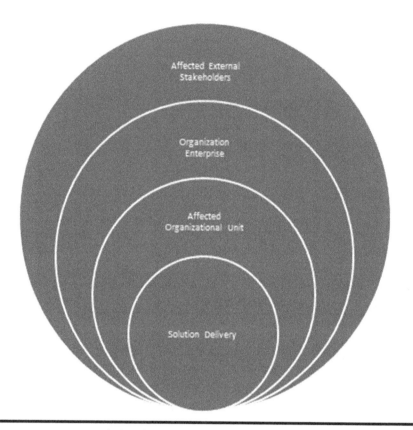

Figure 3.10 Impact on stakeholders.

Table 3.25 RASCI

	Sponsor	Project Manager	Product Owner
Plan stage	A	I	R/C
Approve change request	S	R	C/I

- Address stakeholder perception.
- Identify conflicting ideas and shared views on the problematic situation.
- Clarify key stakeholders' objectives.
- Identifying shared and conflicting objectives.
- Identify their roles.
- Assess performance in each role.
- Identify gaps and overlaps.
- Develop criteria for assessing linkage.
- For each stakeholder list their information needs.
- For each stakeholder check whether stakeholders receive the information they need Indicate the likely gains or losses.

3.11 Align All Work to the Strategy

A strategy expresses how a business competes in the market against the competition and constitutes a set of ends with accompanying means. The portfolio is an application of those means where initiatives are generally the primary tool to actualize the overall goals and ultimately the business strategy. The portfolio is thus crucial for the implementation of strategy and the alignment is essential to the realization of organizational value through the portfolio. The portfolio is regarded as the manifestation of business strategy and should reflect the relative emphasis on technologies, markets, and products the business pursues. Strategic alignment is often cited as one of the main goals of the portfolio and as a main benefit. The connection between the portfolio and business strategy is well documented and its importance is broadly stressed. When made a priority, the portfolio can be an effective means to fulfilling strategy and ought therefore to be considered in the strategic management process, whose effectiveness is a prerequisite for strategic alignment. Backlog management in line with strategy positively correlates to the performance of the portfolio, and it is associated with both customer satisfaction and financial results. Also, the more strategic alignment you have in the portfolio, the more autonomy you can grant, which is increasingly important in an agile environment.

Strategic alignment is usually discussed as the act of ensuring initiatives provide movement in the overall strategic direction. Some (Dietrich and Lehtonen, 2005) talk about the concept of strategic fit, which considers the initiatives alignment with strategy and how well the portfolio mirrors the business strategy. This means in practice that the backlog periodically needs to be reviewed to ensure its alignment with strategy.

Table 3.26   Align All Work to the Strategy High-Level Overview

	Strategic Planning		*Initiative/Operations*		
Portfolio Life-Cycle Stages	*Initiation*	*Planning*	*Executing*	*Optimization*	*Monitoring and controlling*
Portfolio Kanban	Funnel	Review/ analyzing	Portfolio backlog	Implementation	Done
Projectized	3.11 Align All Work to the Strategy				
Recurring					

3.11.1 Core Concepts of Strategy Alignment

Strategy alignments focus on strategic vision/planning, aligning all work in the backlog to the strategy. Various terminology exists, some starting with strategies which are aligned with objectives and key results (OKRs) that consist of initiatives found in the backlog. In Section 3.18 on metrics, we discuss going from vision/strategy/goals/objectives to critical success factors to key performance indicators to metrics. OKRs are important to create clarity about what represents value for the business and its customers.

The book *Executing Your Strategy*, published by Harvard Business School Press (2008), explains strategy by taking outset in the purpose as illustrated in Figure 3.11.

On a more practical level, the strategic alignment model in Figure 3.12 illustrates how a value/mission is divided into goals (A, B, and C). The goals are then split into objectives (1,2,3,4, and 5). The objectives are then applied for creating projects or initiatives.

The following illustrate some techniques to ensure strategic alignment in an agile portfolio.

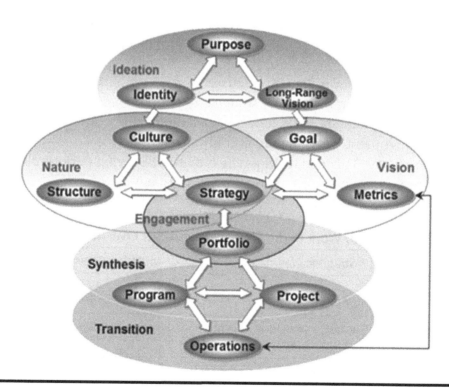

Figure 3.11   Executing your strategy.

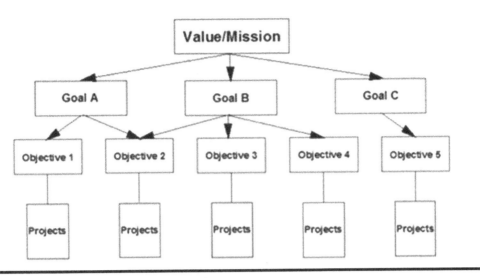

Figure 3.12   Strategy alignment model.

3.11.2 *Hoshin Planning*

Hoshin Kanri is the Japanese term for policy deployment. Hoshin is composed of two characters: *Ho* means "method or form", *Shin* means "shiny needle or compass". Taken together, Hoshin means a "methodology for strategic direction setting" and Kanri means "management" or "control", short for Hoshin planning which:

- Provides a step-by-step planning, implementation, and review process for managed and sustainable change
- Facilitates a set of coordinated processes to accomplish the core objectives of the business
- Clarifies annual target policies derived from long- and medium-term policies that encompass the long-term visions of the company
- Translates organizational goals to actions based on priorities determined by management
- Aligns goals of individuals teams and functions to those of the organization
- Tracks resource allocation to tasks and goals

3.12 Estimation of Initiatives

Agile estimation is the fine art of guessing, and is about setting expectations (Stellman et al., 2011), and about the time required by each participant,

Table 3.27   Estimation of Initiatives High-Level Overview

Portfolio Life-Cycle Stages	Strategic Planning		Initiative/Operations		
	Initiation	Planning	Executing	Optimization	Monitoring and controlling
Portfolio Kanban	Funnel	Review/ analyzing	Portfolio backlog	Implementation	Done
Projectized	3.12 Estimation of Initiatives				
Recurring					

including the stakeholders, the team members, and the organization's management to complete the work. If those expectations are not realistic from the beginning of the initiatives, the stakeholders will not trust the portfolio management and delivery team. Estimation is all about reducing the uncertainty to a minimum, measuring the effort needed to complete the initiatives in the portfolio, and at the same time, taking the complexity of the initiative into account.

In the Agile Manifesto for Software Development, the value and principle of individuals and interactions over processes and tools has a strong emphasis on communication, management, and commitment, which are utilized during estimation process.

Principles of agile estimation emphasize that estimates in knowledge work are almost never accurate but can assist in planning and forecasting team efforts. Estimates are completed exceedingly early in the process, which results in a higher degree of uncertainty, while estimates during development of the work are far less uncertain. This is called the "cone of uncertainty". The cone of uncertainty reminds us of how greatly our estimates can vary at different stages throughout the initiative.

Given that an agile approach is best suited and best applied toward initiatives where uncertainty is the norm and change is an expected part of the delivery process, the agile enterprise seeks to value accuracy over precision. This means that the organization must learn to make commitments at higher levels of abstraction and set delivery windows that reflect the inherent uncertainty in the process. When cost and date considerations are the primary concerns, care must be taken to help the organization converge on the optimal business outcomes possible, given the rate of change.

3.12.1 Agile Estimation Is Based on the Relative Size of the Increments of Value Under Consideration

The concept of agile estimation uses techniques and estimation granularity appropriate for each level of planning. Agile estimation techniques rarely use the past to estimate and predict the future of a knowledge work item, due to the nature of our work. However, it is important to find methods for resolving estimation conflicts within the portfolio or the delivery team when estimates are substantially different. Working agile implies a constant stream of new information and learning which puts heavy emphasis on the constant need for re-estimating. Re-estimating may change the organization's expectations around re-estimation and how to manage new emerging estimates against promised deadlines.

Traditional or plan-based estimating techniques are based upon absolute estimates while agile estimating is mostly based upon relative estimation. The benefits of relative estimating are:

■ Estimating is faster
■ Good for comparing
■ Consensus driven
■ Relative size does not change
■ Unit measure does not matter

3.12.2 Core Concepts of Estimation Techniques

This section contains a wide range of estimation techniques which can be applied to an agile portfolio for estimation of initiatives, epics or, later, the team level.

3.12.3 Relative Sizing

Relative sizing is an agile estimating method of estimation of scales. Some practitioners prefer to apply relative sizing using Fibonacci numbers, i.e., 0,1,2,3,5,8,13,21,34,55,89,144; but options on this scale are many. The concept of relative sizing is to estimate the size of an initiative, epic, or user story based on the size of another one.

Let me illustrate this using the example of cars. This example includes four types of cars; Tata Nano, Toyota Prius, McLaren F1, and the Bugatti Veyron Super Sports, which we had sequenced in relative cost, meaning the

Tata Nano is the cheapest car while the Bugatti is the most expensive car of the four. Then we need to consider how much more expensive the Toyota Prius is as compared to the Tata Nano where our estimate is, say, 14 times. The same goes for the other car which we are comparing to the Tata Nano. Then, if we estimate that the Tata Nano costs US$5,000 and takes five days to build, then we will know that the Toyota Prius would cost US$5,000 × 14 = US$70,000 and take 70 days to build. Our estimate is a quick relative sizing of items compared to the other items.

3.12.4 Wideband Delphi

The original version of the Delphi method was first applied in the 1960s. The concept was to ask a range of experts for an estimate. The experts were not located in the same place and could not communicate and influence the other experts' estimates. This method clearly had some strengths and weaknesses that the later method of Wideband Delphi tried to overcome.

One of the issues with the original Delphi method was the wide range of assumptions the experts used to estimate. Because the experts were unable to communicate with one another, all estimates may have had different assumptions, potentially weakening the estimates. The Wideband Delphi is a process which enables a group of people to generate an estimate. The portfolio manager appoints an estimation team, and gains consensus from that team on the results. Wideband Delphi is a repeatable estimation process because it consists of a straightforward set of steps that can be performed in the same way each time:

- Team selection
- Kickoff meeting
- Individual preparation
- Estimation session
- Tasks assembly

Exercise 3.4 Wideband Delphi

A variant of the Wideband Delphi method is the triangular distribution (simple average) and beta distribution (weighted average) variant where the triangular distribution is the optimistic, pessimistic, and realistic all added up and then divided by three. This team is using the triangular distribution. What is their estimate?

1. Estimate 3 ____
2. Estimate 8 ____
3. Estimate 5 ____

_____

_____

_____

Answers: 5 (3+5+8/3)

The weighted average or beta distribution gives higher value to the realistic estimate which is multiple by four and the sum of the six estimates are then added up and the total is divided by six. This team is using the weighted average. What is their estimate?

1. Estimate 3 ____
2. Estimate 8 ____
3. Estimate 40 ____

_____

_____

_____

Answers: 13 (3+(4×8)+40)/6

3.12.5 Results Review

After the team of estimators is chosen, a kickoff meeting takes place where the story points or items to estimate are discussed, along with any assumptions or other considerations. After this meeting, all estimators have time for individual preparation where the actual initial estimates are completed by the estimators without the influence of the other estimators. All estimators then assemble in an estimation session where they discuss their estimates. This may complete the process if estimates are close and can be agreed upon. If not, the process may run again to narrow down the estimates. The Delphi technique is also good for agile teams because it uses:

- An iterative process which is repeated
- An adaptive process based upon feedback
- A collaborative process based on team participants

3.12.6 Agile Portfolio Poker aka Planning Poker

Planning poker is one of those agile estimation methods that may cause some veteran traditional portfolio managers to smile a bit, as it is an estimation made while playing cards. Agile portfolio poker utilizes the portfolio members' experience (multiple expert opinions), applies other methods such as brainstorming (averaging individuals), fosters communication (live dialogues), increases learning within the group – and don't forget it is fun! Agile portfolio poker is a highly effective Delphi approach that works in the following way:

- Individual stories are presented for estimation.
- After a session of discussion, each participant chooses from his or her own deck the numbered card that represents his or her estimate of how much work is involved in the story under discussion.
- All estimates are kept private until each participant has chosen a card.
- Finally, all estimates are revealed, and discussion resumes.

Like relative sizing, agile portfolio poker is an estimating technique used to achieve consensus on estimates. The estimators use a set of cards with Fibonacci numbers of 0,1,2,3,5,8,13,21,34,55,89,144. An initiative, epic or item is presented for the group of estimators. They discuss the content of the units. Cards are shown and the estimators are asked to come to an agreement on the relative size of the units.

Exercise 3.5 Planning Poker

Estimate the size in acres of the following countries. Egypt is 5 as a starting point. The planning pokers card in this exercise has the following values: 0,1,2,5,8,20,40, and 100.

1. Mexico ____
2. France ____
3. Yemen ____
4. Canada ____
5. Fiji ____

_____

_____

_____

Answers: 8, 2, 2, 40, 0

3.12.7 Affinity Estimating – High-Level Sizing

Affinity estimating aims at triangulation and is an easy method to remember because it reminds us of T-shirts, buckets, or coffee cups that range in size

Table 3.28 Story Range

Story points	S	M	L	XL	XXL
T-shirt sizes	2	3	5	8	13

from S, M, L to XL aligned with units as illustrated in Table 3.28. Affinity estimating applies to relative sizing, as two small stories may require as much time as a medium-sized story, while two medium-sized stories may require the same as one large story and so forth. Whether a story takes x number of hours is irrelevant, as it is all about relative sizing. In the end, the team must decide the number of stories to be conducted during a sprint such as four XL stories that are composed of several smaller stories.

An alternative estimation technique by Lowell Lindstrøm is also suitable for arriving at a high-level estimate of a big feature list (product/portfolio backlog) or initiatives that contains more than 20 items. The steps are:

■ Silent relative sizing
■ Wikipedia-like editing of wall
■ Placement of items into relative size buckets
■ Product owner "challenge"
■ Documentation in an electronic tool

The first step in the process is the silent relative sizing where team members in silence take a subset from the product backlog and place it on the board in ascending order. This step may take five to ten minutes. The second step is an editing process where the backlog is read again for discussion and possible changes are made in order. This step may take 20 to 40 minutes to complete.

Now the items on the board will be placed in buckets of varying size, i.e., small, medium, or large. The product owner challenge is an exercise where the product owner and his or her supporters play the devil's advocate role. This involves asking all kinds of questions about the content of the board and having the team rethink their order. The questions should not be disrespectful; they should simply challenge the decisions and order on the board. If the team decides upon the challenge to reorder, they can do so. This step may take up to an hour. The last step is documentation of the results, often with the help of an electronic tool.

Elatta (2013) has developed a variation of affinity estimation using complexity buckets as a consistent way of sizing stories. Each story is valued in terms of user interface, business logic, data/integration, and testing. The values of each story are ranked from low, medium, high to complex, which is designated with values of none, 1, 2, 3, and 4. A complex story, in terms of user interface, is given the value of 4. Each story receives points ranging from none to 16, which are divided into buckets of various sizes and the bucket with the total score of 3 possibly being called medium.

Exercise 3.6 Affinity Estimating – High-Level Sizing

Estimate the richest people in the world based upon 2014 data from Forbes. The measurements are T-shirt sizes and Warren Buffett is size M. The T-shirt sizes in this exercise are S, M, and L.

1. Carlos Slim Helú ____
2. Larry Ellison ____
3. Lakshmi Mittal ____
4. Bill Gates ____
5. Bernard Arnault ____

_____
_____
_____

Answers: L, S, S, L, and M.

3.12.8 Estimation of Initiatives with Fixed Scope

The portfolio may contain a fixed scope of initiatives that need to be completed. In that case, we may have 200 units, and teams with a collective velocity of 50, meaning initiatives need to be divided into four sprints as 200/50 = 4. Based upon size, i.e., 200 units, we derive duration, if velocity is known.

3.12.9 Estimation of Initiatives with Fixed Schedule

The portfolio may contain 200 units of initiatives, and teams with a collective velocity of 50; however, only two sprints (fixed schedule) are available to conduct these initiatives meaning that 100 units may be developed. In that circumstance the portfolio management needs to consider which initiatives should be developed and which will not be done.

3.12.10 Disaggregation

Disaggregation refers to splitting a story or feature into smaller, easier-to-estimate pieces. If the user stories, included in the projects, are mostly two to four days in duration, it may be difficult to make an estimate. On the other hand, we do not want all stories to be broken down to micro user stories, as it would be difficult to manage. Disaggregation is just a break-down of the user stories or features into the lowest possible and meaning-ful sizes.

3.12.11 Analogous Estimating

Analogous estimating is using actual duration or cost of previous assign-ments or initiatives as the basis for estimating the current initiative, com-bined with historical information and expert judgement. This method is used to estimate total duration when there is a limited amount of detailed information about the project. To illustrate this, the team will compare an older version with a newer version of the same system. The teams estimate that the new system is twice the size in terms of functionality of the old sys-tem, which was completed with five story points. This means that the anal-ogy estimate will be ten story points.

Exercise 3.7 Analogue Estimating

The team is going to work on similar tasks to what they previously have been working with; however, they are aware that these new tasks need 50% more effort than previous due to various factors. Fewer story points per sprint means a 20% higher cost of the team than previously. What would the following estimates look like if they were based upon analogue estimation?

1. Story point 5 _____
2. Story point 3 _____
3. Story point 8 _____
4. Budget of US$10,000 _____
5. Budget of US$20,000 _____

_____
_____
_____

Answers: 8, 5, 13, US$12,000, and US$24,000.

3.12.12 Parametric Estimating

Parametric estimating is an estimation model, which is based on cor-relation of cost and variables such as weight, size, type of assembly, etc.

The benefits are that this method can produce higher levels of accuracy depending upon the sophistication and underlying data. In addition, it can be applied to a total project or to segments of a project. However, parametric estimating, in most cases, would be more accurate than analogous estimating. Nevertheless, there is a risk that historical data may not accurately represent the current business case. For example, the price of a house is US$12,000 per square metre. The new house has a size of 300 square metres resulting in an estimate of US$3,600,000. Combining this with a regression analysis and the tools may work wonders for your business case.

Exercise 3.8 Parametric Estimating

You know the cost of one team of seven people is US$10,000 per week. A sprint is two weeks. Cadence is five sprints. What is the cost of?

1. Two weeks, one team? _____
2. Four weeks, two teams _____
3. Full cadence for seven teams _____

_____
_____
_____

Answers: US$20,000, US$80,000, and US$700,000.

3.12.13 Expert Judgement

Expert judgement is simply a method to ask someone who is familiar with, and knowledgeable about the application area, and the technologies, to provide an estimate. Research shows that experts' judgement in practice tends to be based on analogy.

3.12.14 Programme Evaluation and Review Technique (PERT)

The programme evaluation and review technique (PERT) is a three-point estimation method based upon an optimistic and, most likely, a pessimistic estimate. The findings may be divided by three or in some cases, multiply the most likely estimates by four and then divide the result by six. To illustrate this, let us have three estimates of 15, 30, and 60 which equals 32.5 using the modified PERT technique. The Alpha method just adds them up and divides them by three, giving 35. If optimistic or pessimistic was significantly higher/lower, it would impact the result.

3.12.15 *Fist of Five or Roman Voting*

Sometimes you want people to confirm the estimation using Fist of Five or Roman Voting. Roman Voting means thumps up for confidence or thumbs down for lack of confidence while Fist of Five uses all the fingers as explained below.

The number of fingers used to vote indicates the level of agreement and desire for discussion:

■ One finger: I disagree with the group's conclusion and have major concerns.
■ Two fingers: I disagree with the group's conclusion and would like to discuss some minor issues.
■ Three fingers: I am not sure and would like to go with the group's consensus conclusion.
■ Four fingers: I agree with the group's conclusion and would like to discuss some minor issues.
■ Five fingers: I wholeheartedly agree with the group's conclusion.

Exercise 3.9 Fist of Five and Roman Voting

Think about Exercise 3.5 and if I were saying that Argentina is five story points, using Fist of Five how many fingers would you give me? If you are using just one, make sure it is the right one.

_____

_____

_____

Answers: One or two fingers.

Okay, you are right. Argentina is not five story points. I have done some research and it turned out that it is story point 21. Using Roman Voting, would you give thumbs up or thumbs down? Thumbs up, if you agree, thumbs down if you disagree.

_____

_____

_____

Answers: Thumbs down, Argentina is 13 story points.

Table 3.29   Portfolio Prioritization High-Level Overview

	Strategic Planning		Initiative/Operations		
Portfolio Life-Cycle Stages	*Initiation*	*Planning*	*Executing*	*Optimization*	*Monitoring and controlling*
Portfolio Kanban	Funnel	Review/ analyzing	Portfolio backlog	Implementation	Done
Projectized	**3.13 Portfolio Prioritization**				
Recurring					

3.13 Portfolio Prioritization – Sorting/Ranking the Portfolio

Portfolio prioritization is important to ensure that the list of things to build is prioritized so that the delivery team is working on the items that deliver the highest value first. Portfolio management needs to understand and experience techniques to prioritize the list of things to build. Initially techniques such as storyboards, user story mapping ("walking-skeleton") are useful; other methods of backlog prioritization are illustrated next. Prioritization needs to include concepts such as MMF (minimum marketable feature set) and MVP (minimum viable product). See Chapter 3 that combines to deliver value for one or more stakeholder groups.

3.13.1 Core Concepts of Portfolio "Backlog" Prioritization

When it comes to backlog prioritization a range of techniques exist with various criteria for prioritization.

3.13.2 Customer-Valued Prioritization (Business Value Versus Risk)

Customer-valued prioritization may have emphasis on business value and risk; if business value is high and risk is low, then it is a sure thing, however if business value is low and risk is high it is something to be avoided. High business value and high risk might be expected but it depends on what else is in the portfolio. Often, we seek to spread the risk.

3.13.3 Customer-Valued Prioritization (Business Value (Impact) Versus Effort)

Business value versus effort prioritization is like business value versus risk. If business value is high and effort is low, then it is good to do, while low business value and high effort hardly has a chance. If business value is high and effort is high, then we wait and see what else we got. Some use the term relative return on investment or RROI for this as it calculates business value divided by effort.

3.13.4 Dot Voting

Dot voting is the process where stakeholders and other key portfolio members simply vote once, twice, or three times with a dot from a pen on the initiative or epic to be prioritized. The initiative or epic with the most dots receives the highest ranking.

3.13.5 Relative Prioritization

Everything in agile is relative. We compare things. Should this initiative have a higher prioritization than that initiative? Perhaps, that's relative prioritization.

3.13.6 Ranking

Ranking is simply a list where all the initiative or epics are ranked from the highest to the lowest. The list may vary in length and may be ranked, based on a range of objective or subjective criteria.

3.13.7 Top Ten

A variation of the ranking technique is the Top Ten, which is similar in process. It, however, results in only the top ten initiatives or epics.

3.13.8 Single-Criterion Classification.

Single-criterion classification may be based on the amount of work it takes to complete the item, its costs, quality, or risk. The result would be a list of items ranked on a single-criterion classification.

3.13.9 Points

Various models using points exist for prioritization of a backlog. The typical concept is that key stakeholders and portfolio managers receive a certain amount of points which can be used to buy initiatives and epics. If an initiative or epic is bought, then it is prioritized for the upcoming period of work. Some techniques are called 100-points, buy-a-feature, and monopoly money.

3.13.10 Weighted Shortest Job First

This technique has become popular due to its application in scaled agile framework. Weighted shortest job first or WSJF using the factors of user value, time value, and risk reduction which are scored using the Fibonacci scale. The result is then divided by size/duration.

3.13.11 Position in the Marketplace (Early Adopters)

Some products may have a better position in the market for various reasons. This technique applies this position to rank upcoming initiatives and epics.

3.13.12 Prioritizing Using Business Value Buckets (Grouping)

You may recall affinitive estimation from Section 3.12.7 where items were placed in groups. Prioritizing using business value buckets is similar. We may use high-, medium-, and low-value buckets. We do initiatives or epics from the high-value bucket first and so forth. This is just a variant of MoSCoW.

3.13.13 MoSCoW Prioritization

According to *A Guide to the Business Analysis Body of Knowledge*, version 2.0, section 6.1.5.2, the MoSCoW categories are as follows.

Table 3.30 Weighted Shortest Job First (WSJF)

Initiative	User Value	Time Value	Risk Reduction	= Cost of Delay	Size/ Duration	Score	Ranking
Epic 1	3	8	5	16	13	1.23	3
Epic 2	5	3	3	11	5	2.2	1
Epic 3	5	5	2	12	8	1.5	2

- M – MUST: Describes an initiative or epic that must be satisfied in the final solution for the solution to be considered a success.
- S – SHOULD: Represents a high-priority item that should be included in the solution if it is possible. This is often a critical requirement but one which can be satisfied in other ways, if strictly necessary.
- C – COULD: Describes an initiative or epic which is considered desirable, but not necessary. This will be included if time and resources permit.
- W – WON'T: Represents an initiative or epic that stakeholders have agreed will not be implemented in each release but may be considered for the future.

3.13.14 Kano Analysis Classification

The Kano classification (Pohl et al., 2011) contains dissatisfiers, satisfiers, and delighters.

- Dissatisfiers – must be fulfilled by the system; completely fulfilled dissatisfiers help to avoid massive discontent, dominantly influenced by existing systems.
- Satisfiers – consciously known and explicitly demanded, fulfilled satisfiers bring contentment and satisfaction; any missing property can lead to product unacceptability. Satisfaction decreases with each missing satisfier.
- Delighters – properties of a system are recognized only on using the system.

3.13.15 Karl Wieger's Relative Weighting

Karl Wieger's relative weighting prioritization matrix is like the Kano. Both include the relative benefits of a feature present and the negative impact

Table 3.31 MoSCoW Prioritization

Initiative	User Value	Prioritization
Epic 1	3	MUST
Epic 2	5	MUST
Epic 3	5	SHOULD
Epic 4	8	COULD
Epic 5	5	WON'T

or relative penalty of a feature not present. Relative Weight may include all kinds of weights.

3.14 Bottlenecks and Cost of Delays

An agile portfolio should be a smooth-running Kanban machine with initiatives and epics with small batch sizes coming in; queues are managed and WIP is constrained and suchlike by Reinertsen (2009) descriptions. We seek to avoid large initiatives in a portfolio backlog which creates queues or bottlenecks. However, that is easier said than done. When multitasking, some sort of processing bottleneck happens in a person's brain. Some might have tried the coin game or the Multitasking Name Game (Kniberg, 2011) where we measure how long it takes to write a name. When no one waits (all at the same time) taking one letter at a time (no customer waits) or taking one at a time (one customer at a time) the rest will have to wait. Bottlenecks, queues, multitasking, task switching, overloads and suchlike is waste. Something organizations changed prioritizes and focus on something else, often a whole new and fancy topic, technology, opportunity, goal, or strategy, it is also called the "shiny object syndrome.

Many product developers assume that higher utilization leads to faster development. They neither measure nor manage the invisible queues in their process. Consequently, they underestimate the true cost of overloading their processes. Such overloads severely hurt all aspects of development performance.

going into detail, we need to recognize the importance of cost of delay. Cost of delay is a way of communicating the impact of time on the outcomes we hope to achieve. More formally, it is the partial derivative of the total expected value with respect to time. Cost of delay combines urgency and value – two things that humans are not particularly good at

Table 3.32 Bottlenecks and Cost of Delays High-Level Overview

	Strategic Planning		Initiative/operations		
Portfolio Life-Cycle Stages	Initiation	Planning	Executing	Optimization	Monitoring and controlling
Portfolio Kanban	Funnel	Review/ analyzing	Portfolio backlog	Implementation	Done
Projectized	3.14 Bottlenecks and Cost of Delays				
Recurring					

distinguishing between. To make decisions, we need to understand not just how valuable something is, but how urgent it is.

3.14.1 Core Concepts of Cost of Delays

Examining the cost of delay, we ask the question: How does the cost of delay influence the order of our initiatives? Let us turn to Kenneth Rubin (2013) who states different portfolio scheduling principles. The categories are cost of delay, duration/size, and scheduling approach. Table 3.33 is adapted based upon his work. Depending on whether it is the same or different across the products, then various scheduling approaches are recommended.

> **Exercise 3.10 Calculating the Cost of Delay**
>
> This exercise has been created by Planview (2020) and is adapted here. The options are no priority (do everything at once and complete them all at the same time), duration priority (tackle the backlog based on delivery duration, starting with the shortest duration), value priority (tackle the backlog based on value, starting with the highest value feature), or cost of delay priority (tackle the backlog based on CD3, starting with the highest cost of delay).
>
> If you work on all the features at once, it will be 23 weeks until you see any value. Therefore, you eat the value of each feature for the full 23 weeks. That means you lose the entire US$18,000 each week for 23 weeks, for a total of US$414,000 cost of delay. Which options to choose and why? Support your answer with data (**Table 3.34a–d**).

The next step is the cost of delays profile as costs over time varies. One profile is large, fixed costs meaning that cost is high and constant. Initiatives with this cost of delay profile should be prioritized high while initiatives with intangible cost of delay profile would take much longer to reach the same high cost of the large fixed-cost cost of delay profile. The various cost of delay profiles are illustrated in Figure 3.13 which is adapted from

Table 3.33   Different Portfolio Scheduling Principles

Cost of Delay	Duration/Size	Approach
Same across all initiatives	Varies across initiatives	Shortest job first
Varies across initiatives	Same across all initiatives	High delay cost first
Varies across initiatives	Varies across initiatives	Weighted shortest job first

Table 3.34a   Exercise – Calculating the Cost of Delay

Feature	Duration	Value	Cost of Delay
A	4 weeks	US$1,500	0.375
B	2 weeks	US$2,000	1
C	10 weeks	US$8,500	0.85
D	7 weeks	US$6,000	0.857
Total	23 weeks	US$18,000	N/A

Table 3.34b   Exercise – Calculating the Cost of Delay (Duration Priority)

Feature	Duration	Value	Costs
B	2 weeks	US$2,000	2 × US$2,000 = US$ 4,000
A	4 weeks	US$,500	6 × US$1,500 = US$ 9,000
D	7 weeks	US$6,000	13 × US$6,000 = US$ 78,000
C	10 weeks	US$8,500	23 × US$8,500 = US$ 195,500
Total			US$286,500

Table 3.34c   Exercise – Calculating the Cost of Delay (Value Priority)

Feature	Duration	Value	Costs
C	10 weeks	US$8,500	10 × US$8,500 = US$ 85,000
D	7 weeks	US$6,000	17 × US$6,000 = US$ 102,000
B	2 weeks	US$2,000	19 × US$2,000 = US$ 38,000
A	4 weeks	US$1,500	23 × US$1,500 = US$ 34,500
Total			US$259,500

Table 3.34d   Exercise – Calculating the Cost of Delay (Cost of Delay Priority)

Feature	Duration	Value	Costs
B	2 weeks	US$2,000	2 × US$2,000 = US$ 4,000
D	7 weeks	US$6,000	9 × US$6,000 = US$ 54,000
C	10 weeks	US$8,500	19 × US$8,500 = US$ 161,500
A	4 weeks	US$1,500	23 × US$1,500 = US$ 34,500
Total			US$254,500

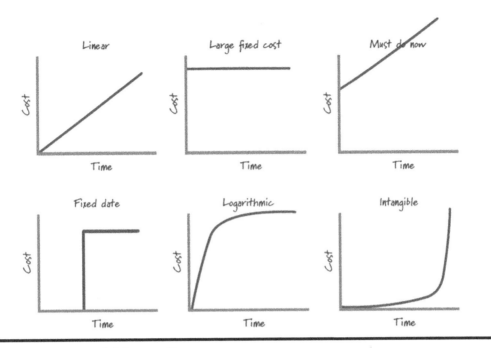

Figure 3.13 Cost of delay profiles.

Table 3.35 An Example That Could Be a Real Case Study

Week	1	2	3	4	5	6	7	8	9	10	11	12	13	14	15
Value Add	X								X						X
Risk Reduction		X							X						
Wait Waste			X	X	X	X	X			X	X	X	X	X	

Rubin (2013). The cost of delay profile is just an additional technique to rank the portfolio and supplement the techniques found in this chapter.

In the example in Table 3.34d, the cost of delay for this feature was more than US$100,000 per week! So, the ten weeks that this opportunity spent waiting in various queues cost the organization nearly US$1m in lost revenue.

3.15 Qualify Ideas for Portfolio Inclusion – the Agile Business Case

A business case says: "Here is what needs to be done" and backs it up with evidence. More neatly stated the business case provides justification for

Table 3.36 Qualify Ideas for Portfolio Inclusion High-Level Overview

	Strategic Planning		Initiative/Operations		
Portfolio Life-Cycle Stages	*Initiation*	*Planning*	*Executing*	*Optimization*	*Monitoring and controlling*
Portfolio Kanban	Funnel	Review/ analyzing	Portfolio backlog	Implementation	Done
Projectized	**3.15 Qualify Ideas for Portfolio Inclusion**				
Recurring					

undertaking an initiative, epic, or similar. It evaluates the benefit, cost, and risk of alternative options and provides a rationale for the preferred solution.

The business case is important for various reasons. Its document, the justification for the undertaking of the work, assesses the estimated costs of development and implementation and the risks versus the anticipated business benefits and savings to be gained. In addition, the business case provides the management commitment and approval for investment in business change, through rationale for the investment and enables us to monitor and measure the realization of the benefits of the initiative.

We can go one step further and align the business case with policies and strategies to document their spending objectives and deliver benefits. The business case, both as a product and a process, provides decision-makers, stakeholders, and the public with a management tool for evidence-based and transparent decision-making and a framework for the delivery, management, and performance monitoring of the resultant scheme. The business case document initiatives represent best value for money, are viable, affordable, and achievable. The business case does all that by answering all the key questions: Why, What, How, When, Where, and Who?

We have worked with the business case concept since the 1960s (Bradley, 2010) where the focus was on reducing costs, and with agile, years later, came the focus on added value. The dismal state of the business case process today is described by Gartner, who says: "Business cases are generally viewed only as documents for gaining funding. Once approved they are put away … few track the business benefits the projects actually achieve".

Some may argue our business case is obsolete; however, for many organizations we need to meet the organization return and variance threshold as funding is conditional. New information is constantly used to recalibrate return expectations and each business case needs to continuously compete with other business cases, so the business case is still needed.

This section has emphasized on the business case; however, in some organizations it may be possible to qualify ideas with less, a statement, ranking criteria, just as an epic or.

3.15.1 Core Concepts of the Agile Business Case

Many practitioners are familiar with the concept of a business case; however, we are rarely talking about the same kind of business case. It is not right or wrong, it is just that content, application, format, and size vary a lot. In some organizations a business case is comprehensive and highly detailed, sometimes more than 100 pages; others are just 20 to 30 pages, or a page, or a slide. This section will illustrate this by three approaches.

3.15.2 Old-fashioned Heavy Business Case

The old-fashioned extensive business case is a legacy from the plan-based approach where we try to examine and document all kinds of details. The common elements found in a business case are listed below:

- Project description/context
- Strategic alignment
- Financial case
- Risk assessment
- Alternative evaluation
- Project plan
- Economic case
- Stakeholder analysis
- Accountability
- Monitoring performance
- Approval and challenges
- Executive summary
- Commercial case
- Change management

3.15.3 Light Business Case

The light business case is an extensive business case but described on a few pages as common in SAFe and similar frameworks. Initiatives are based upon business cases which typically include the following content:

- Problem/opportunity
- Benefits
- Impact/opportunity missed if not done
- Description
- Scope (in, out, NFR)
- Decision factors (return, investment)
- Risk management
- Success criteria
- Sponsors
- User or market affected
- Estimation
- Dependencies

3.15.4 Better Business Case – the Iterative Development

The better business case is the model for public sector (HM Treasury, 2012) spending in the UK. The interesting part here is that it is iterative, which is a concept to be included in other formats as well. The UK approach include five sections:

- The strategic case
- The economic case
- The commercial case
- The financial case
- The management case

Each section contains a vital part of the business case. What is important here is that the first version focuses heavily on the strategic element and less on the other areas. If it is approved, then more content is added on other areas and so forth. That means if you reject a business case, little effort has been put into it and you expand the relevant content as it moves closer to approval.

3.16 Visualize and Present the Portfolio Values

Earlier chapters have illustrated how the portfolio value is identified, assessed, strategy is aligned and planned, while this chapter will emphasize delivering the portfolio value, confirming, and tracking portfolio value.

Table 3.37 Visualize and Present the Portfolio values High-Level Overview

	Strategic Planning		*Initiative/Operations*		
Portfolio Life-Cycle Stages	*Initiation*	*Planning*	*Executing*	*Optimization*	*Monitoring and controlling*
Portfolio Kanban	Funnel	Review/ analyzing	Portfolio backlog	Implementation	Done
Projectized					
Recurring	**3.16 Visualize and Present the Portfolio Values**				

3.16.1 Delivering the Portfolio Value

The portfolio Kanban section 3.4 illustrates how initiatives journey from the funnel to the implementation. At the implementation it is vital to keep focus on the supporting elements of delivering value. Using the portfolio Kanban board is of great use and techniques such as work-in-progress limits and suchlike may be helpful to reduce the number of bottlenecks when delivering.

3.16.2 Confirming the Portfolio Value

We can do all kinds of calculations, i.e., total cost of ownership or return on investment on the portfolio value based upon financial metrics found in the business case; however, some may still question how we demonstrate value. Besides the business case we may confirm value based upon productivity, performance against target, service quality, business impact, or customer satisfaction.

Customer satisfaction could imply:

- Usage metrics
- NPS (net promotor score)
- Customer and user interviews
- Social media sentiment
- Direct observation
- Profitability of the product
- Inbound customer feedback
- Prototypes
- Simulations
- Demonstrations

- IKIWISI (I will know it when I see it)
- Customer-valued prioritization

3.16.3 Tracking and Reporting on the Portfolio Value

Planning value also means tracking, articulating, or reporting on the portfolio value as organizational value is derived through multiple initiatives across multiple time horizons. Selecting which initiatives to fund is a key to maximizing outcomes. It is important to know the variety of tools for selecting which initiatives to fund, which to discard, and when to change strategic direction. This could mean enterprise architecture and other strategic frameworks, while on the initiative level focus could be on earned value management, cumulative flow diagram, risk burndown chart, and the use of the portfolio Kanban board.

3.17 Managing Portfolio Risks

If there's no risk on your next project, don't do it.

(Demarco et al., 2003)

Agile risk management is integrated into everything the team does, to maximize business value by reducing risk by guiding the team to do the hard things first. The basic problem of software development is risk (schedule slips, business misunderstood, defect rate, etc.). These risks act as a multiplier on your estimates, doubling or tripling the amount of time it takes to finish your work.

Table 3.38 Visualize and Present the Portfolio Values High-Level Overview

	Strategic Planning		Initiative/Operations		
Portfolio Life-Cycle Stages	Initiation	Planning	Executing	Optimization	Monitoring and controlling
Portfolio Kanban	Funnel	Review/ analyzing	Portfolio backlog	Implementation	Done
Projectized					
Recurring	**3.17 Managing Portfolio Risks**				

The essence of risk management lies in maximizing the areas where we have some control over the outcome while minimizing the areas where we have absolutely no control over the outcome and the linkage between effect and cause is hidden from us.

Today, risk management is more important than ever before and remains an essential discipline when managing the portfolio. The reason for this is that initiatives, to some degree, are built on assumptions, which is why the likelihood of their results becomes questionable by the management. The management would then be looking at all the factors that may influence the end results and need to be watched for, and all these factors are included under risk management.

> Risk comes from not knowing what you're doing.
>
> **Warren Buffet**

In general, the portfolio process should identify all the risks associated with the proposal, indicate the people who will have to bear those risks, and propose practical means to manage those risks. The recommended course of action that needs to be followed in order to reduce the risks is highlighted by assessing the risks in advance. Every initiative is a calculated gamble and the developer's role in writing the initiative is to articulate what is at stake (the cost), the payback (revenue), and the odds (risks). The goal of risk management is, then, to minimize the risk of a decision, not to hide away the possible risks involved within a proposal.

Risk management guides the planning of risk management activities in a structured and professional manner. Some of the first activities in this regard involve the planning of risk management, including the identification of the risks in the initiative, as well as contemplating the risks of implementing the initiative. All the possible risks need to be managed in a qualitative and quantitative approach, so that they can be analyzed accordingly. With the help of risk management, the identified risks need to be mitigated.

3.17.1 Definition of Risk

Currently we do not have a common definition of risk. Tables 3.39, 3.40, and 3.41 illustrate the negative, neutral, and broader definitions on risks accumulated by David Hillson (2004) in *Effective Opportunity Management for Projects*.

Table 3.39   Negative Definitions of Risks

Standard Documents	Definitions
British standards BS8444-3:1996	"[O]f occurrence and the consequence of a specified hazardous event".
Norges Standardiseringforbund NS5814:1991	"[T]he danger that undesirable events represent".
UK Construction Industry Research and Information Association: 1996	"[C]hance of an adverse event".
Canadian Standards Association CAN/CSA-Q85-97:1997	"[T]he chance of injury or loss".
UK CCTA MSP 1999	"Events or situations that may adversely affect the direction of the programme, the delivery of its outputs or achievement of its benefits".
US DOD DSMC 2000	"[P]otential inability to achieve overall programme objectives".
IEEE 1540:2001	"[T]he likelihood of an event, hazard, threat, or situation occurring and its undesirable consequences; a potential hazard".

Table 3.40   Neutral Definitions of Risks

Standard Documents	Definitions
UK Association for Project Management Guide 1997	"[A]n uncertain event or set of circumstances which, should it occur, will have an effect on achievements of … objectives".
Standards Australia/New Zealand AS/NZS 436:1999	"[T]he chance of something happening that will have an impact upon objectives".
British Standard PD 6668:20	"[C]hance of something happening that will have an impact upon objectives".
British Standard BS IEC 62198:2001	"[C]ombination of the probability of an event occurring and its consequences for project objectives".

Thus, we define a risk as an event that may happen, that will affect negatively or positively the success of a project. A risk, in other words, is just a future event with a probability of occurrence between 1% and 99%. On the other hand, if the probability or likelihood of an occurrence is 0% or 100%, it is not a risk, as the result is already known. Aside from the probability of its occurrence, the other aspect of risk is its impact, which can be measured in percentage or monetary values, such as US dollars.

Table 3.41   Broad Definitions of Risks

Standard Documents	Definitions
British Standard BS ISO 1006:1997	"Potential negative events and ... opportunities for improvement ... the term risk covers both".
UK Institute of Engineers Guide 1997	"[A] threat (or opportunity) which could affect adversely (or favourably) achievement of the objectives".
British Standard BS6079-1:2002 and BS6079-2000	"[C]ombination of the probability ... of a defined threat or opportunity and the magnitude of the consequences".
Project Management Institute PMBOK 2000	"[A]n uncertain event or condition that, if it occurs, has a positive or negative effect on a project objective ... includes both threats to the project's objectives and opportunities to improve on those objectives".
British Standard BSI PD ISO/IEC Guide 73:2002	"[C]ombination of the probability of an event and its consequences ... consequences can range from positive to negative".
UK Office of Government Commerce MOR 2000	"Uncertainty of outcome, whether positive opportunity or negative threat".
UK MOD Risk Management Guidance 2002	"[A] significant uncertain occurrence ... defined by the combination of the probability of an event occurring and its consequences on objectives ... the term 'risk' is generally used to embrace the possibility of both negative and/or positive consequences".

Today I tried to be positive, but it did not work.

The reasons for this thinking were illustrated by the Risk Doctor David Hillson, using Maslow's hierarchy of needs, where the basic physiological needs, safety needs, and the needs for love and belonging must be satisfied, in a form of risk management to reduce the threats and fears associated with unfulfilled needs. When the threats have been reduced or when the basic needs have been satisfied, the higher needs of esteem and self-actualization can be realized with the help of positive or negative opportunities. However, if only the basic needs are covered, portfolio managers would not seek to include higher opportunities, as they are already struggling with all the basic-level threats. For portfolio managers, a risk is a negative event that the portfolio managers seek to avoid, which is correct in most cases. However, a risk may also be a positive opportunity, which in our case, may strengthen the initiative.

3.17.2 Risk-Adjusted Backlog Reflects the Portfolio Decisions

The main principle behind a risk-adjusted backlog is to have a smart blend of value-generating business features and risk-reduction actions. This means risk-adjusted backlog equals what needs to be done and risks. The first step is to develop a prioritized list of what needs to be done using a ranking technique, i.e., MoSCoW as illustrated in Table 3.42.

3.17.3 Identifying Portfolio-Level Risks

The former United States Secretary of Defense, Donald Rumsfeld, gave a talk in 2002, to the United States of Defense, which later became known as the "known knowns", which are illustrated in Table 3.43 as the Rumsfeld matrix.

The most important part of risk management within the portfolio is identifying the risks. Some risks, the portfolio managers identify as risks that they know. Other risks, the portfolio managers know that they do not know, and some of them the portfolio managers are lucky enough to cover during various activities, but the portfolio managers are unaware of the fact that they know them. However, the challenge is how to manage the risks the portfolio managers do not know that they do not know. Unknown unknowns have some similarities with the black swan theory which is a metaphor for events that comes as a surprise and have a major effect.

Risk identification is usually based on three perspectives: past, current, and future. The past perspective lays emphasis on techniques using historical reviews, while the current perspective employs current assessments. The future perspective, on the other hand, typically involves creative techniques. Table 3.44 explains some of the techniques for risk identification along with their varying perspectives.

Table 3.42 Risk-Adjusted Backlog

Must have	Must have	Must have	Should have	Should have	Could have	Could have
Scope	Scope 1	Scope 3	Scope 2	Scope 6	Scope 4	Scope 5
ROI	US$500	US$800	US$500	US$400	US$100	US$700
Probability	20%	20%	20%	20%	10%	10%
Impact	US$200	US$200	US$300	US$300	US$50	US$400
Scope value	US$460	US$760	US$440	US$340	US$95	US$660

Table 3.43   The Rumsfeld Matrix

	Level of Observability	
Level of Risk	Known knowns (Things we know we know)	Unknown knowns (Things we do not know we know)
	Known unknowns (Things we know we do not know)	Unknown unknown (Things we do not know we do not know)

3.17.4 Assessing Portfolio-Level Risks

Assessing portfolio-level risks mainly consists of a qualitative risk analysis, but in some circumstances a quantitative assessment is also used. Table 3.45 illustrates how the risk management effort is scaled from single-point adjustment to the qualitative assessment. It also shows how, in some cases, when risks have a high-risk probability or impact which may extend the risk tolerance, the quantitative risk analysis is conducted. However, working agile implies a high degree of uncertainty.

Initially, the qualitative risk assessment or risk analysis will consider the risks identified and assess them according to the risk matrix illustrated in Table 3.46. Within this matrix, the two main variables are probability and impact. The probability is the chance or likelihood of the risk's occurrence, whereas the impact describes the consequences or damage/benefits. In this case, the risk matrix includes a scale from one to five, where five is extremely high and one is extremely low. This means that a risk with a probability and impact of five is extremely dangerous or hugely beneficial, as it is highly likely to occur and the impact is extreme.

Applying the qualitative risk management assessment matrix is an easy and quick-to-use technique to sort the possible risks into three buckets. In some circumstances, however, it can be difficult to assess the risk probability or impact score; and the more people involved in the assessment, the more variation will be found in the results. To counter this, the risk assessment matrix should be expanded with financial details or explanations, so that the impact of all the scores is clearly defined and easily understood by all. Tables 3.47 and 3.48 from the University of London (2014) illustrate how probability and impact can be described and applied in a uniform approach.

Certain risks are identified for further assessment due to: a high score on probability or impact on the qualitative assessment; high expected monetary value; or key stakeholders' or decision-makers' requirements. Whatever the reasons may be, quantitative risk management consists of a wide range of techniques.

Table 3.44 Techniques for Portfolio Risk Identification

Technique	Description	Perspective
Brainstorming	Brainstorming is a group based or individually performed creative technique, through which efforts are made to find a conclusion to a specific problem, by gathering a list of ideas spontaneously contributed by all the member(s) participating in the technique	Future
Brainwriting	A written form of brainstorming, where each participant writes one risk on a piece of paper before passing it on	Future
Interviews	One-on-one interviews on risk identification	Current
Root Cause	See above	Current
Delphi	The original version of the Delphi method was first applied in the 1960s. The concept was to ask a panel of experts to identify risks. The experts were all placed in different isolated locations so that they were unable to communicate with one another. This helped in reducing the influence of one expert's views on the other's responses	Current
Delphi, Wideband	The Wideband Delphi is a process that a team can use to identify risks. The project manager chooses an estimation team, and gains consensus from that team on the results. Wideband Delphi is a repeatable process, because it consists of a straightforward set of steps that can be performed the same way each time	Current
SWOT analysis	See above	Current
Pre-mortem	The team imagines that a project or organization has failed or succeeded, and then works backward to determine what potentially could lead to the success or failure of the project or organization	Current
Change of perspective – Edward de Bono's *Six Thinking Hats*	White hat – factual view of the subject of discussion Red hat – emotional, allows one's emotions to run wild Black hat – finds negative aspects and risks (pessimist) Yellow hat – discovers positive aspects (optimist) Green hat – creative, searches for alternatives (usual brainstorming) Blue hat – controlling and organization of the thinking process Sequence of methods for the identification of risks and opportunities: Clarification of the problem	Current

(Continued)

Table 3.44 (Continued)   Techniques for Portfolio Risk Identification

Technique	Description	Perspective
	Putting on the white hat to collect facts and figures relevant to the topic (flipchart, post-it on pin wall) Similarly, putting on all hats, one at a time, to think accordingly about the risks. For instance, putting on the black hat, for e.g., to identify risks	Past
Document centric techniques	Investigate documentation for risks, i.e., software requirement documentations, contracts, legacies, and other such documentations.	Current
Survey techniques	Interviews, qualitative and quantitative surveys	Past
Analogy techniques	The basis of the analogy technique is to describe (in terms of several variables), the project for which the risk identification is to be made, and then to use this description to find other similar projects that have already been completed	Current
Observation techniques	Field observation and apprenticing	Current
Storyboarding/Prototypes	Build a prototype or create a storyboard from which risks can be derived	Current
Focus groups or facilitation	Structured interviews of several participants in a facilitated manner	Past
Artefact risk identification	Risk identification based upon solid artefacts, i.e., former car model or item sold	Current
The Crawford Slip Method	Step 1 Explain the process Step 2 Define the terms Step 3 Ground rules Step 4 Pass out the sticky notes before asking the question Step 5 Ask the question Step 6 Evaluate your answers Step 7 Stick the answers on the wall and arrange these responses into Categories Step 8 Go through the categories Step 9 Next steps	
My worst nightmare	Draw your worst risk and explain it to your team	Current

Table 3.45   Scalability of the Risk Management Effort

	Full analysis	*<–>*	*Light analysis*
Uncertainty	Quantitative analysis	Qualitative analysis	Single-point adjustments

Table 3.46   Risk Matrix

Probability	5	GREEN	YELLOW	YELLOW	RED	RED
	4	GREEN	GREEN	YELLOW	YELLOW	RED
	3	GREEN	GREEN	YELLOW	YELLOW	YELLOW
	2	GREEN	GREEN	GREEN	GREEN	YELLOW
	1	GREEN	GREEN	GREEN	GREEN	GREEN
		1	2	3	4	5
				Impacts		

Table 3.47   Probability

Score	*General Description*	*Frequency Description*	*Probability Description*
1	Rare: this will probably never happen	Occurs once every few years (or less) in any three-year period.	1/1000 chance or less
2	Unlikely: this is not expected to happen, though it remains a possibility	Occurs less than annually in any three-year period	Between 1/1000–1/100 chance
3	Possible: this happens occasionally	Occurs about once per year in any three-year period	Between 1/100–1/10 chance
4	This will probably happen, but it is not a constant occurrence	Expected to occur several times per year in any three year period	Between 1/10–5/10 chance
5	This will undoubtedly happen, possibly quite frequently	Expected to occur in more months than not	1/2 chance or more

The quantitative risk assessment broadens the scope for risk management, as some methods, like the sensitivity analysis, assess the initiatives assumptions and illustrate the findings with Tornado diagrams; while other quantitative risk management assessments, such as the decision tree, emphasize scenarios, which illustrate the broader application of the qualitative risk management assessment in the initiative.

Table 3.48 Impact

Score	Description
1	financial loss <£250K / no significant adverse publicity / minor operational impact
2	financial loss £250K–£500K / limited unfavourable media coverage / service disrupted but key activity not delayed
3	financial loss £500K–£750K / unfavourable local or short-term media coverage / sporadic provision of key activity
4	financial loss £750K–£1M / significant public, media concern / key activity unavailable delaying processes, wasting resources
5	financial loss >£1M / adverse national, prolonged media coverage / key activity unavailable for more than one week

The following list includes a range of techniques and tools used to apply quantitative risk assessment:

- Sensitivity analysis
- Spider plot
- Tornado diagram
- Analytical hierarchy process
- Decision trees
- Monte Carlo analysis
- Probability trees and charts
- Waterfall chart
- Assumptions analysis
- Influence diagram
- Fault tree
- Path convergence
- Force field
- Latin hypercube
- Multipoint probability analysis

However, this list is far from comprehensive, as there are numerous other quantitative risk management tools and techniques available for the business case team.

3.17.5 Mitigating and Managing Portfolio-Level Risks

At this stage, risk has been assessed and the risk response or mitigation needs to be conducted. It involves strategies for negative risks, which need to be avoided, transferred, mitigated, or accepted to lower probability and/or impact. Meanwhile, positive risk mitigation strategies are also developed, which include exploitation, sharing, enhancement, and acceptance, where probability and/or impacts seek to be increased for positive opportunities.

Table 3.49 demonstrates the positive risk responses with exploitation strategy, as being an almost certain or 100% chance for positive impact, which is often not possible. The sharing response implies sharing the risk with others: mostly business units, vendors, or subject matter experts, to increase the probability and/or impact. The enhancement strategy is like the sharing strategy, as here; the portfolio managers seek to increase the probability and/or impact by doing things differently, adding resources or similar kind of initiatives for further positive responses. However, sometimes, the portfolio managers do not have the means and resources to do anything more. This is when the acceptance strategy is applied.

The negative risk responses are remarkably like the positive responses with a reserve outcome, as the portfolio managers seek to decrease probability and/or impact, instead of increasing it, as is the case with the positive risk responses demonstrated in Table 3.50. The avoidance strategy seems to eliminate the risk, reducing the probability and/or impact to close to 0%. This can be done by removing an element from the initiative. The transfer strategy implies transferring the impact of the negative risk to another party, like an insurance vendor, or similar partner. The mitigate strategy involves decreasing the probability and/or impact, to make it less likely

Table 3.49 Positive Risk Responses

Risk Responses	Descriptions
Positive	Possible event that may positively impact a project
Exploitation	Increased opportunity by making the cause more probable
Sharing	Retain appropriate opportunities or part of opportunities instead of attempts to transfer them to others
Enhancing	Increase probability or impact of occurrence
Acceptance	Do nothing

Table 3.50 Negative Risk Responses

Risk Responses	Descriptions
Negative	Possible event that may negatively impact a project
Avoid	Eliminate the threat of a risk by eliminating the cause
Transfer	Assign the risk to someone else by subcontracting or buying insurance
Mitigate	Reduce probability or impact of occurrence
Acceptance	Do nothing or create a contingency plan

Table 3.51 Negative Risk Response Strategies

High Impact	Transfer	Avoid
Low Impact	Accept	Mitigate
	Low Probability	**High Probability**

to happen, and if the risk occurs, the consequences are less than before the mitigation. The acceptance strategy can be conducted passively, as the portfolio managers do nothing other than accepting the possibility with an open mind or a positive viewpoint, as mitigating it is too expensive or out of our reach.

The use of the negative risk responses depends to some degree on the impact and possibilities, where a high probability and high impact should be handled with the "avoid" responses, while the low impact and low probability risks can be accepted, as illustrated by Table 3.51, based upon Geiger (2007).

"As low as reasonably practicable" (ALARP) is the concept that describe at what level of risk resource ought to be used to mitigate the risk until a certain point when it is too costly and less effectiveness to continue to mitigate. Figure 3.14 illustrates this, as ALARP is the point of mitigation.

Playing it safe is the riskiest choice we can ever make.

Sarah Ban Breathnach

3.17.6 Risk Burndown Chart for the Portfolio

A chart where the risk to project success associated with the scope is displayed is illustrated in Figure 3.15. The project risk will burn down and

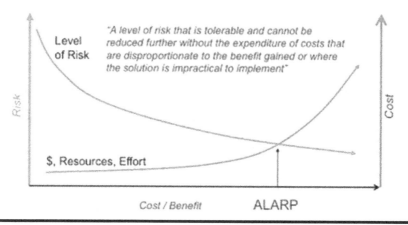

Figure 3.14   ALARP.

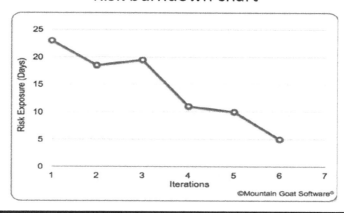

Figure 3.15   **Risk burndown chart (Cohn, 2012).**

decrease as the project progresses and the functionality is completed. The chart in Figure 3.15 demonstrates how the risk reduces as the project proceeds. The risk exposed is on the Y axis and the number of iterations is on the X axis. Risk burndown charts are easy to create and make communication within the team a lot easier and can be found on the information radiator.

3.17.7 Applying Risk-Based Spike on Initiatives in the Portfolio

In agile, a spike is like a fork in the road. The team or customer, or both, may be uncertain of the way ahead – often a user story that cannot be estimated. Spikes often become a technical, architectural, and development investigation between sprints to research an answer to a problem. Risk-based spikes underlay the concept of failing fast, as spikes are quickly tested, and resolution is drawn. This means that risk-based spikes are quick time-boxed experiences used to help the team answer a question and determine a path forward.

3.17.8 Why Use Risk-based Spikes?

Spikes, another invention of XP, is a special type of story used to drive out risk and uncertainty in a user story or other project facet. Spikes may be used for several reasons:

- Spikes may be used for basic research to familiarize the team with a new technology of the domain.
- The story may be too big to be estimated appropriately and the team may use a spike to analyze the implied behaviour so they can split the story into estimable pieces.
- The story may contain significant technical risk and the team may have to do some research or prototyping to gain confidence in a technological approach that will allow them to commit the user story to some future time-box.
- The story may contain significant functional risk, in that although the intent of the story may be understood, it is not clear how the system needs to interact with the user to achieve the benefit implied.
- Spike solutions are a learning technique based on performing small, concrete experiments.
- If something does not work as expected, is it because your understanding of the technology is wrong? Is it due to an unseen interaction with the production code or test framework? Standalone spikes eliminate this uncertainty.
- For stories that you cannot estimate accurately, an alternative to scheduling a spike story is to provide a high estimate. This is risky, because some stories will take longer than your highest estimate, and some may not be possible at all.
- Another option is to research problems by reading about the underlying theory and finding code snippets in books or online. This is often a good way to get started on a spike, but the best way to really understand what is going on is to create your own spike.

3.18 Portfolio Metrics Worth Tracking – Measuring Progress and Value

Lord Kelvin should have said: "When you can measure what you are speaking about, and express it in numbers, you know something about it, when you cannot express it in numbers, your knowledge is of a meager and unsatisfactory kind; it may be the beginning of knowledge, but you have scarily, in your thoughts advanced to the stage of science".

Many years later, we have the short version by Peter Drucker "If you can't measure it, you can't improve it". Before going into details, let us get the bearing right. We start out with the vision, strategy, goals, objectives, and suchlike, which is found in this chapter. What must happen to achieve the vision, strategy, goals, objectives are critical success factors (CSF). Critical success factors (CSF) are underpinned by key performance indicators, i.e., a number of standard changes which are supported by metrics such as various types of standard changes.

These are some of the considerations for portfolio metrics in general:

■ The agile principles are based upon the agile manifesto where one of the 12 principles emphasizes "Working software as the primary measurement for progress" which we should honour.

■ When working with metrics it is also important to consider which metrics are worth tracking and if data is "good enough".

■ Selecting metrics will send a strong message to the organization and may change the behaviour of people working within the organization, as if metrics are taken seriously they drive what people do. Some researchers call these value-driven metrics where metrics such as output, or productivity is a different value-driven metric than measuring

Table 3.52   Portfolio Metrics Worth Tracking High-Level Overview

	Strategic Planning		Initiative/Operations		
Portfolio Life-Cycle Stages	*Initiation*	*Planning*	*Executing*	*Optimization*	*Monitoring and controlling*
Portfolio Kanban	Funnel	Review/ analyzing	Portfolio backlog	Implementation	Done
Projectized					
Recurring	**3.18 Portfolio Metrics Worth Tracking**				

outcome or value. Do you just measure velocity, or do you measure deployment time?

- Some organizations argue the need to rethink performance metrics, as traditional metrics can have an adverse impact and incentivize the wrong behaviours in agile organizations, while understanding how to identify relevant metrics for rewarding team performance, focusing on value, and driving high performance is more important in an agile portfolio.
- For a start, it is important to consider what you are using the portfolio metrics for. Think about DevOps and the three ways by Gene Kim (2013). The first way emphasizes flow, the second, feedback, while the third way, learning. Each way has a unique set of metrics which could be useful. We are doing DevOps, we have emphasis on the three ways, so is our metrics.

In 2014, Gartner developed the DevOps Metric Pyramid which neatly highlights various steps of metrics from operational efficiency to business performance. It is not a maturity model but gives a good understanding on how various metrics are needed to do other or perhaps more advanced metrics on something more relevant to the portfolio. In the agile portfolio it is vital to involve the entire team in construction of goals to ensure the organization measures up, down, and across in a meaningful way, and establish a bunch of disciplines of cross-functional and interdependent metrics.

Metrics on team level are constructed by the team, for the team. On the portfolio level the organization needs to keep in mind the right number of metrics and who the customers or stakeholders are. Nobody likes to measure something that is wrong, not used, requires a lot of work just for the sake of the metrics, or sending the wrong message, i.e., individual metrics.

On the quest for the most meaningful metrics, it is vital to consider whether the organization is using lagging or leading metrics or a combination. Lagging metrics are "outcome" indicators, slow to change, and looking back in time. This is our past performance. Leading metrics are forward-looking, change quickly, are early warnings, have immediate and actionable feedback, avoid unwanted outcomes, and suchlike. These describe what is going on right now. Perhaps we want some of these on our portfolio Kanban. Dynamic/static metrics are similar, where the dynamic metric is rapidly changing.

Table 3.53 illustrates some of the common portfolio metrics to be applied. Currently no standard groping exists and some people may argue it is all about performance but varies aspects.

Table 3.53 Metrics

Product Metrics	Process Metrics	Speed/Stability Metrics
Size Complexity Performance Reliability	Effort Time Effectiveness Defects Maturity Feedback loops Agility	Lead time Cycle time Mean time to detect incidents
Project Metric	**Quality Metrics**	**Project Success Metrics**

Number of people
Actual cost
Schedule
Productivity
Velocity
Story points
Burnup/down
Earned value management
  Cumulative flow
Costs of delays
Progress or obstacles
  preventing progress
	Defect
	Code coverage
	Total number of defects
	Ratio of total number of
	  test cases to open defects
	Unit-test code coverage
	Total number of unit tests
	Escaped defects
		Outcome, not activities
		Time to market
		Customer value
		Epic delivered
		User satisfaction
		Boomerangs – things
		  that bounce back from
		  delivered solutions

Culture Metrics	**Other Metrics**	
Retention Loyalty Moral Knowledge sharing	Team morale Collaboration Employee engagement	

Stettina and Gregory have researched the use of reporting in agile portfolios. Table 3.54 illustrates how various organizations are driven by various elements and the results of its reporting on the portfolio.

3.19 The Agile Project Management Office (PMO)

To fully grasp how an agile PMO works let's first have a common understanding of what a traditional, predictive, or plan-based project management office (PMO) does. From a Project Management Institute (PMI) perspective from the *PMBOK Guide* 6th edition the primary function of the PMO is to

Table 3.54 Identified Portfolio Reporting Approaches

	PMO-Driven	*Cadence-Driven*	*Tool-Driven*
Organization Size	Large	Large to Medium	Large
Driving Element	PMO	Cadence	Tooling
Predominant PPM Approach	Phase-gate	Portfolio review	Portfolio review
Metrics	Qualitative and quantitative	Qualitative	Quantitative
Agile Maturity	Low	Low to medium	Medium to high

Table 3.55 The Agile Project Management Office High-Level Overview

	Strategic Planning		*Initiative/Operations*		
Portfolio Life-Cycle Stages	*Initiation*	*Planning*	*Executing*	*Optimization*	*Monitoring and controlling*
Portfolio Kanban	Funnel	Review/ analyzing	Portfolio backlog	Implementation	Done
Projectized					
Recurring	3.19 The Agile Project Management Office				

support the project managers in managing shared resources across projects, identifying and developing project management best practice and standards, coaching, training, and oversight, monitoring compliance with project management standards, policies, etc., via project audits, developing and managing project policies and procedures, and coordinating communication.

The PMO functions may expand into the role of being supportive, controlling, or directive. Supportive means providing methodologies, procedures, templates, best practices, training, and other resources, while controlling implies establishing procedures to ensure adherence to methodologies, through monitoring metrics and performance reporting to management. Directive means leading the recruiting of project management staff, assignment of resources to projects (including project managers themselves), project selection in alignment with the organization strategy, cancellation of failed projects, resource management across projects.

An alternative approach to PMI is the PMO value ring which has identified more than 26 functions and benefits which need to be tailored to the PMO and processes. Each PMO needs to figure out what they will do and how they can provide value to the organization. The selected functions and processes are then supported with KPIs, maturity, performance, ROI, and such measurements to support the ongoing activities and development of the PMO.

The value that an "agile PMO" provides is essentially the same as the value any PMO can provide consistent with the definition of processes across an organization – a means of providing expertise and promoting excellence in the planning and execution of projects, and a pool of trained resources on which to draw. The agile PMO simply supports a different (agile) process, or a broader array of processes, including classic "plan-driven" and new agile processes, as appropriate.

However, it is important to realize that the impact of an "agile mindset" goes beyond the definition of specific functions and processes. The development of agile processes was driven by the need to manage projects that are plagued by rapid changes in business needs, and the high and irreducible uncertainty around requirements and the effort required to implement them. These drivers have forced a shift away from efficiency and schedule minimization to adaptability and risk mitigation.

If you recall the agile manifesto, the challenge is then that the traditional PMO is focused on delivering the right side of the agile manifesto which is not the part we valued highest. The agile approach values the left side higher than the right side which the agile PMO should support and emphasize. The DSDM Consortium Guide on the agile PMO states this as the following needs:

- Close to business
- Responsiveness to business change
- Ensuring incremental delivery
- Small chunk of works
- Continuous support
- Empowered
- Responsive
- Proactive
- Facilitative
- Collaborative

As the agile PMO promotes the agile approaches, functions and processes need to vary from the traditional PMO as most things are different. Just think about the less-precise agile business case, the need for tooling and such.

Portfolio Management is analogous to managing the "product back-log" of an agile project

We may consider taking your agile PMO to the next step which some label agile value management office. Consider the section on value management and then combine it with the benefits of business agility. This implies decomposing large projects into smaller units of business value, achieving a continuous flow of value to the business, within the constructs of the traditional project structure and suchlike.

The agile PMO needs to be able to support and foster *being* agile, not just *doing* agile.

3.20 Exploring EDGE

In 2020, Jim Highsmith, Linda Luu, and David Robinson published the book: *EDGE: Value-Driven Digital Transformation*. EDGE is an operating model with concepts, practices, and principles. Principles like value-based prioritization are straightforward for many organizations while autonomous teams require a bit more work. EDGE aims to answer the following three questions:

■ How should we work together?
■ How should we invest?
■ How can we adapt fast enough?

Part of this is portfolio-related as EDGE includes the portfolio perspective which to some degree nicely highlights several concepts from Chapter 3. In EDGE, the concept is to apply the Lean value tree or LVT (see Figure 3.16).

Table 3.56   Exploring EDGE High-Level Overview

	Strategic Planning		*Initiative/Operations*		
Portfolio Life-Cycle Stages	*Initiation*	*Planning*	*Executing*	*Optimization*	*Monitoring and controlling*
Portfolio Kanban	Funnel	Review/ analyzing	Portfolio backlog	Implementation	Done
Projectized					
Recurring	3.20 Exploring EDGE				

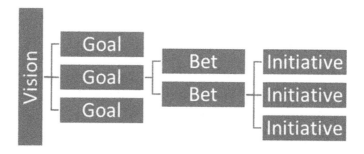

Figure 3.16　Lean value tree.

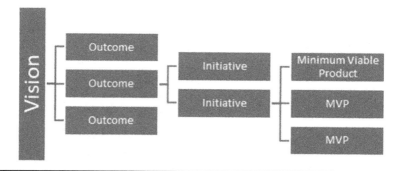

Figure 3.17　Lean value tree.

This implies that the vision sets the guiding direction for all investments. A vision contains various goals. A goal could be "look and feel great" and could be supported by a description – success measures and challenges/opportunities. A goal is divided into bets which are specific ways goals can be realized. In our case, "look and feel great", the bets could be: "eat less" and "train more". The bets are then divided into initiatives. In our example that could be "start running" or "eat less sugar". You might say a goal is a portfolio of bets. An alternative terminology is illustrated in Figure 3.17.

If we base the funding allocation on Figure 3.17, then our initial funding (let us say US$1,000,000) would be shared between the outcome, such as 40%, 30%, and 30%. The 30% of the outcome (US$300,000) could imply 50% for each initiative (US$150,000). The 50% from the initiative could then be split 40%, 40%, and 20% between the minimum viable products (MVP). Each MVP would in this case receive between US$30,000 and US$60,000.

Some organizations may prefer to use categorizations to balance the investments. One approach is the McKinsey (see Figure 3.5) or use various buckets like geographic area, product, or suchlike. Measures of success is important in EDGE (see Section 3.18 for more details for measurements). The concept is to measure each level, so measure the bet, e.g., "exercise more".

The measure could be hours of exercise per week and with a target of two to ten hours of exercise per week.

The estimation and prioritization of EDGE nicely sums up several concepts already discussed. The concept in EDGE is to estimate relative value and relative effort using the Fibonacci scale which is remarkably like weighted shortest job first (WSJF) as many may recall from, e.g., SAFe (Chapter 4 for details). In EDGE this can be combined with the cost of delays (see Section 3.14 for more details). So far EDGE has been helpful recapping some of the key issues discussed. On a final note, EDGE introduces the value realization team which replaces the traditional PMO. The value realization team's aim is to foster agility and embrace value delivery which is discussed in Section 3.19 as the agile PMO and suchlike.

3.21 Transformational Leadership for a Successful Portfolio

Transformational leadership is the ability to inspire and motivate people with shared values and sense of purpose. This drives people toward a common goal while facilitating a wide-scale transformational change which is required for a successful agile portfolio adaptation. People need to identify with the organizations and work with them. In agile we tend to highlight servant and adaptive leadership, which are explained later in this section; however, they are not the same as transformational leadership. Servant leadership focuses mainly on people performance and development which is good for the portfolio Scrum master while adaptive leadership is closer to traditional leadership, so it can be applied for the portfolio product owner; however, from top management, who are ultimately in charge of the agile

Table 3.57   Transformational Leadership for a Successful Portfolio High-Level Overview

Portfolio Life-Cycle Stages	Strategic Planning		Initiative/Operations		
	Initiation	Planning	Executing	Optimization	Monitoring and controlling
Portfolio Kanban	Funnel	Review/ analyzing	Portfolio backlog	Implementation	Done
Projectized					
Recurring	3.21 Transformational Leadership for a Successful Portfolio				

portfolio, we need transformational leadership, which is all about common goals and a sense of purpose for everyone in the agile portfolio.

In 2017, the *State of DevOps Report* explained transformational leadership as:

- Vision: Has a clear concept of where the organization is going and where it should be in five years.
- Inspirational communication: Communicates in a way that inspires and motivates, even in an uncertain or changing environment.
- Intellectual stimulation: Challenges followers to think about problems in new ways.
- Supportive leadership: Demonstrates care and consideration of followers' needs and feelings.
- Personal recognition: Praises and acknowledges achievement of goals and improvements in work quality; personally, compliments others when they do outstanding work.

Learning culture and job satisfaction are discussed in Section 2.6 on the culture and work environment. The last piece of the puzzle was transformational leadership as all three (learning culture, job satisfaction, and transformational leadership) are the set of capabilities that drive higher software delivery and organizational performance. These capabilities were discovered by the DORA State of DevOps research (2020) programme, an independent, academically rigorous investigation into the practices and capabilities that drive high performance. These capabilities are also needed for empowering teams, which are needed for autonomous teams and Lean product management, so it is all related.

3.21.1 Adaptive Leadership (for the Portfolio Product Owner)

In agile, we embrace change. This requires adaptive leadership that deals with change and problem-solving. Adaptive leadership focuses on team management from building self-organized teams for developing servant leadership style. In agile, the leaders engage the teams while the team members solve the tasks. In recent years, adaptive leadership has received the attention of Harvard academics, with Ronald A. Heifetz as one of the main exponents. Adaptive leadership explores why responsiveness is critical to success. Adaptive leadership refers to everyday dealings with changes and problem-solving – these tasks are at the core of what leaders and managers must be able do. In teams, most challenges are technical challenges, where they are the experts. However, sometimes adaptive challenges arise where someone outside the team must show leadership or the team will suffer. Six principles of adaptive leadership are:

- Get on the balcony
- Identify the adaptive challenges
- Regulate distress
- Maintain disciplined attention
- Give the work back to people
- Protect the voice of leadership from below

The principle of getting on the balcony implies that leaders must be able to view patterns and not get too involved in the field of action to have an overall view on the situation and the work at hand. Leaders must identify the adaptive challenges by understanding themselves, their people, and potential sources of conflict. Adaptive work generates distress which must be regulated to maintain a productive level of tension and motivate people without disabling them. A leader must have the emotional capacity to tolerate uncertainty, frustration, and pain, which puts the emphasis back on emotional intelligence. To maintain disciplined attention, leaders must have an open mind to learn and gather input, while at the same time keep focus. People need leadership to help them maintain their focus on tough situations. Disciplined attention is the currency of leadership.

The principle of giving the work back to people means that when people do not apply their special knowledge and capabilities, businesses fail to adapt and succeed. Leaders must provide the impetus to motivate people to do what they are best at. People will act, if they have the right amount of knowledge, information, and sense of urgency, but only when the adaptive leaders facilitate this. Protecting the voice of leadership from below refers to the need for adaptive leaders to give a voice to all people. An organization that is willing to listen and learn from all its workers is one that is based on a firm foundation.

3.21.2 Case Study – Doing Adaptive Work at KPMG in Netherland

Harvard Business Review posted an article in 1997 entitled as "The Work of Leadership". Part of the article tells the story of leadership as learning and aligning people with the vision through adaptive work; Ruud Koedijk was chairman at KPMG in Netherlands and doing extremely well. He saw new markets and opportunities but could also see from the balcony that the very structures of KPMG needed change to reach them. The chairman knew that a sense of autonomy could be used to develop talents, but the culture of KPMG was one of not making mistakes and billing as many hours as possible, so there was little motivation to change. Cultural changes were needed, but even the chairman could not mandate behavioural change. However, Koedijk could change conditions. The strategic initiative started out with a meeting where the chairman recounted the history of KPMG and explained the business situation to all employees. Next, he began with a strategic initiative through dialogue and quickly created trust. Among the initiatives, he allowed the partners and employees to use 60% of their time to solve strategic challenges and do adaptive work. This was a rare situation for employees at KPMG. The change had ups and downs and conflicts as well. Concerns were voiced and employees faced adaptive challenges. But in the end, the initiative created a collective understanding and stands as a prime example of leadership as learning and the need to align people with the vision.

3.21.3 Servant Leadership (for the Portfolio Scrum Master)

Servant leadership is a philosophy and set of practices that enriches the lives of individuals, builds better organizations, and ultimately creates a more just and caring world. While servant leadership is a timeless concept, the phrase "servant leadership" was coined by Robert K. Greenleaf in "The Servant as Leader", an essay that he first published in 1970.

Larry Spears, Executive Director of the Robert K. Greenleaf Center for Servant-Leadership, succinctly defines servant leadership as "A new kind of leadership model – a model which puts serving others as the number one priority. Servant-leadership emphasizes increased service to others; a holistic approach to work; promoting a sense of community; and the sharing of power in decision-making" (Greenleaf, 1996).

Servant leadership can be defined as a theoretical framework that advocates a leader's primary motivation and role as service to others, which implies a comprehensive view on the quality of people, work, and community spirit. Servant leadership emphasizes core personal characteristics and beliefs over any specific leadership techniques. The core characteristics of being a servant leader are:

■ Listening
■ Empathy

■ Healing
■ Awareness
■ Persuasion
■ Conceptualization
■ Foresight
■ Stewardship
■ Commitment to the growth of people
■ Building community

It is no coincidence that the phrase "servant leadership" places the word "servant" before "leader". The order reflects the underlying philosophy of servant leadership. Firstly, we act as servants for the team, and secondly, we act as leaders. The characteristics of being a servant leader listed above emphasize the development of team members and ensure all are doing well. Servant leadership works well in an agile team with roles like coach, portfolio scrum master. or just Scrum master, as they are concerned to support and enhance the team and the wellbeing of its members.

Servant leadership lacks a formal, confirmed framework for application and has not yet been empirically linked to organizational performance. Consequently, servant leadership relies heavily on personal styles of leadership.

Exercise 3.11 Stand and Deliver

Get up and recap what you have learned in this chapter and how you are going to apply it.

_____

_____

_____

_____

Answers: No right or wrong answers.

Chapter 4

Agile Portfolio Management Frameworks

Figure 4.1   Overview.

Organizations have varied reasons for adopting a framework for agile portfolio management. The common reasons for framework adoptions are the need for a well-proven public structure (widespread use – adopted by others like our organization), market demands, and means to faster delivery and a framework to scale more people. Sometimes may consultants trained (selling training and implementation) in the frameworks, case studies and similar recommendation do their part in creating a viable option. Still, we also see some organizations adopting a framework for no discernible reason.

4.1 Agnostic Agile Portfolio Management

Agnostic Agile is an organization created years ago when they saw the

> importance of being agnostic with agility at any level. This means
> one size does not fit all, one framework is not the answer, and the
> "what" and "how" should be suited to customer context and to a
> wider strategic vision.
>
> Our work is to help our customers attain the right level of agil-
> ity that meets their needs, our work is not to create framework
> lock-ins nor to limit how agility can be applied to the organisation,
> whether at team levels or at scale.
>
> This means we as agile practitioners must strive to be masters of
> our craft, understand and practice at least two formally established
> frameworks or methods, uphold good conduct between ourselves
> and others, and help to nurture and grow our community of agile
> practitioners.
>
> **(Agnostic Agile, 2021)**

Agnostic Agile is based upon the following principles:

- To put my customer first, making them independent
- To do my best, complementing theory with practical experience
- To tailor agility to context
- To understand hindering constraints and work to remove them
- To share, learn, and improve
- To respect frameworks and their practitioners
- To acknowledge unknowns and seek help
- To never mislead and to never misrepresent
- To remember that agility is not the end goal
- To acknowledge that dogmatism is non-agile
- To recognize that there is more to agile than agile
- To give to the community as it has given to me

4.2 Agile Portfolio Management

Chapter 3 contains a description of the common benefits of adopting agile
portfolio management. The benefits of the frameworks are aligned and

would encompass quality, transparency, collaboration, productivity, and strategy alignment among the common illustrations in the literature and the trade press.

It is not necessarily easy to implement or adopt a framework for agile portfolio management. Chapter 9 includes some of the challenges and pitfalls identified by researchers, and commonly witnessed in practice, and provides suggestions on how to mitigate them. The major challenges of adoption of a framework are commonly: change resistance, moving away from/to agile, controversies with the framework, programme increment challenges, and agile-release-train challenges, just to highlight a few.

The transformation steps or implementation would most likely include the need for a cultural shift, trainings and workshops, transformation teams, value-streams mapping, team formations, integration of waterfall and non-development units to agile and suchlike. See Chapter 9 for more details.

Organizations have adopted a framework and not obtained the expected benefits, changed framework, ended the agile journey, and suchlike, so it is not an easy task, and, as you will witness in this chapter, several of the frameworks are comprehensive and with various degrees of maturity. Combine these facts with the need for tailoring the frameworks and the ability to deliver quality fast, and you, as an organization, are faced with a dire task.

Some organizations apply analysis methods like "Readiness and Fit Analysis (RFA)" from the Software Engineering Institute (SEI) that allow the profiling of a set of practices to understand their cultural assumptions and then use the profile to support an organization in understanding its fit with the practices. This example includes the cultural assumption, business, and acquisition, organizational climate, project, and customer environment, practices, system attributes, and the technology environment. The question here is not which framework to choose but to emphasize the need to do some initial assessment/analysis before engaging on adopting an agile framework for agile portfolio management as it is going to be a major change with major consequence for the organization, so due diligence is highly needed.

Exercise 4.1 Turn and Talk

Turn and talk with others about what you know about agile portfolio management frameworks.

Answers: No right or wrong answers.

This chapter aims at providing you with an understanding of the various frameworks that exist in the market, so will help with making an enlightened decision if your organization is selecting or working with a framework for agile portfolio management. The frameworks would, for the most part, contain information on:

- Scaling practices for more teams, e.g., planning agile-release trains
- Scaling engineering practices across the iterations, e.g., synchronized sprints, bi-weekly meets, quarterly meets, hardening sprints
- Scaling roles, e.g., area product owners, proxy product owners (PPOs)
- Scaling artefacts, e.g., portfolio management, backlog management
- Scaling frameworks: SAFe, LeSS, DAD
- Scaling architecture

Some of these scaling practices are illustrated in Figure 4.2 as a subway map of scaling practices. The colours of the map represent various frameworks,

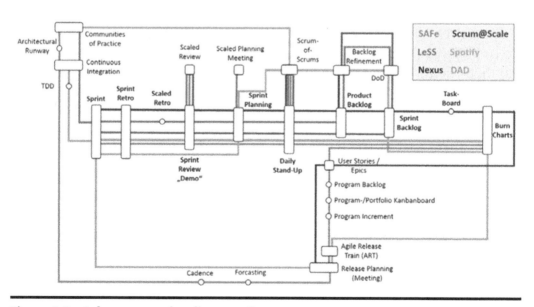

Figure 4.2   Subway map of scaling practices.

e.g., black for Nexus and a range of practices, e.g., scaled retro(spectives) and artefacts, e.g., sprint backlogs, which are illustrated. This shows some degree of similarity between the frameworks and the differences which are just single or fewer colours. Also, it brings backs memories for those who remember the train map by the agile alliance for team level back in the day.

4.3 Scaling Frameworks for Agile Portfolio Management

The Crystal Methods were developed by Alistair Cockburn in 1992. He believed that one of the major obstacles facing product development was poor communication and modelled the Crystal Methods to address these needs. Cockburn explains his philosophy:

> To the extent that you can replace written documentation with face-to-face interactions, you can reduce the reliance on written work products and improve the likelihood of delivering the system. The more frequently you can deliver running, tested slices of the system, the more you can reduce the reliance on written "promissory" notes and improve the likelihood of delivering the system.

The Crystal (clear, yellow, orange, red, maroon, diamond, and sapphire) family in 1992 was the first to focus on large agile teams with more than 50 developers. In the years following came a range of frameworks; however, few emphasized multiple teams and the portfolio layer. An example was the dynamic system development method (DSDM), which was created in 1994, while the agile portfolio management approach was included much later in 2018.

Most of the scaling agile frameworks for agile portfolio management are from within the last ten years and have had a major increase in popularity over the last five years, so it is still a relatively new discipline. While all frameworks include similar structures such as cross-functional and self-organizing teams, there are significant conceptual differences between the frameworks, so choose carefully.

4.3.1 Core Concepts of the Scaled Frameworks for Agile Portfolio Management

The classic theory would classify approaches for projects, programmes, and portfolios whereas our emphasis is on the agile portfolio management which is the interface with the non-agile organizations. A fair number of frameworks exist for agile on the team/project level with Scrum the most popular and applied according to "the 14th annual State of Agile" (VersionOne, 2020). Some of these frameworks have an inter-team focus, meaning that they can handle several teams but do not necessary include the portfolio level. Examples of these would be Crystal, Nexus, Spotify, PRINCE2 Agile, Scrum Lean in Motion, and suchlike. On the portfolio level, some frameworks have a more transformational focus, which can be either process, i.e., agile culture model, or progress, i.e., agile maturity model, agile maturity map, Scrum capability ratings, and suchlike. For portfolio application we need the enterprise focus, however frameworks, sets of principles, or sets of methods such as enterprise agility, enterprise unified process, and the Iacocca Model have been deselected while Scrum of Scrums, LeSS, and DSDM are included due to the level of maturity and possible agile portfolio management application. In general, a fair number of frameworks for agile portfolio management exist but few are used – this may change soon. Selection of a scaling method or approach is often not done systematically but based upon popularity. To illustrate this, the most common and applied scaled agile frameworks with portfolio management capabilities are listed in Table 4.1 and covered in this chapter. The table contains basic information, the latest data on use from "the 14th Annual state of agile" combined with information on contributions, cases, applications, documentation, training, certification, community, forum, blogs, and suchlike which gives a subjective maturity score of low, medium, or high.

Few works exist on highlighting various methods, differences, and similarities; Figure 4.3, which is adapted from Alqudah and Razali (2016), highlights team size, training, methods and practices, technical practices, and organization types for DAD, SAFe, LeSS, Spotify, Nexus, and RAGE.

Similar to Figure 4.3 is Figure 4.4 by Uludag (Uludag et al., 2012) and others who investigated the role of architects in scaled agile frameworks. It also gives some background information on the agile portfolio management frameworks.

4.4 The Scaled Agile Framework (SAFe®)

The scaled agile framework version 1.0 was introduced to the market in 2011, however it started years earlier and at least in 2010 when Dean Leffingwell published the book *Agile Software Development* which

Table 4.1 Scaling Agile Frameworks

Scaling Agile Frameworks	Methodologist	Publication Date	14th State of Agile	Category	Maturity
Disciplined agile/ disciplined agile Delivery (DA)	Scott Ambler and Mark Lines	2012	4%	Framework	High
Recipes for agile governance in the enterprise (RAGE)	Kevin Thompson	2013	1%	Framework	Low
Scaled agile framework (SAFe)	Dean Leffingwell	2011	35%	Framework	High
Scrum@Scale	Jeff Sutherland and Alex Brown	2014		Framework	Low
Scrum of Scrums	Jeff Sutherland and Kenn Schwaber	2001	16%	Mechanism	High
XSCALE	Peter Mecel	2014		Set of Principles	Low
Dynamic system development method (DSDM)	Arrie van Bennekum	1994		Framework	Medium
Large-scale Scrum (LeSS)	Craig Larsen and Bas Vodde	2008	4%	Framework	High
Enterprise Scrum	Mike Beedle	2014	4%	Framework	Low

introduced the agile enterprise big picture which later was to become a central part of the scaled agile framework. Version 1.0 was created by chief methodologist at scaled agile, Dean Leffingwell, and with help from a few contributors, one being Drew Jamilo, today SAFe fellow. At that time, SAFe focused on Lean product development which later also included agile development, DevOps, and system thinking. The first version of SAFe was released in 2011, then came versions 2.0, 3.0, LSE, 4.0, 4.5, 4.6, and the latest version, 5.0, which was released January 2020. SAFe has become more and more popular, which has been supported by data from the annual state of agile surveys where there has been increasing popularity for years. Scaled agile states that 70% of the Fortune 100 in the US and more than 700,000 people have certified their products, which is a major accomplishment since its first release of version 1.0 in 2011.

TABLE II							
Methods Differences And Similarities							
Criteria	**DAD**	**SAFe**	**LeSS 1**	**LeSS 2**	**Spotify**	**Nexus**	**RAGE**
Team size	200 people or more. It also supports small and medium teams.	Large Enterprise includes more than 1 release trains (50 to 124 people in each release trains)	Up to 70 people or 10 SCRUM teams, 7 stakeholders in each team	Any large projects, More than thousand people on one product	Any large projects, Normally 250 to 300 people at Spotify (30 teams)	Three to nine SCRUM teams	No specific size but it support different size for enterprises
Training and certificate on	Workshops to explain the idea of DAD, Book of DAD is available	Training is needed and there should be certified, coaches	Seven companies in six countries are available for coaching	Seven companies in six countries are available for coaching	Lack of training	Scaled Professional SCRUM Training is needed	Training is conducted by webinar and presentation slides
Methods and practices adopted	Kanban Practices (mainly visualizing Work and limiting work in progress), SCRUM (almost all SCRUM practices), Agile Modeling which is the source for DAD's modeling and documentation practices, the Unified Process, XP, TDD and Agile Data.	SCRUM, Lean, Kanban, SCRUMban, DevOps and some practices of XP	SCRUM was fully adopted including additional practices for large projects	SCRUM was fully adopted including additional practices for large projects	Allow Kanban, SCRUM, DevOps and Lean Startup	SCRUM with additional practices in solving the dependency-related issues in multiple teams	Allow SCRUM, Kanban, Plan-Driven development and Hybrid approaches
Technical Practices required	High (Need to adopt many technical practices which require high technical skills)	Medium but should understand the use of portfolio management tools	Medium and low for SCRUM adopters	Medium and low for SCRUM adopters	Medium but teams should be able to communicate well	Medium and low for SCRUM adopters	Medium and low for SCRUM adopters
Organization Type	Multiple Organization and Enterprise practicality	Enterprises and portfolio level	Large Traditional organization	Enterprises	Enterprises specifically similar to Spotify	Portfolio level for medium project	Traditional and Agile Enterprises

Figure 4.3   Methods differences and similarities.

				Descriptive Information				Maturity				
	Methodologist	**Organization**	**Publication Date**	**Category**	**Contributions**	**Cases**	**Documentation**	**Training Courses and Certifications**	**Community Forum or Blog**	**Rating**		
Crystal Family	Alistair Cockburn	-	1992	Set of Methods	17	1	Yes	No	Yes	◗		
Dynamic Systems Development Method Agile Project Framework for Scrum	Arie van Bennekum	DSDM Consortium	1994	Framework	28	4	Yes	Yes	Yes	◕		
Scrum-of-Scrums	Jeff Sutherland and Ken Schwaber	Scrum Inc.	2001	Mechanism	27	2	Yes	No	Yes	◗		
Enterprise Scrum	Mike Beedle	Enterprise Scrum Inc	2002	Framework	4	-	Yes	Yes	Yes	◗		
Agile Software Solution Framework	Asif Qumer and Brian Henderson-Sellers	University of Technology	2007	Framework	2	2	No	No	No	○		
Large Scale Scrum	Craig Larman and Bas Vodde	LeSS Company B.V.	2008	Framework	29	22	Yes	Yes	Yes	●		
Scaled Agile Framework	Dean Leffingwell	Scaled Agile Inc	2011	Framework	35	35	Yes	Yes	Yes	●		
Disciplined Agile 2.0	Scrott Ambler	Disciplined Agile Consortium	2012	Framework	27	4	Yes	Yes	Yes	●		
Spotify Model	Henrik Kniberg, Anders Ivarsson, and Joakim Sundén	Spotify	2012	Model	11	1	Yes	No	Yes	◔		
Mega Framework	Rafael Maranzato, Marden Neubert, and Paula Heculano	Universo Online S.A	2012	Framework	2	1	No	No	No	○		
Enterprise Agile Delivery and Agile Governance Practice	Erik Marks	AgilePath	2012	Set of Practices	1	-	Yes	No	Yes	◔		
Recipes for Agile Governance in the Enterprise	Kevin Thompson	Cprime	2013	Framework	4	1	Yes	Yes	No	◔		
Continuous Agile Framework	Andy Singleton	Maxos LLC	2014	Framework	3	-	Yes	No	Yes	◔		
Scrum at Scale	Jeff Sutherland and Alex Brown	Scrum Inc.	2014	Framework	9	-	Yes	Yes	Yes	◗		
Enterprise Transition Framework	-	agile42	2014	Framework	1	2	Yes	Yes	Yes	◗		
ScALeD Agile Lean Development	Peter Beck, Markus Gärtner, Christoph Mathis, Stefan Roock and Andreas Schliep	-	2014	Set of Principles	2	-	Yes	No	Yes	◔		
eXponential Simple Continuous Autonomous Learning Ecosystem	Peter Merel	Xscale Alliance	2014	Set of Principles	3	-	Yes	Yes	Yes	◗		
Lean Enterprise Agile Framework	-	LeanPitch Technologies	2015	Framework	0	-	Yes	Yes	Yes	◗		
Nexus	Ken Schwaber	Scrum.org	2015	Framework	5	-	Yes	Yes	Yes	◗		
FAST Agile	Ron Quartel	Cron Technologies	2015	Set of Methods	2	-	Yes	No	Yes	◔		

Figure 4.4   Methods differences and similarities.

The core concepts of the scaled agile framework are illustrated in the following sections mainly based on version 4, so there might be minor changes to how SAFe is applied today as it has constantly undergone major updates.

4.4.1 Core Concepts of the Scaled Agile Framework (SAFe)

Scaled agile framework, or just SAFe, is for enterprise-scale Lean-agile development. The foundation of SAFe is built upon Lean-agile leaders, communities of practice which align around value streams and SAFe core values (alignment, built-in quality, transparency, and programme execution). SAFe contains the Lean-agile mindset which underpins the understanding and embracing thinking of Lean and agility. It is also here that you find the SAFe "House of Lean" which include principles such as "Respect for people and culture, Flow, Innovation, Relentless improvement". SAFe also contains nine principles which are discussed in Chapter 3. One of the principles is: decentralize decision-making.

The big picture of SAFe (version 4) reveals three, optionally four, organizational levels, the foundation, and the Spanning Palette which supports the development.

4.4.2 Team Level

Team level is the lowest level of SAFe. This is the power of the agile release trains (ART). The team level is much like Scrum/XP with a twist of the Kanban method. We have agile teams who are on the trains (ART) and work on the trains. Teams works with a product owner and a Scrum master. The product owner focuses on backup of product management of what needs to be done while the Scrum master ensures the process runs smoothly, removes impediments, and suchlike. The core roles work with a team backlog where all things are included whether its functionality, non-functional requirements, and suchlike. During the iteration (same as sprints in Scrum) tasks are worked on, on the team board/Kanban. The meetings or rituals include iterations, iterations planning, iteration execution, iteration retrospective, and team demo. The team demo is the first of several as SAFe also includes Solution demo for the ART and system demo for all teams. Team-level functionality is described in stories, also called user stories. The team may break user stories into features which are tracked on the team Kanban board. Each iteration has one or more goals, which are high-level business and technical goals.

4.4.3 *Programme Level*

In SAFe, the programme level is a virtual structure composed of 5 to 12 teams. This is an agile release train (ART) which is a portion of a value stream. The programme may consist of several of these ARTs. These trains are run by a Release Train Engineer (RTE) who makes sure the process is running. The RTE is supported by system architect/engineering and product management. Product management is the programme-level product owner while the RTE to some degree is the Scrum master for the whole train. We do not have teams on the programme level. On the programme level, what needs to be done is handled in the programme backlog and virtualized on the programme Kanban. A programme runs as programme increments (PI) which is a cycle containing x iterations. The PI may include 5 iterations of 4 weeks each, totally 20 weeks PI. A programme increment requires some planning which is conducted in the PI planning meeting. Think Sprint planning for multiple teams and sprints. A PI, like an iteration, is governed by an objective – the PI objectives which are specific business and technical goals. Another new meeting is the system demo which at the end of each iteration gathers work from all teams and demos it. Think Sprint review for multiple teams if you are familiar with Scrum. What needs to be done comes in several flavours. We have features which are one or more user needs, capabilities which are higher-level behaviours, epics, user stories, and nonfunctional requirements. Enablers are stories, features, capabilities, or epics which we need to do to provide something else, like a functionality. A key SAFe tool is weighted shortest job first (WSJF) which is used to calculate the cost of delay. The formula takes business value, time criticality, risk reduction, and duration into account, which makes it an effective tool for rankings. Each PI includes an innovation and planning iteration which is space for innovation and time to plan the next PI.

4.4.4 *Value-Stream Level*

The value-stream level is optional and used with large and complex solutions. The new role here is the value-stream coordination which focuses on cadence and synchronization among other tasks. This level describes the solution intent/context and applies various tools for modelling requirements such as model-based systems engineering and set-based design. The new meetings are solution demo, which is the sum of multiple ARTs demoed, and a pre- and post-PI planning due to the complexity at hand. The roles of supplier and customer are included on this level.

4.4.5 *Portfolio Level*

The portfolio level (think agile portfolio management) is the highest level of concern. This ties development and operation together with the enterprise. The work is governed by strategic themes which connect the portfolio to the strategy of the enterprise. On this level the roles are programme portfolio management, epic owners (driving epics), and the enterprise architect. On the portfolio level we have a portfolio backlog with business and enabler epics (high-level requirements/significant initiatives) which are managed on the portfolio Kanban which illustrates the flow of epics. On the portfolio level we find the budget and various types of expenses, i.e., CapEx and OpEx (capital and operating expenses) and value streams (flow of value to a customer) as we need to consider which value streams to fund. See Chapter 3 for more details.

4.4.6 *The Spanning Palette*

The spanning palette is a range of supporting teams, tools, and suchlike to make everything work. This includes DevOps, system team (special dedicated team), release management, shares services, user experience, vision, roadmap, metrics, milestones, and releases.

4.4.7 *Research Insights*

Grundler and Westner (2019) investigated various agile frameworks and conducted a project portfolio management evaluation which resulted in a conformity rating for each of the frameworks. The scores from SAFe are found in Table 4.2. SAFe is the framework with the highest score of all the investigated frameworks.

4.4.8 *SAFe Key Terms*

The key terms of this chapter are found in Table 4.3 and are structured around the various levels.

4.5 More with Large-Scale Scrum (LeSS)

When you think about large-scale Scrum or LeSS for short, you should think about Craig Larman and Bass Vodde as the inventors and driving forces. It

Table 4.2 Conformity Rating for SAFe

Objective	Conformity	Operationalization	Hierarchy level
Portfolio Structuring			
Selection and prioritization	YES	Selection and prioritization on portfolio Kanban and backlogs	Portfolio and programme level
Re-evaluation	YES	Epic review and specification workshop	Portfolio level
Portfolio Steering			
Monitoring	YES	Kanban as centralized view Metrics	Portfolio level for epics
Re-adjusting	MAYBE	Re-adjusting in backlogs	Programme and team level
Resource Management			
Resource planning	YES	Roadmaps PI Planning Lean budgets	Portfolio, programme and team level
Reactive allocation	NO	Stable team of teams (ART)	N/A
Organizing learning	MAYBE	PI as PDCA cycle of an ART	Programme level

started in 2002 when Craig Larman wrote, and a year later, published the book *Agile & Iterative Development: A Manager's Guide*, which kickstarted the journey. At that time, the impression was that Scrum was for small teams. In the years following, Craig Larman and Bass Vodde worked with Nokia, Cisco, and suchlike, where it become evident that LeSS worked with many teams. Part of the findings were published in 2008 in the book *Scaling Lean & Agile Development: Thinking and Organizational Tools for Large-Scale Scrum* and a few years later in 2010 with *Practices for Scaling Lean and Agile Development: Large, Multisite and Offshore Product Development with Large-Scale Scrum*. The focus in the later books was more on the experimental part explained in the core concept section. In 2011 they published *Feature Team Primer* which was a bit under the radar until the 2017 book *Large-Scale Scrum*, which nicely sums up a lot of the knowledge accumulated on LeSS. The theory on LeSS is well documented and an active

Table 4.3 Levels of SAFe

Objective	Conformity	Operationalization	Hierarchy Level
Portfolio Structuring			
Selection and prioritization	YES	Selection by the Product Owner Prioritization of the Product Backlog	Product management
Re-evaluation	YES	Review of the direction every sprint	Product management
Portfolio Steering			
Monitoring	NO	No centralized view	Teams track progress
Re-adjusting	YES	Re-adjustment of the overall product backlog every LeSS Sprint	Product management
Resource Management			
Resource planning	YES	Short-term resource planning via Sprint planning 1 and 2 No mid- or long-term planning	Product management Teams
Reactive allocation	NO	Stable teams of teams	N/A
Organizing learning	YES	Team and overall retrospective	Product management Teams

community exists; however, the big breakthrough in market applications is still not happening.

4.5.1 Core Concepts of LeSS

What is LeSS? Large-scale Scrum, or LeSS, is Scrum. LeSS is Scrum applied to many teams working together on one product. LeSS is a scaled-up version of one-team Scrum, and it maintains many of the practices and ideas of one-team Scrum. In LeSS, you will find a single product backlog (because it is for a product, not a team), one definition of done, for all teams, one potentially shippable product increment at the end of each sprint, one product owner, one sprint, and many complete, cross-functional teams (with no single-specialist teams). In LeSS, all teams are in a common sprint to deliver a common shippable product, every sprint.

LeSS consists of two frameworks: LeSS and LeSS Huge. Less is two to eight teams or up to eight teams (of eight people each) while LeSS Huge is more than eight teams and up to a few thousand people on one product. Both frameworks include one product owner, product backlog, sprint, and product increment.

Central components of the frameworks are the principles which are extracted from experience with LeSS adaptations, the LeSS Guides which are optional and should be considered as a moderate set of guidelines, and LeSS experiments, which are optional things to try out in various situations.

The principles, guides, and experiments are all listed below; however, they are not so much explained as self-explained and recognized from the agile environment.

The LeSS principles are:

- Queuing theory
- Empirical process control
- System thinking
- Lean thinking
- Continuous Improvements
- Customer-centric
- Whole-product focus
- More with less
- Transparency

The LeSS Guides are:

- LeSS structure
- Adoption
- Organize by customer value
- Management
- Scrum masters
- Less product
- Product
- Product owner
- Product backlog
- Definition of done
- LeSS sprint

- Product backlog refinement
- Sprint planning
- Coordination and integration
- Review and retrospective

The LeSS experiments are:

- System thinking
- Lean thinking
- Queueing theory
- False dichotomies
- Be agile
- Feature teams
- Teams
- Requirements areas
- Organization
- Large-scale Scrum
- Scrum primer
- Test
- Product management
- Planning
- Coordination
- Requirements and PBIs
- Design and architecture
- Legacy code
- Continuous integration
- Inspect and adapt
- Multisite
- Offshore
- Contracts

If we examine the LeSS structure, it is remarkably like Scrum, which is great. Most of the teams are customer-focused feature teams. Each team is self-managing, cross-functional, co-located, and long-lived. We have full-time Scrum masters who can serve one to three teams and is responsible for a well-working LeSS adoption. The Scrum master's focus is toward the teams, product owner, organization, and development practices. The product owner is as in Scrum, however, there is just one for multiple teams. In LeSS, managers are optional, but if managers do exist, their role is likely to change.

Their focus shifts from managing the day-to-day product work to improving the value-delivering capability of the product development system.

LeSS is different from Scrum in various ways:

- Sprint planning: In addition to the one product owner, it includes people from all teams. Let team members self-manage to decide their division of product backlog items. Team members also discuss opportunities to find shared work and cooperate, especially for related items.
- Sprint planning: This is held independently (and usually in parallel) by each team, though sometimes, for simple coordination and learning, two or more teams may hold it in the same room (in different areas).
- Daily Scrum: This is also held independently by each team, though a member of team A may observe team B's daily Scrum, to increase information-sharing.
- Coordination: Teams, or rotating representatives from each, may hold an open space, town-hall meeting, or Scrum of Scrums regularly to increase information-sharing and coordination.
- Product backlog refinement (PBR): The only requirement in LeSS is single-team PBR, the same as in one-team Scrum. But a common and useful variation is multi-team PBR, where two or more teams are in the same room together, to increase learning and coordination.
- Sprint review: In addition to the one product owner, it includes people from all teams, and relevant customers/users and other stakeholders. For the phase of inspecting the product increment and new items, consider a "bazaar" or "science fair" style: a large room with multiple areas, each staffed by team members, where the items developed by teams are shown and discussed.
- Overall retrospective: This is a new meeting not found in one-team Scrum, and its purpose is to explore improving the overall system, rather than focusing on one team. The maximum duration is 45 minutes per week of sprint. It includes the product owner, Scrum masters, and rotating representatives from each team.

For the agile portfolio aspects, we need to turn our focus to LeSS Huge. LeSS Huge still just includes one product owner who has overall responsibility for the product or portfolio. But at this point we may include several area product owners who, together with the product owner, makes up the product owner team. The product owner still has just one product backlog on the portfolio level however it is structured, so each area product owner has an area product backlog, all of which are part of the overall product backlog. Each area product owner then has four to eight teams within a requirement area. That means the portfolio product backlog and management of it is very much treated as an ordinary product backlog, prioritized, and shared with the area product owners who manage the execution of the area requirements.

4.5.2 Research Insights

Grundler and Westner (2019) investigated various agile frameworks and conducted a project portfolio management evaluation which resulted in a conformity rating for each of the frameworks. The scores from LeSS are found in Table 4.4. LeSS is not the framework with the highest score of all the investigated frameworks.

LeSS is scaling Scrum for more than one team, using single-team Scrum practices, e.g., backlog refinement, sprints, retrospective for multiple teams.

Exercise 4.2 Visual Notetaking

Turn your notes from this chapter into a visual representation.

_____

_____

_____

_____

_____

Answers: No right or wrong answers.

4.6 Agile Portfolio Management by Agile Business Consortium

The UK-based DSDM consortium, a not-for-profit organization with focus on business agility, was created in 1994 as one of the first agile organizations. Among other things, the organization took part in the development of the agile manifesto in 2001, however its focus was beyond the world of IT. Besides conferences, publications, and suchlike, the organization founded a range of certifications, the DSDMs. In 2016 the organization changed its name from the DSDM Consortium to the Agile Business Consortium (ABC) Limited which in 2017 published the agile portfolio management framework.

Table 4.4 Conformity Rating for LeSS

Team Level	Programme Level	Value-Stream Level	Portfolio Level	The Spanning Palette
Agile teams	Agile release train (ART)	Value-stream coordination	Enterprise strategic themes	DevOps
Product owner	Release train engineer and value-stream engineer	Economic framework	programme Portfolio management	system team
Scrum master	System and solution architect/engineering	solution intent	Epic owners	release management
Team Kanban	Product and solution management	Model-based systems engineering	Enterprise architect	shares services
Team backlog	Weighted shortest job first (WSJF)	Set-Based design	portfolio Kanban	User experience
Iterations	Programme and value-stream Kanban	Agile architecture	Portfolio Backlog	Vision
Iterations planning	Programme and value-stream backlog	Solution demo	Portfolio vision	Roadmap
Iteration execution	Nonfunctional requirements	Pre- and post-PI planning	Solution Investments by horizon	Metrics
Team demo	Programme increment	Supplier	Budget	Milestones
Iteration retrospective	PI planning	Customer	CapEx and OpEx	Releases
Stories	Business owners	Solution	Value streams	
Iterations goals	PI objectives	Solution Context	Epics	
Built-in quality	System demo		Portfolio sync	
	Features and capabilities		Strategic Portfolio Review	
	Enablers		Participatory budgeting guardrails	
	Innovation and Planning iteration		Portfolio canvas	
	Inspect and adapt			

4.6.1 *Core Concepts of Agile Portfolio Management*

The agile portfolio management framework is a framework for business agility which scales from agile project management to agile programme management and, lastly, the value-focused agile portfolio management. The framework consists of six core behaviours, which are:

■ Focus on the creation of value.
■ Review the portfolio continuously.
■ Involve the right people to shape and manage the portfolio.
■ Clearly and continuously demonstrate that the portfolio is delivering optimum value.
■ Encourage innovation and creativity.
■ Encourage collaboration and empowerment.

The portfolio process is based upon a set of innovation hubs which are steps needed to be done to move forward. The first two steps are "Confirm drivers" and "Confirm foundations", which is where the framework is set up. When the portfolio is up and running the steps are "Deliver change", which is the ongoing activities of delivery value, while "Keep it current" makes sure it is continuously relevant and updated with retrospectives and suchlike.

An initiative that is going to "Deliver change" goes through a maturity process within the portfolio. The steps are:

■ Unformed
■ Immature
■ Ready (to be worked upon)
■ Current (ongoing)
■ Completed (done)
■ Reality (benefits are obtained)

The initiatives are in the past (done), today (current), and to be current in the near-term view and the longer-term view.

The framework is supported by a range of roles. The roles of business change ownership and business innovation leadership are the leading roles for the portfolio and for setting the stage. The business change ownership for each initiative and the change coordinator for each initiative ensures work is done and benefits are obtained. The role of idea generation is bringing new ideas into the portfolio while expert guidance, change analysis, change coordinator, and change support are the core change participants making it all work and run day to day.

The agile portfolio management framework is supported by agile governance which consists of five principles:

- Ensure value drives priority (do the right things).
- Never compromise quality (do things in the right way).
- Decide with the initiatives, do not manage them.
- Give clear, considered direction.
- Stay informed.

4.7 The Nexus Framework for Scaling Scrum

In 2014, the Nexus framework was created by Ken Schwaber in collaboration with key contributors from scrum.org.

4.7.1 Core Concepts of The Nexus Framework for Scaling Scrum

The definition of a Nexus is "a relationship or connection between people or things" which leads to the applied definition of Nexus being "a framework that extends Scrum to enable multiple Scrum teams to use a single Product Backlog to deliver an integrated product. It enables organizations to apply Scrum's iterative and incremental approach to product delivery to deliver large, complex products".

(Bittner et al, 2018)

Scaled Scrum is still Scrum. The Nexus framework is simply an extension of Scrum. Ken Schwaber describes it as an "Exoskeleton, that protects and strengthens Scrum Teams". The general rule for scaling is, do not do it unless you cannot avoid it. The Nexus framework has applied this lesson, as it states, "Simplicity is the Key to Scaling".

The Nexus framework consists of roles, events, artefacts, and rules that bind and weave together the work of approximately three to nine Scrum teams working on a single product backlog to build an integrated increment that meets a goal. One of the aims is also to handle the dependencies that relates to requirements, domain knowledge, software, and test artefacts.

The meetings, rituals, or events include some common, some new, and others which are removed. The ones still applied are refined into the product backlog, development work, the sprint, sprint planning, daily Scrum, and sprint retrospective. The new and extra events are Nexus sprint planning, Nexus daily Scrum, Nexus sprint retrospective, Nexus sprint review, and the Nexus sprint goal. This means the sprint review is gone. The common events are existing Scrum events which are conducted as previously while the Nexus events are new and additional events to cover communication, dependencies, and suchlike when scaling.

The Nexus roles are still the product owner, Scrum master, and team members; however, a new Nexus integration team is introduced where we need the Scrum core roles to be represented as Nexus integration team members. The Nexus integration team or (NIT) is accountable for maximizing the value of the integrated product.

The Nexus artefacts are almost the same as Scrum, with a product backlog, sprint backlog, and integrated increment. The Nexus sprint backlog is a new artefact which contains the product backlog items that have cross-team dependencies.

The Nexus framework also includes practices which serve as techniques and ideas for various situations. One practice is using the exposition (science fair) format for Nexus sprint review to make running large sprint reviews more effective and to engage between the development teams and stakeholders. This is just an example of a set of related techniques that can help to improve the sprint review at scale by letting stakeholders see what they want/need to see, on demand, during the Nexus sprint review.

4.8 Disciplined Agile (Delivery) (DA/DAD)

The framework was originally developed at IBM Rational from early 2009 to June 2012. The IBM team worked closely with business partners, including Mark Lines, and was led by Scott Ambler. The DA 1.0 release occurred in June 2012 with publication of the first DA book, *Disciplined Agile Delivery: A Practitioner's Guide to Agile Software Delivery in the Enterprise.* Ownership of the DA framework intellectual property effectively passed over to the Disciplined Agile Consortium in October 2012, a fact that was legally recognized by IBM in June 2014. The focus was on the software delivery process. Disciplined agile 2.x focuses on describing a flexible, context-sensitive approach to the entire IT process.

Disciplined agile 3.x was released in August 2017 to introduce a fourth layer, disciplined agile enterprise (DAE), to address the full process range required for business agility. In December 2018, disciplined agile 4, now referred to as the disciplined agile toolkit, was released. It focused on a completely revamped description of DAD and a team-based improvement strategy called guided continuous improvement. In August 2019, disciplined agile was acquired by Project Management Institute. (Wikipedia, 2021)

Major changes were done to the certification programmes, among others.

4.8.1 Core Concepts of Disciplined Agile Delivery

Disciplined agile delivery is a hybrid framework with a high-level life cycle including concept, inception (nine process goals/outcomes), construction (five process goals/outcomes), transition (two process goals/outcomes), production, and ongoing (six process goals/outcomes), e.g., grow team members. The life cycle includes phases which disappear over time. This goal-driven framework also includes six adapted life cycles such as basic/agile, lean, continuous delivery, exploratory, programme, and suchlike. Disciplined agile delivery is also supported by a robust set of roles, five primary and five supporting. A primary role is a stakeholder or product owner while a supporting role could be a specialist or integrator. There are clearly some interesting aspects to the DAD framework. DAD is a hybrid approach which extends Scrum with proven strategies from agile modelling (AM), extreme programming (XP), unified process (UP), Kanban, Lean software development, outside-in development (OID), and several other methods. DAD is a non-proprietary, freely available framework. DAD extends the construction-focused life cycle of Scrum to address the full, end-to-end delivery life cycle from project initiation all the way to delivering the solution to its end users. It also supports lean and continuous delivery versions of the life cycle: unlike other agile methods, DAD does not prescribe a single life cycle because it recognizes that one process size does not fit all. DAD includes advice about the technical practices such as those from extreme programming (XP) as well as the modelling, documentation, and governance strategies missing from both Scrum and XP. But, instead of the prescriptive approach seen in other agile methods, including Scrum, the DAD framework takes a goals-driven approach. In doing so, DAD provides contextual advice regarding viable alternatives and their trade-offs, enabling you to tailor DAD to effectively address the situation in which you find yourself. By describing what works, what does not work, and more importantly why, DAD helps you to increase your chance of adopting strategies that will work for you.

4.8.2 Team Level

- Inception
- Form initial team
- Explore initial scope

4.8.3 Programme Level

- Process decision framework for enterprise IT
- Process blades (programme management, product management, EA, IT governance, release management)
- Programme management external workflow

4.8.4 Portfolio Level

- Portfolio management disciplined agile workflow
- The portfolio management process blade addresses how an IT organization goes about identifying, prioritizing, organizing, and governing their various IT endeavours

4.8.5 Processes

Disciplined agile portfolio management seeks to do this in a lightweight and streamlined manner that maximizes the creation of business value in a long-term sustainable manner. IT endeavours typically include solution delivery initiatives/projects, stable product development teams, business experiments (along the lines of a Lean startup strategy), and the operation of existing IT-based solutions. Each process includes goals and factors such as default options and preferences, e.g., envision the future or develop business case, so it is more accessible. The portfolio management processes are:

- Identify potential value (envision the future, obtain customer feedback, monitor business environment).
- Explore potential endeavours (run a small experiment, run a focus group, evaluate alternatives, estimate ROI, estimate market impact, develop business case).

- Prioritize potential endeavours (legislated/regulatory requirements, business value, risk, WSJF, due date, dependency).
- Manage portfolio budget (rolling wave budgeting, stable team budgeting, annual budgeting, ad-hoc budgeting).
- Initiate endeavours (experiment team, product team, project/programme team).
- Finance endeavours (provide initial funding, provide ongoing funding, monitor fund usage).
- Plan IT capabilities (plan IT delivery capability, plan IT operational capability).
- Manage vendors (monitor contracts, identify potential vendors, award contracts, close contracts).
- Govern the portfolio (monitor IT finances, monitor delivery teams, monitor production systems, assess portfolio health, develop portfolio metrics, develop guidance).

4.8.6 Research Insights

Grundler and Westner (2019) investigated various agile frameworks and conducted a project portfolio management evaluation which resulted in a conformity rating for each of the frameworks. The scores from DAD are found in Table 4.5. DAD is not the framework with the highest score of all the investigated frameworks.

4.9 Portfolio Management Using Scrum (Scrum of Scrums)

The history of Scrum goes back to 1986 and the publication by Hirotake Takeuchi and Ikujiro Nonaka (1986) in the *Harvard Business Review* (January–February 1986) titled "The New Product Development Game", where they introduced a new holistic approach to the sport of rugby, where the whole team "tries to go to the distance as a unit, passing the ball back and forth". At the same time, work by William Deming on "Plan-Do-Check-Act" gave rise to new ideas.

In 1993, Jeff Sutherland, John Scumniotales, and Jeff McKenna implemented Scrum at Easel Corporation, which is one of the first well-known implementations. Later IDX was said to have more than 500 people doing Scrum.

Ken Schwaber and Jeff Sutherland presented "The SCRUM Development Process" *at* the Object-Oriented Programming, Systems, Languages &

Table 4.5 Conformity Rating for DAD

Objective	Conformity	Operationalization	Hierarchy Level
Portfolio Structuring			
Selection and prioritization	YES	Selection and prioritization in process factor number 1–3	Portfolio management
Re-evaluation	NO	N/A	N/A
Portfolio Steering			
Monitoring	YES	Centralized view not described Process factors govern the portfolio	Portfolio management
Re-adjusting	NO	N/A	N/A
Resource Management			
Resource planning	YES	Resource planning in process factor 7,8	Portfolio management
Reactive allocation	NO	N/A	N/A
Organizing learning	YES	Guidance to and from continuous improvement Community	Continuous improvement Process blade

Applications (OOPSLA) Conference '95 in Austin, Texas, which may be the first public appearance of Scrum. In 2001 Ken Schwaber and Jeff Sutherland, among others, took part in the development of the Agile Manifesto which is covered in Chapter 3.

Scrum then erupted into various Scrum organizations or bodies of knowledge, such as Scrum Alliance, Agile Alliance, scrum.org, and others, which is very much the market we see today. The Scrum of 1995 did not consider the scaling aspects which later were included. Several of the Scrum organizations have introduced new methods for this: Nexus (see Section 4.5), Scrum @Scale, Scrum of Scrums (ibid.), and suchlike, are just a few to mention.

4.9.1 Core Concepts of Scrum

Scrum is not just Scrum, as each Scrum body of knowledge adds its own flavours and guidelines on what Scrum is and how to use it. However, most

Scrum organizations do agree that Scrum is based upon five Scrum values which are:

- Commitment
- Focus
- Openness
- Respect
- Courage

Some Scrum organizations include aspects which are like themes or knowledge areas and include:

- Organization
- Quality
- Risk
- Business justification
- Change

This division is not that common, but the content within the themes is found in most Scrum applications.

4.9.2 Team Level

Scrum at team level starts with the business case which is a tool to justify the work and to select the product owner. The product owner writes, based upon the business case, the product vision statement and onboards the Scrum master to fit with the vision and underlying business case. They select the Scrum team which sums up the Scrum core roles. Most Scrum frameworks have a common understanding of which core roles are doing what, with minor variations. This means the product owner focuses on business justification and value, the Scrum master removes impediments and ensures the Scrum flows is going well, while the Scrum team focuses on delivering the actual work. The so-called ceremonies or meetings may be initiated by the optional release planning meeting which builds the initial product backlog (list of things to do) with the first epics (high-level requirements). The product owner may elaborate on the epics and decompose them into user stories (who, what, and why). When the product backlog is ready (user stories – definition of ready), the product owner meets up with the Scrum team to conduct the sprint planning. The sprint goal is set, user stories are estimated using planning poker, affinity estimation, or similar, then the committed (by the Scrum team) work is placed in the sprint backlog which is broken down from user stories into tasks by the Scrum team and arranged on the Scrum board or information radiator. The amount of committed work is based upon the Scrum team's velocity, which is a measure of how much work they can do in a period. The Sprint commerce and the Scrum teams works on delivering the tasks. Each day, the Scrum team meets up for the daily Scrum to discuss the three questions. During the sprint, the burndown/burnup chart may be updated on user stories completed or left. While the Scrum team is Scrumming, the product owner works on the product backlog, which is called backlog refinement or backlog grooming. At the end of the sprint, often two to four weeks, the Scrum review is arranged where the Scrum team presents the output (if definition of done is completed) of the sprint for the product owner and possible key stakeholders. Tasks are approved if they pass the acceptance criteria or rejected if not the case. If rejected, the user stories are put back into the product backlog. The approved tasks are the increment of the sprint. After the sprint review the Scrum teams hold the Scrum retrospective where the sprint is discussed, and improvements are made.

4.9.3 *Programme Level*

Scrum is just Scrum and work is conducted on the team level; however, in most frameworks of Scrum the programme level introduces additional roles. Some frameworks have a chief product owner and chief Scrum master who is required to coordinate and make decisions in case of multiple teams and core roles. In addition, some frameworks have a programme product owner (area product owner) and programme Scrum master where content of the roles are like the team level, except on the programme level. The programme product owner manages the programme backlog, which is a product backlog, except on the programme level. The programme backlog is then shared with the product owners on the team level and each takes their share of the work. The core team may be expanded to have a large core team with members from all Scrum teams, Scrum masters, products owners, and the chiefs. The only new meeting is the Scrum of Scrums where four questions are covered to managed dependencies, ongoing work, and impediments. Some Scrum frameworks also introduce a wide range of artefacts and meetings such as environment plan meetings, release readiness plans, collaborations plans, and resource planning.

4.9.4 Portfolio Level

Scrum at the portfolio level is the management of one common backlog, now the portfolio backlog. The portfolio backlog needs constant work – portfolio backlog refinement/grooming (e.g., two hours, bi-weekly). The inputs into the portfolio backlog sounds are traced to the company mission/vision and suchlike (see Chapter 3 on strategy). At this stage, the content of the portfolio backlog is initiatives, like small projects or epics, not user stories at the portfolio level. Some Scrum frameworks uses the same core roles as on the team level, just the portfolio version such as portfolio product owner or portfolio Scrum master, while others talk about portfolio master or portfolio manager. The meetings are like the team level, as illustrated in Table 4.6.

As illustrated in Table 4.6, the structure is very much the same as on the team level; however, different work is to be done at this level. Some Scrum frameworks introduce minimum done criteria, which are the criteria which must be followed by the programme and team level, i.e., compliance requirements.

4.9.5 Research Insights

Grundler and Westner (2019) investigated various agile frameworks and conducted a project portfolio management evaluation which resulted in a conformity rating for each of the frameworks. The scores from Scrum are found in Table 4.7. Scrum is not the framework with the highest score of all the investigated frameworks.

Table 4.6   Scrum Meetings at Team and Portfolio Levels

Team Level	Portfolio Level
Sprint planning	Portfolio planning
Sprint review	Portfolio review
Sprint retrospective	Portfolio retrospective
Backlog refinement grooming	Portfolio backlog refinement grooming
Product backlog	Portfolio backlog

Table 4.7   Conformity Rating for Scrum

Objective	Conformity	Operationalization	Hierarchy Level
Portfolio Structuring			
Selection and prioritization	YES	Selection of epics by the enterprise action team	Highest level executive
Re-evaluation	NO	N/A	N/A
Portfolio Steering			
Monitoring			
Re-adjusting	NO	N/A	N/A
Resource Management			
Resource planning	NO	N/A	N/A
Reactive allocation			
Organizing learning			

Scrum of Scrums can be described as a basic mechanism for scaling Scrum.

4.9.6 Scrum Key Terms

The key terms of this chapter are found in Table 4.8 and structured around the various levels.

4.10 XSCALE Alliance (XA)

The XSCALE alliance is like the Linux of the agile world – a learning ecosystem of independent coaches and consultancies based on a kernel of proven agile practice patterns. Like Linux, the XSCALE alliance wraps this kernel in independent commercial distributions of coaching and training. XSCALE is a set of principles based upon patterns constructed by Peter Merel, an Australian coach back in 2014. Later this work became the XSCALE alliance (XA), which has grown some but still waits on its big breakthrough.

Table 4.8   Levels of Scrum

Team Level	Programme Level	Portfolio Level
Core roles Scrum team Product owner Scrum master	Chief product owner Chief Scrum master Programme product owner (area product owner) Programme Scrum master Core team and large core team	Portfolio product owner Portfolio Scrum master Portfolio master Portfolio manager
Release planning Sprint Refinement/grooming Sprint planning Daily Scrum Scrum review Scrum retrospective	Scrum of Scrums	Portfolio planning Portfolio refinement/ grooming Portfolio review Portfolio retrospective
Sprint goal Sprint Increment Timebox Product backlog Sprint backlog Epic User Stories Tasks Definition of done Acceptance criteria Velocity Impediments Burndown chart Scrum board, information radiator	Programme backlog Environments plan Meetings Release readiness plan Collaborations plans Dependencies Resource planning	Company mission/vision Portfolio backlog Refinement/grooming Minimum done criteria Epics Impediments log Dependencies

4.10.1 Core Concepts of XSCALE Alliance (XA)

The purpose of XSCALE is to provide patterns to descale organizations. XSCALE is built upon four descaling values and 12 principles. These are the four descaling values:

- Autonomy in alignment over command and control
- Throughput accounting over cost accounting

- Pull-based delivery and change over push-based
- Learning ecosystems over training hierarchies

4.10.2 Autonomy in Alignment over Command and Control

In XSCALE a portfolio has 10 to 80 squad members. The work is structured value streams where product and feature squads of four to eight members are onboard the value systems. They are supported by the system squads. All squads are supported by various chapter leaders with two to ten members. The aim is to create a self-directing portfolio of self-managing streams of self-organizing teams of the client's own staff through self-propagating transformation. To support this endeavour, three descaling metrics are applied: a ceremony size limit, which focuses on the amount of team members; a collaboration loop limit, which is like communication channels; and a feedback frequency limit, which is the maximum period after which any plan priority or work product goes unreviewed. This is supported by "leadership as a service" and techniques such as "Round council" and the "Camelot Model".

4.10.3 Throughput Accounting over Cost Accounting.

The concept is that throughput accounting continuously identifies and prioritizes the bottleneck that dominates throughput per stream and per portfolio in contrast to the classic approach. This value emphasizes the product manager's role versus the PMO role which is considered a waste. The 3D Product Management and suchlike contain various techniques that can be useful in various cases such as:

- Pirate Canvas shows you which market bottleneck your product must attack next.
- Impact Mapping questions the business value of your epics.
- Behaviour Mapping starts with tools for mapping epics to features.
- Acceptance Matrix compiles the output of Behaviour Mapping breadth-first.
- Business Bingo generates quick consensus on actionable numbers for feature cost, business value, risk, and priorities.
- Release Refactoring maximizes ROI across multiple value streams for multiple release goals.
- Leadership as a Service is a protocol that eliminates politics and speeds the flow of learnings between teams and streams.

- Throughput Accounting uses the components of ecosystem growth, rather than cost minimization, as the basis for feature prioritization.
- Set-Based Design is a collaborative method for exploring the design space breadth-first.
- CRC Carding aligns the remaining choices with architectural constraints and user experiences.

4.10.4 Pull-Based Delivery and Change over Push-Based

This value focuses on delivery and change when conducting an agile transformation. The concept is that "A team can't change faster than its most resistant member. Nor a stream than its most resistant team. Pushing change on existing groups builds resistance and compromise, making things harder & risker over time" (Xscale, 2021 – their website). This is supported by triple-loop learning and suchlike which means the teams needs to *pull* the transformations rather than being *pushed* in their direction. You need to be using agile to roll out agile, you need to go to France to learn to speak France: that is the general idea illustrated.

4.10.5 Learning Ecosystems over Training Hierarchies

At the heart of XSCALE and the XSCALE Alliance is the Shu Ha Ri training hierarchies and Mu Hin Shu learning communities inspired by various Japanese sources. The idea is to create an ecosystem thinking using coaches, stewards, and suchlike rather than the training and certification hierarchies often applied in agile organizations. The four decaling values are supported by the 12 principles which are illustrated below. Keep in mind, as with the four descaling values, that these 12 principles are not the same as the organismal 12 principles from the people who created the agile manifesto.

- Directly responsible individuals: business, design, and tech stakeholders make decisions together as peers to build solutions that meet each other's constraints.
- Capture and store learning in small, self-organizing teams: as these work with current constraints, they become capable of opening future bottlenecks.
- Work on outcomes: teams continuously prioritize the current bottleneck, quantify their contributions to top line business throughput, and minimize work in progress.

- Align small groups of teams into self-managing business streams that continuously adapt their work priorities to changing market feedback.
- Reward mutual benefit across business streams to reduce silos, waste, and missed opportunities, and share resources, services, and learning.
- Mercilessly refactor business streams: reuse, recycle, or reduce all the resources a stream produces so all contribute to the top line throughput and none go to waste.
- Design breadth-first. Step back to see patterns in and between markets and value streams. These inform designs we can only detail as we learn more.
- Collaborate rather than delegate: people and teams are in the right relationships when conversations evolve to support each other's work and learning.
- Take time to simplify and automate solutions: simple, automated systems cost less than big manual ones, taking less work to maintain business outcomes.
- Use and value experimentation: experiment to reduce risk and adapt each product to the changing constraints of your business streams and markets.
- Enrich interfaces to serve underserved markets: spaces between market segments are where most opportunities for innovation and productivity occur.
- Transform to embrace change: continuously adapt your organization's patterns to changing market conditions and opportunities to open new markets.

4.11 Enterprise Scrum

Enterprise Scrum was created by Mike Beedle who started his journey in June 1995 where he became good friends with Ken Schwaber and Jeff Sutherland. The same year, Mike Beedle implemented Scrum at William M. Mercer. Years followed with various presentations and papers until 2000, when Mike Beedle developed and released "XBreed: Scrum with engineering practices and release management". In February 2001, the Agile Manifesto was developed with Mike Beedle as one of the co-writers. From 2001 Enterprise Scrum as a company and framework was marketed and more than 3,000 instances of the product with Scrum were implemented. In 2001, Mike Beedle and Ken Schwaber published *Agile Software Development with Scrum* which is one of the first books with Scrum or Agile on its title. The first version of Enterprise Scrum was published on 29 March 2014. In 2017, Enterprise Scrum Definition 3.0 was released while the current version, 4.0, was released the following year.

4.11.1 Core Concepts of Enterprise Scrum

Enterprise Scrum is developed to "quickly delivers the most business value and balanced benefits to all people involved" (Mike Beedle). It is to some degree an abstraction of Scrum. It is built upon the ideas of generalization, extension of Scrum, parametrization, explicit techniques (i.e., Lean startup, blue ocean strategy), iterative-incremental, scalable, and all-in-all framework.

The enterprise Scrum concepts and names are the same as Scrum; however, there are a fair number of changes. The enterprise Scrum values are the same, being:

■ Commitment
■ Openness
■ Focus
■ Respect
■ Courage

Roles are enterprise scrum team, business owner (can be shared), and coach (can be shared). The Enterprise Scrum Team has the same tasks as other Scrum teams. They are Self-DMOS meaning self-directed, self-managed, self-organized, and self-selected. The business owner has the same functions as a product owner; however, the role may be shared among many people, including team members. The same concept is applied with the coach, who has the same functions and tasks as a Scrum master; once again it can be shared and multiplied. The opportunity to share roles opens up for scalability but at the cost of complexity. Rituals or meetings play a minor part in the guide; however, common Scrum meetings are expected. The process is simplified with a vision, then identified as to value, followed by cycles or sprints.

The guide applies the Business Canvas techniques which help with adoptions together with the Enterprise Scrum Configuration Guide by which each adaptation or implementation can be tailored to the needs of the organization.

For the portfolio level, the concepts are as illustrated, and the number of business owners defines the vision and identifies/prioritizes the value list before work can commerce. It is stated what tasks each role should perform but there is little information on how to perform them except for the various techniques which are mentioned, so you need to join the dots.

4.12 Recipes for Agile Governance in the Enterprise (RAGE)

Recipes for Agile Governance in the Enterprise (RAGE) were documented in 2013 by Kevin Thompson while working for cPrime, an Alten Group Company.

4.12.1 Core Concepts of Recipes for Agile Governance in the Enterprise

This approach includes recipes for agile governance. The term agile governance refers to an agile style of governance, not specifically to the governance of projects that use agile processes. Although we use the term governance, we rarely define it or have a common understanding of it. In RAGE, governance includes the following:

- Creating a vision
- Securing resources
- Defining clear roles and responsibilities
- Establishing benchmarks for performance
- Monitoring the benchmarks
- Accounting to key stakeholders for the organization's direction and performance

RAGE applies three primary levels of granularity for the work of an organization: portfolio, programme, and project. Governance is important at all levels.

The portfolio governance process contains three roles, two ceremonies, and four artefacts. The roles are portfolio owner, area product owner, and programme manager, which are described below.

4.12.1.1 Portfolio Owner

This role has authority over initiative selection and prioritization. Most business units have only one portfolio manager (who often has VP or COO as a job title).

Responsibilities include:

■ Reviewing business cases for initiatives (usually developed by area product owners)
■ Setting priorities (and sequencing) of initiatives
■ Making decisions about whether to carry out, re-prioritize, or cancel initiatives

4.12.1.2 Area Product Owner

The sole authority over product requirements for the product and the intended content of the release. Responsibilities include:

■ Working with customers and stakeholders to identify needs, solutions, and business value
■ Working with team product owners to develop sufficient detail about requirements and cost (based on development and testing effort) to support useful ROI estimates
■ Develop business case for product releases, for use in portfolio planning
■ Monitor changes in business needs, and work with team product owners to revise the planned product release content as needed
■ Provide ongoing guidance to team product owners regarding cross-team priorities and trade-offs

4.12.1.3 Programme Manager

Works closely with teams' Scrum masters or project managers to ensure that cross-team collaboration is effective in achieving the product's release goals. Responsibilities include:

■ Enforcing agreements on how cross-team collaboration is done
■ Facilitating cross-team meetings
■ Monitoring cross-team dependencies, and ensuring that these are planned and addressed effectively

- Assessing impact of development issues and scope changes on cross-team dependencies and overall execution
- Monitoring progress of the product release
- Ensuring that risks are addressed effectively during planning and execution
- Removing obstacles to effective cross-team collaboration

The two ceremonies are portfolio grooming meeting and portfolio planning meeting. Portfolio grooming refers to the process of developing a business case while a portfolio planning meeting is where the portfolio owner commonly facilitates this meeting, as well as providing the final decision regarding proposed or in-process initiatives. The ceremonies are so-called governance points which are illustrated in Table 4.9.

The four artefacts are:

- Business case
- Agile charter
- Decision matrix
- Portfolio backlog

The decision matrix is a multicriteria analysis, while the other artefacts are as they are commonly applied.

The programme level is mainly like scaled Scrum with minor variations while the team level is Scrum or Kanban which makes it easy to apply as it

Table 4.9 RAGE Governance

WHEN	PARTICIPANTS	DECISIONS AND ACTIONS
Portfolio grooming meeting	Area product owner, team product owners, programme managers	Area product owner gets feedback on quality and completeness of business cases. Programme manager provides effort estimate, but often after follow-up consultation with Scrum masters and Scrum teams.
Portfolio planning meeting	Portfolio owner, area product owners	Each area product owner describes business cases for initiatives. All discuss to clarify understanding, and possibly adjust estimates. Portfolio owner adds items to decision matrix, makes decisions about whether/when to start new initiatives. Portfolio owner may also decide to terminate ongoing initiatives.

fits in most organizations. Besides the governance, RAGE includes practical recipes for new governance and the principles that apply across them.

4.13 The Spotify Model

We have included the Spotify model as it is often included when frameworks for scaling agile is assessed however it is not a framework. The Spotify model "is a people-driven, autonomous approach for scaling agile that emphasizes the importance of culture and network" (Kniberg and Ivarsson, 2012). In the Spotify model we believe engagement increases value and value increases engagement.

"Alistair Cockburn (one of the founding fathers of agile software development) visited Spotify and said, 'Nice – I've been looking for someone to implement this matrix format since 1992 so it is really welcome to see'" (Kniberg and Ivarsson, 2012).

The Spotify model was published by Henrik Kniberg and Anders Ivarsson in 2012 after working with Spotify (30 teams in 3 cities), the innovative music service which was launched in 2008. The Spotify model includes a structure of squads, tribes, chapters, and guilds. Table 4.10 describes the content of the structure.

Table 4.10   The Spotify Model Structure

Structure: Squad	A squad is the basic unit of development at Spotify. A squad is like a Scrum team. They are cross-functional, co-located, organized around a business capability.
Structure: Tribe	A tribe is a collection of squads that work in related areas. Squads in a tribe are located the same place (co-located). They have a fair/high degree of autonomy and freedom. Tribe size is max. 100 members. Tribes meets now and then for informal meetings and such.
Structure: Chapter	The chapter is your small family of people having similar skills and working within the same general competency area within the same tribe.
Structure: Guilds	Community of Interest/shared interests like cycling, coffee drinking, or engineering related like C++. Works well for standardization, common problem-solving, onboarding new people, and suchlike. Most guilds have regular meetings. Some guilds are more formal than others. Guilds can be sponsored by management and self-proclaimed.

The Spotify model includes four main roles: the product owner, chapter lead (line manager), tribe lead (senior technical leader), and agile coach; however, additional roles were used at Spotify, these being guild coordinator, system owner, and chief architect (Table 4.11).

Just after implementation, the employee satisfaction was high, 4.4 out of 5. But it did not continue. In 2020, Henrik Kniberg went back and examined how the Spotify model worked at Spotify in Sweden which was published (Smite et al., 2020) in the "Communications of the ACM" March 2020. It not really working anymore (see Figure 4.5). Members of the teams were fine with meeting with close team/squad members; however, when it came to taking part in tribes, chapters, and guilds the attendance and output was minimal. People did not have the time to dedicate to the model and the organization support and prioritizations changed. Also increased diversity among the team members made it more difficult to find common ground for guilds, which decreased the value of engagement. As a respondent noted: "Guilds seem bloated and diluted. There could be a need for a guild-like forum on a smaller scale" (Smite et al., 2020). One of the major problems was the growth (fragmentation) of the company which in the years from 2012 to 2020 increased from a few hundred to many thousands of employees across six global locations. Scaling causes detachment and makes a sense of common community, networking, and suchlike much more difficult.

Table 4.11   The Spotify Model Roles

Role: Product Owner	The squad has a dedicated product owner that prioritizes the work and takes both business value and tech aspects into consideration.
Role: Chapter Lead	The chapter lead is line manager for his chapter members, with all the traditional responsibilities such as developing people, setting salaries.
Role: Tribe Lead	Overall, responsibly for the tribe
Role: Agile Coach	The squad has an agile coach that helps them identify impediments and coaches them to continuously improve their process.
Role: Guild Coordinator	Basic coordination like sharing info, enrollment, and such.
Role: System Owner	All systems have one or more system owners. Technical and architectural expert on the system.
Role: Chief Architect	High-level architecture.

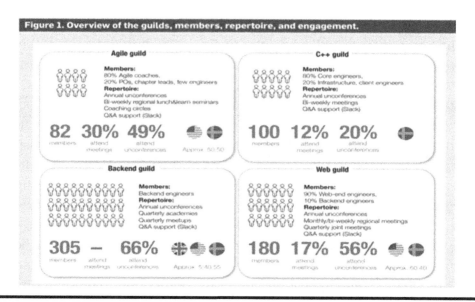

Figure 4.5   Overview of the guilds, members, repertoire, and some engagement at Spotify.

Still, you can offer support with the agile portfolio framework, with the Spotify model for increased emphasis on networking and culture; however, it is not without problems.

Exercise 4.3 Walk and Talk

Take a walk and talk about what this chapter has been all about, what you have learned, and how you are going to use it back at work.

_____

_____

Answers: No right or wrong answers.

Chapter 5

Project Portfolio Management Versus Agile Portfolio Management

Figure 5.1   Overview.

Many practitioners have been working with project portfolio management for years and might be familiar with the financial approach to project portfolio management which is discussed in Chapter 1. Fewer practitioners have extensive experience with the software development approach to agile portfolio management, which is covered in Chapters 2, 3, and 4 when we discussed the consequences of scaling, the generic topics on agile portfolio management, and the specific frameworks which can be applied for agile portfolio management.

This chapter is designed to foster an understanding of the similarities and differences between project portfolio management coming from a financial approach and agile portfolio management which comes from agile software development, two very much different approaches to solving the same kind of problems.

One of the best global practice standards for project portfolio management is the "Management of Portfolios" (MoP) from Axelos where the current 2011 edition applies to the project portfolio management approach. The project portfolio management approach is then compared with the agile portfolio management approach based upon Chapters 2 and 3, in the following tables.

Table 5.1 contains the five portfolio management principles, the portfolio definition, and portfolio delivery cycles which in the "Management of Portfolios" (MoP) global standard are supported by 12 practices. Table 5.2 contains the key activities commonly conducted at the outset in the MoP standard while Table 5.3 contains the major roles applied in MoP; finally, Table 5.4 includes the documentation (artefacts) applied in "Management of Portfolios". After each table an analysis is conducted on the table, and the findings will be discussed.

The second part of this chapter contains guidelines to consider if your organization is going to make a choice between project portfolio management or agile portfolio management, hopefully confirming that the right choose of portfolio management approach has been made (and for the right reasons).

The first table, Table 5.1, includes the "Management of Portfolios" in the left-hand column and agile portfolio management in the right-hand column. The MoP sets the topics while the agile portfolio management column aims at explaining how similar concepts would be applied in an agile setting. On the agile setting, the concepts mentioned refer to Chapters 2 and 3. Often one or two concepts found in project portfolio management need several concepts to be explained in the agile portfolio management approach, which to some degree highlights some of the differences between the two approaches. They may sound similar on the overall portfolio level but digging deeper shows some major differences.

High-level portfolio management, whether it is project portfolio management or agile portfolio management, seems to solve many of the same tasks, just done differently. In general, project portfolio management is less principle-driven than agile portfolio management. "Management of Portfolios" contains five principles while agile is built upon Lean; additional principles and values are then added from the agile manifest, the declaration of interdependence, and suchlike, which makes it extensively principle-driven

Table 5.1 High-level Portfolio Management

Project Portfolio Management	
Management of Portfolios (MoP)	*Agile Portfolio Management*
Five portfolio management principles **Senior management commitment**	Agile principles Lean thinking and Lean portfolio Management Adaptability vs. predictability
Five portfolio management principles **Governance alignment**	Agile principles Lean thinking and Lean portfolio Management Agile level of governance Explaining roles and responsibilities
Five portfolio management principles **Strategy alignment**	Agile principles Lean thinking and Lean portfolio Management Align all work to the strategy
Five portfolio management principles **Portfolio office**	Agile principles Lean thinking and Lean portfolio Management The agile project management office (PMO)
Five portfolio management principles **Energized change culture**	Agile principles Lean thinking and Lean portfolio Management
Portfolio definition cycle **Practice 1 – Understand**	Align all work to the strategy Agile requirements levels (scope decomposition)
Portfolio definition cycle **Practice 2 – Categorize**	Identify the portfolio value in an initiative Estimation of initiatives Qualify ideas for portfolio inclusion – the agile business case
Portfolio definition cycle **Practice 3 – Prioritize**	Portfolio prioritization – sorting/ranking the portfolio
Portfolio definition cycle **Practice 4 – Balance**	Bottlenecks and cost of delays
Portfolio definition cycle **Practice 5 – Plan**	Visualize and present the portfolio values Continuous planning
Portfolio delivery cycle **Practice 6 – Management control**	Explaining roles and responsibilities Agile level of governance

(Continued)

Table 5.1 (Continued)   High-level Portfolio Management

Project Portfolio Management	
Management of Portfolios (MoP)	*Agile Portfolio Management*
Portfolio delivery cycle **Practice 7 – Benefit management**	Qualify ideas for portfolio inclusion – the agile business case Identify the portfolio value in an initiative Visualize and present the portfolio values Benefit management and communicative the portfolio values
Portfolio delivery cycle **Practice 8 – Financial management**	Agile portfolio budgeting and resources
Portfolio delivery cycle **Practice 9 – Risk management**	Managing portfolio risks
Portfolio delivery cycle **Practice 10 – Stakeholders engagement**	Portfolio-wide stakeholder analysis
Portfolio delivery cycle **Practice 11 – Organizational governance**	Explaining roles and responsibilities Agile level of governance
Portfolio delivery cycle **Practice 12 – Practice-resource management**	Agile portfolio budgeting and resources

and one of the key drivers for making agile portfolio management work. Both portfolio management approaches include a wide range of practices where titles like risk management or resource management may look similar, but content varies in application. In the project portfolio management, the activities of each project, programme, or operation are funded individually (financial management), while in agile portfolio management we tend to fund the whole portfolio, so funding and resources are fixed, while in project portfolio management they are flexible. In the agile column of Table 5.1 transparency and collaboration could have been included for most parts as they are central themes whatever work is done in the agile portfolio management; to a degree this is far from the same in the project portfolio management approach, where transparency and collaboration have much less emphasis. Risk management and stakeholder's engagement are areas of similarity in mindset and techniques; however, when it comes to execution, the approaches are different. In the agile portfolio management approaches,

Table 5.2 Key Activities

	Project Portfolio Management (MoP)		Agile Portfolio Management
Key Activity	Purpose	Portfolio Life Cycle	
Understand the environment	Developing a clear understanding of your organization's strategic objectives, culture, and environment	Portfolio definition cycle	Align all work to the strategy
Portfolio planning	Ensuring visibility of the portfolio-level journey and integrating plans at strategic, portfolio, programme, and project delivery level	Portfolio definition cycle	The portfolio Kanban aka agile portfolio planning Kanban Wall Visualize and present the portfolio values
Prioritization	Ensuring an ongoing prioritization mechanism that provides a clear view of which projects and programme are the most important to your organization	Portfolio definition cycle	Portfolio prioritization – sorting/ranking the portfolio
Managing benefits	Embedding a robust investment process that ensures that benefits are effectively defined, planned, and delivered. Ensuring any deviation from the agreed return of investment is managed transparently and effectively	Portfolio definition cycle	Qualify ideas for portfolio inclusion – the agile business case Identify the portfolio value in an initiative Visualize and present the portfolio values Benefit management and communicative the portfolio values
Categorization	Grouping the projects and programme into common types to help understand where you are investing your resource and contributes to your strategic objective	Portfolio definition cycle	Identify the portfolio value in an initiative Estimation of initiatives Qualify ideas for Portfolio inclusion – the agile business case

(Continued)

Table 5.2 (Continued)   Key Activities

Key Activity	Project Portfolio Management (MoP)		Agile Portfolio Management
	Purpose	Portfolio Life Cycle	
Optimizing and balancing	Juggling all the elements of time, resources, finance, risk, and creating the most suitably balanced portfolio with particular focus on dependency management	Portfolio definition cycle	Bottlenecks and cost of delays
Establishing a portfolio management office	A highly skilled team operating at executive level providing the standard across the organization for effective portfolio investment, planning, prioritization, collaboration, and delivery of change	Portfolio office principle	The agile project management office (PMO)
Managing risk	Ensuring that there are an overall understanding and appropriate mitigation of risk that could impact the portfolio at all levels	Portfolio delivery cycle	Managing portfolio risks
Applying governance	Developing a governance structure that adds value and facilitates information flow at all levels enabling effective, timely, and confident executive decision-making	Governance portfolio principle	Agile principles Lean thinking and Lean portfolio management Agile level of governance Explaining roles and responsibilities
Engaging with stakeholders	Engaging in conversation with the right people at the right time whilst curating the development of an energized and collaborative portfolio delivery community	Portfolio delivery cycle	Portfolio-wide stakeholder analysis

risk management and stakeholder's engagement are often conducted by a few product-owner type of roles, while in project portfolio management is a general concept to consider for many roles.

Some of the major topics of Table 5.1 are broken down in Table 5.2 into key activities, explained as the purpose of the activity, place in the portfolio life cycle, and then compared to agile portfolio management.

Table 5.2 illustrates some of the same tendencies as witnessed in Table 5.1, except with additional details and explanations. Another aspect to highlight is how the various meetings or rituals applied in the agile portfolio management system are made to work, e.g., retrospectives, demos, and suchlike, which are not highlighted here, as the project portfolio management approach provides the headlines with which it is compared.

Most of the roles found in "Management of Portfolios" representing project portfolio management would, in an agile setting, be covered mostly by a portfolio-level product-owner type of role. This makes the comparison with reference to Table 5.3 less interesting; however, what should be highlighted is which roles seem to be missing in the project portfolio management approach that are central in the agile portfolio management approaches. To some degree, the portfolio level Scrum master, or facilitation of the process on the portfolio level, is extraordinarily little emphasized in project portfolio management while it is central on most frameworks for agile portfolio management. Agile focuses mainly on software development while project portfolio management covers all kinds of projects. Due to this, we have a lot of software-development–specific roles in agile portfolio management such as test, infrastructure, architects, DevOps, and suchlike which are

Table 5.3   Role Descriptions

Project Portfolio Management	
Management of Portfolios (MoP)	*Agile Portfolio Management*
Portfolio direction group or Investment committee	Explaining roles and responsibilities
Portfolio progress group or change delivery committee	Explaining roles and responsibilities
Business change director or portfolio director	Explaining roles and responsibilities
Portfolio manager	Explaining roles and responsibilities
Portfolio benefits manager	Explaining roles and responsibilities

little mentioned in the project portfolio management approaches as roles are more generic and put less emphasis on the technical disciplines. You might say that agile portfolio management frameworks are already tailored to initial software development while using project portfolio management frameworks for software development would require a bit more work, which is discussed in Chapter 8 on tailoring and its importance.

Table 5.4 contains the common portfolio documentation applied in project portfolio management. In an agile setting the term artefact is used for all kinds of documentation, but using different names and quite different content. The extensive documentation illustrated in Table 5.4 is, in that form, not used in the agile portfolio management approach. In the agile portfolio management approach, most of the subjects are included but in a quite different form and format, often limited to part of an agile charter, business case, and suchlike. The project portfolio management is much more document-driven, and more upfront documentation is complete, while the agile portfolio management approach documents are iterative (minimum upfront) when needed and less document-intensive. The main difference is in the portfolio dashboard, where use in project portfolio management is to some degree limited while the agile portfolio management approach heavily

Table 5.4   Portfolio Documentations (Artefacts)

Project Portfolio Management	
Management of Portfolios (MoP)	*Agile Portfolio Management*
Portfolio management framework	Portfolio artefacts
Portfolio strategy	Portfolio artefacts
Portfolio delivery plan	Portfolio artefacts
Portfolio benefits management framework	Portfolio artefacts
Portfolio benefits realization plan	Portfolio artefacts
Portfolio financial plan	Portfolio artefacts
Portfolio resource schedule	Portfolio artefacts
Portfolio stakeholder engagement and communication plan	Portfolio artefacts
Portfolio dashboard	The portfolio Kanban aka agile portfolio Planning Kanban wall Visualize and present the portfolio values

replies on the Kanban board and similar for transparency, collaboration, and such key functions. Chapters 3 and 4 include various artefacts or documentation applied in agile portfolio management which are not found in project portfolio management and are therefore hidden in this table's alignment.

5.1 Which Portfolio Management Approach to Choose and Why?

In research or business practice it is not possible to pinpoint just one framework that can support us in our decision as to whether to work with project portfolio management or agile portfolio management; however, several frameworks and models exist which can guide organizations and practitioners in making that decision on the team, rather than the portfolio, level.

One set of techniques for the team level is also illustrated in Chapter 2, that is, Cynefin (Snowden) and the Stacey Matrix (Stacey) which states that if projects or initiatives are best practice or simple, then project portfolio management would be the best choice, whereas situations that are complex or complicated would entail agile portfolio management.

Another set of techniques for team-level decisions are models where decisions are based upon a range of criteria. In PRINCE2 Agile they apply a model called the "Agilometer" to assess whether to work plan-based, equal to project portfolio management, or agile, equal to agile portfolio management. The "Agilometer" applies the following six factors:

- Flexibility on what to deliver
- Level of collaboration
- Ease of communication
- Ability to work iterative and deliver incremental
- Advantageous environmental conditions
- Acceptance of agile

The general view is that if you are scoring low, then project portfolio management and the plan-based approach would work well, while scoring high would foster an agile, or agile portfolio management, approach. It makes you wonder why plan-based approaches require so little communication and collaboration, but that is a topic for another day.

An alternative to the "Agilometer" is Table 5.5, containing executive attributes for portfolio management which could help the organization to

Table 5.5   Executive Attributes

Scenarios/Attributes	Agile Portfolio Management	Project Portfolio Management	Hybrid Portfolio Management
Changing requirements	YES		
Unproven technology	YES		
When the product is intended for an Industry with rapidly changing standards or market conditions	YES		
When you have skilled developers, who are adaptable and able to think independently	YES		
Rapid prototyping of the product is more important than the quality of the product	YES		
More than three interfacing systems are involved		YES	
When definitions, not speed, is key to success		YES	
Multi-component programme where infrastructure or some workstreams are well defined while software or user interface are not defined in detail			YES
Significant regulatory compliance and laws need to be followed		YES	YES
Significant infrastructure build required		YES	YES
Complex requirements and design need to be completed upfront		YES	YES
Sponsors are not brought into agile approach; product owners have limited time to work with the development teams		YES	
Releases management process is not mature		YES	
Full-time resource allocation not possible		YES	
Team is experienced in agile	YES		

guide the decision on whether project portfolio management or agile portfolio management would be the best choice for a certain portfolio within the organization. In this case, the table contains "YES", if there is a match. Also in Table 5.5 there is hybrid portfolio management, which is a combination of project portfolio management and agile portfolio management. The hybrid approach is covered in detail in Chapter 6. In some cases, e.g., significant regulatory compliance and laws needed to be followed, several options could work, e.g., project portfolio management or hybrid portfolio management.

It is not easy making the right call. This chapter contains some ideas on what to do. Chapter 7 on implementation also contains ideas on how to implement, and why, where some of the reasons might be similar for choosing one approach over the other. With regard to selecting the right framework, Chapter 4 may also help you and your organization make the right choice. Tough choices are often based upon various criteria, so a combination of various chapters might be the way to go. but that is why it is a tough call.

Chapter 6

Hybrid Portfolio Management

Figure 6.1   Overview.

Now, portfolio management, the classic approach (project portfolio management), which was based upon financial theory and the agile approach to portfolio management is derived from agile software development but working with portfolio management, does not always fit into one of the two categories that have been covered.

Exercise 6.1 Where Do You Stand on Hybrid Portfolio Management?

Discuss and write down your points of view of hybrid portfolio management. Does it work? If not, why not?

_____

_____

_____

_____

_____

Answers: No right or wrong answers.

If you have worked on the team level, you might be using a plan-based or waterfall approach, e.g., PMI or PRINCE2, or you might have worked agile-based upon the spiral development approach, e.g., Scrum. For the last 10 to 15 years, many have observed more and more organizations mixing these, e.g., a plan-based project with agile teams for execution. In theory, these combinations of software development models, e.g., waterfall and spiral model, could be labelled hybrid models. The theory on hybrid models for the team or project level is maturing as we speak. Some clear examples are that it is now part of the new *PMBOK Guide* 7th Edition from the Project Management Institute and has been part of PRINCE2 with PRINCE2 Agile for some time, so hybrid models are more and more discussed in theory and are acceptable as a valid approach rather than just something people actually do in the projects to make it work. The same hybrid concepts can be applied on the programme/many teams or portfolio level. On the portfolio level, hybrid portfolio management is a combination of project portfolio management (PPM) and agile portfolio management (APM). However, it is not always clear how an organization can or should mix these approaches. This is the harsh reality when theory and practice clash and something many organizations need to deal with. Nevertheless, hybrid models on the portfolio level are not a topic that has been extensively researched or documented in practice, but knowledge, practice, and new ideas can be shared in this section.

The project portfolio management approach is effective with plan-based projects on the team level. However, researchers have seen several cases where the project portfolio management approach based upon a Stage-Gate model is used with agile content, even in big agile transformations in the portfolio. However, we rarely see the agile portfolio management approach with anything other than agile content on the team level. These combinations, some common, some more unlikely, are illustrated Table 6.1. It is not known whether it is lack of maturity, risk adversity, culture, or suchlike,

Table 6.1   Hybrid Models for Portfolio Management

		Team Level		
	Portfolio/Team Level	*Plan-Based*	*Agile*	*Combi*
	Project Portfolio Management	Standard PPM	Stage-Gate	Stage-Gate
Portfolio Level	Agile Portfolio Management	N/A	Standard APM	Rarely

but in many organizations the project portfolio management approach is evidently preferred over the agile portfolio management approach, which makes little sense but that is true of the cases that are seen in the market.

6.1 Project Portfolio Management with Agile (PPM Stage-Gate)

Many organizations have several portfolios, often based upon the project portfolio management approach. The project portfolio management approach is in many organizations based upon the Stage-Gate model by Cooper (2016). Figure 6.2 illustrates a Stage-Gate model. This hybrid portfolio management approach was labelled project portfolio management with agile steps as the concept is to keep the project portfolio management model as it is normally performed, while, however, allowing the projects to work agile in the various steps and between the gates. This model still applies the various stages and gates but keeps agile development within the same structure and governance as applied in a project portfolio management approach for plan-based projects. This approach is commonly applied and works well in many organizations; however, it is obvious that the amount of agility can be discussed. It is violating the agile principles, and there is

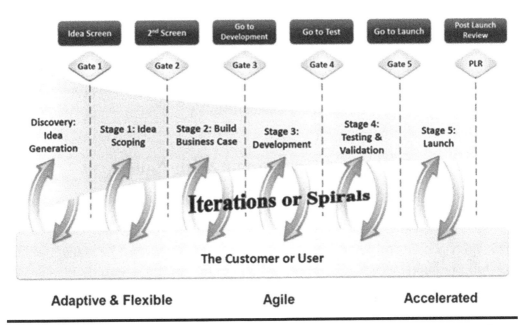

Figure 6.2 Scalable Stage-Gate system to handle projects of different sizes or risk levels.

lack of transparency, adaptability, collaboration, continuous planning, and suchlike, so the amount of agility on the portfolio level in this approach is extremely limited. But it allows you to work agile on the team level.

In research, Sommer, Hedegaard, and others (2015) conducted seven case studies of organizations working agile on the team level but with a project portfolio management approach on the portfolio level. Table 6.2 highlights these findings where the process modifications often resulted in an extra step in the Stage-Gate model and the opportunity to work agile, e.g., Scrum in these steps. This highlights this approach with agile on the team level and plan-based project portfolio management on the portfolio level.

6.2 Project Portfolio Management with Agile teams (Just Like a Project) (PPM Stage-Gate)

In this approach the organization takes all its projects and possible agile teams and places them into a common portfolio based upon the project portfolio management approach. The portfolio level is completely separated from any agility and all agility happens on the team level. This portfolio simply treats agile teams and projects the same way. This is simple governance for the portfolio layer as it is "business as usual", except you need to assess, prioritize, and suchlike both projects and the work of agile teams, which makes it like "apples and pears", but it is still fruit. The challenge is on the team level and for the teams working agile as they need to fit into a plan-based portfolio management approach with stages, gates, increased documentation and lack of interaction and transparency which is filled with waste and possibly worrying for the agile teams.

6.3 Project Portfolio Management with Agile Teams in Plan-Based Projects (Part of the Projects) (PPM Stage-Gate)

This approach is simple governance for the portfolio level. The project portfolio management level works with projects and the way they normally work – "business as usual", so no agility on the portfolio level. In this approach agility is just in the projects and on the team level. How much or little agility is a matter for the projects. The project portfolio management is just "business as usual"; whether the projects execute plan-based or agile, the portfolio work is the same. The challenge is on the team level if they are

Table 6.2   Case Study Process Modifications and Tools Instituted

Process Type	Company	Process Modifications	Tools Instituted
Stage-Gate	WindT	Added 5 steps in stage 4 (product design) of existing 7-stage model	Toolbox including manuals, best practice, and ideas for improvement
	Valves	Added an iteration step in first phase of the existing 5-phase model	Product specifications sheet, idea selection scoreboard
Hybrids	Pharma	Added Scrum in step 4 (product design) of 6-step Stage-Gate model	Scrum board, burndown, daily Scrum, product backlog and similar
	Toys	Added Scrum as alternative to step 3 in a 5-step Stage-Gate model	Scrum
	Electro	Added Scrum for project execution and retaining Stage-Gate model for strategic project management	Scrum
	WindO	Added Scrum for project execution and retaining Stage-Gate model for strategic project management	Scrum
	Power	Added Scrum in step 3 and 4 (requirement and analysis) of a 5-step Stage-Gate model	Scrum

agile as they need to follow and report into a plan-based portfolio management approach which may not fit the way they work on the team level. This is where the PMO needs to step up and ensure proper reporting or you might have an agile uprising due to increased documentation, waste, and similar impediments.

6.4 Project Portfolio Management with an Agile Framework (PPM Stage-Gate)

Researchers have seen more and more organizations applying an agile framework (see Chapter 4) but many of the organizations have not taken the agile portfolio management approach from the framework into use. In several cases, the organizations have tailored their project portfolio management approach to work with an agile delivery organization running as described in a framework, e.g., SAFe. It is SAFe with plan-based project portfolio management. This approach was clearly not intended by the frameworks but is a reality in more and more organizations. The benefits of this approach for the organizations are that they can run their major IT development transformations like other work and governance within the organization. Executives are familiar with this approach; roles and documentation are as "business as usual" which means it is easier to make it work in many large organizations. This might also be an easier approach to accept in organizations which do not want to change their culture and way of working "just" because of a major agile transformation. The problem is that the organizations do not obtain the benefits of working agile on the portfolio level. This approach fosters predictability over adaptability, transparency as the current level instead of transparency on a higher level. Collaboration is kept on the team level not with the portfolio level, so organizations foster fast and effective IT development on the team level without the increased communication and adaptability that is known from agile on the portfolio level.

> You want a racing car, and it seems to be able to drive fast, but you are not driving it to its true potentials.

6.5 Agile Portfolio Management with Fixed Plan-Based Projects (APM with Plan-Based Projects)

This is not yet a viable option.

6.6 Agile Portfolio Management with Fixed Projects and Agile Teams (APM Combi)

This option is not seen anywhere; however, it is possible, as projects can be treated as a team but you do not gain all the benefits of running an agile portfolio management system as only a few teams may solve the project tasks and suchlike.

Exercise 6.2 Hybrid Portfolio Management

Discuss in which cases a hybrid portfolio management approach is preferred over standard project portfolio management or agile portfolio management and why? Come up with examples of the application of the various hybrid portfolio management approaches.

_____

_____

_____

Answers: There is not one right answer.

Chapter 7

Implementing Agile Portfolio Management

Figure 7.1   Overview.

In literature, knowledge exists about why organizations adopt a framework for agile portfolio management but when it comes to implementing the agile portfolio in the most effective manner, it is a different tale. Some organizations implement agile portfolio management based upon semi-proven, public, and widespread use of a framework or approach. They adopt the framework or portfolio management approach in the same ways of working that other well-known organizations have done. This approach is often supported by consultants and/or vendor recommendations which are largely based upon the previous experiences of other clients. Unfortunately, the literature lacks extensive information on challenges and negative traits across large organizations, as there is likely to be an inherent bias to the cases published by the consultants, clients, and vendors. Some organizations implement agile portfolio management based upon no discernibly reasoned approach; it is just "random" or a bit immature, based upon the context or whatever comes to mind during implementation.

Exercise 7.1 Table Talk on Implementing Agile Portfolio Management

Discuss and write down with people at your table how implementing agile portfolio management should be done and your experiences, whether they are good or have room for improvements.

_____

_____

_____

_____

_____

Answers: No right or wrong answers.

It is common in research that some of the predictors for successful outcomes when implementing are about the degree of effort in agile planning. The moderators are quality of the vision/goals, project complexity, and organization experience. The outcomes are overall project success, project efficiency, and stakeholder satisfaction.

Figure 7.2 is adapted based upon research by Kieran Conboy and Noel Carroll (2019). It illustrates how to adopt a large-scale agile framework which includes agile portfolio management. The factors are time (x) and expectations (y). It recommends that an organization completes the steps from left to right, from "pre large-scale agile" to "initial large-scale agile thinking and practice" and so on. Think of it as a maturity model where

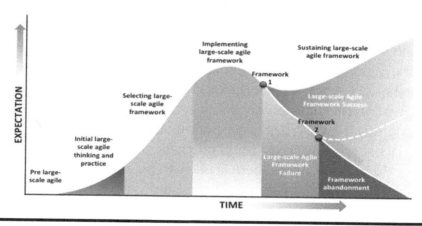

Figure 7.2 Adoption of large-scale agile frameworks.

mindset, knowledge, and practices are matured before implementing a full and large-scale agile framework with major consequences. It is not recommended that organizations implement a major agile portfolio management framework if the organization only has limited experience of working agile in a not-scaled environment, e.g., few teams with the portfolio level.

The research by Kieran Conboy and Noel Carroll (2019) is based upon 13 case studies from companies of various sizes, team locations, and use of frameworks which provides some degree of validity and illustrate the differences. The case studies are illustrated Table 7.1.

The amount of research on how to implement agile portfolio management is highly limited; however, a fair amount of research, from several studies on some of the challenges or high-level pitfalls organizations have encountered in recent years when implementing agile portfolio management, does exist. The top ten challenges for implementing have been identified by several of the studies and are described in the following as a combined list with suggested actions. The list is not ranked or sorted.

7.1 Defining Large-Scale Agile Framework Concepts and Terms

- Spend time reflecting and defining what is meant mean by "agile" and "scale" in your organizational context; before adopting a large-scale agile framework "learn how agile and large-scale agile framework really works".
- Establish clear motivation to scale agile development to meet business needs.
- Develop a common vocabulary to capture the vision and value of large-scale agile transformation.
- Ensure the common vocabulary is accessible, coherent, and promoted across all stakeholders in the early stages of adopting a large-scale agile framework.
- Practice agile at the top (management).
- Early on, address change resistance, e.g., new roles.
- Do not underestimate the need for transformational leadership.

There is a need for organizations to focus on inculcation of an agile mindset and understanding agile principles before any framework or process adoption.

Table 7.1 Case Studies on the Adoption of Large-Scale Agile Frameworks

Organization	Product/Service	Years Studied	Scale (no. developers)	Framework(s) used	Team locations
Accenture	Global management consulting, technology services, and outsourcing	2001–2004	180 to 2,500 across >60 large-scale agile engagements	Mixed/custom frameworks	42 sites –Europe, Asia, Australia
IrishBank*	Financial services	2014–2018	>150	Mixed/custom frameworks	Ireland, UK
TechCo*	Products for software development and project management	2013	>340	SA Fe	Australia, Europe, San Francisco
Dell	Technology solutions services and support	2014–2018	>180	Scrum at Scale	Ireland, India, China
FinanceCO*	Financial services	2006–2018	>1250	Spotify, custom frameworks	Ireland, II.S., India, China
InformationMosaic	Global provider of post-trade securities and corporate actions processing solutions	2010–2018	>200	Mixed/custom frameworks	Ireland
SemiCo*	Industrial engineering systems for power and distribution	2012–2018	>1500	LeSS	Ireland, US, China

(Continued)

Table 7.1 (Continued)   Case Studies on the Adoption of Large-Scale Agile Frameworks

Organization	Product/Service	Years Studied	Scale (no.) developers)	Framework(s) used	Team locations
Ericsson	Network and communication technology innovation and services	2013–2015	>200	Scrum at Scale	Ireland,Sweden
Intel	Technology solutions services and support	2005–2008	>250	Mixed/custom frameworks	Ireland, U.S.
ConsultingCo*	Management consulting, technology services	2001–2018	60 to 1,100 across multiple large-scale agile consulting engagements	Mixed/custom frameworks	>50 sites–Europe, US, Asia, Australia, South America
RevenueCo*	Public sector –tax/customs authority for ELT country	2012–2018	>200	Spotify, SAFe	Anonymous
Rovsing	Software for space and satellite testing and simulation systems	2007–2011	65	Mixed/custom frameworks	Denmark
BankCo*	Financial services	2010–2014	>150	LeSS	Australia

7.2 Comparing and Contrasting Large-Scale Agile Frameworks

- Avoid comparison against methods out of context or without framework-independent criteria to meet organizational-specific requirements.
- Use metrics that are core to an organization's value portfolio to evaluate how each framework contributes to organizational productivity and performance, for example, employee engagement, customer satisfaction, productivity, agility, time-to-market, or quality.
- Use a small number of metrics (one to four), aggregated from other metrics if necessary, to compare large-scale agile frameworks.
- Ensure comparison and justification of framework selection is clear to all key stakeholders in the large-scale agile transformation process.

7.3 Readiness and Appetite for Large-Scale Agile Frameworks

- Conduct an organizational readiness assessment to examine potential barriers of adopting specific large-scale agile transformation frameworks.
- Identify gaps/issues and associated steps to resolve issues, e.g., increased training, organizational structural changes, or new management styles or strategies.
- Use an incremental adoption of a large-scale agile framework in areas of weakness to ensure a smooth transformation process and demonstrate "small wins".

7.4 Balancing Organizational Structure and Large-Scale Agile Frameworks

- Identify what new structural requirements a specific large-scale agile framework imposes on an organization.
- Evaluate how new agile framework structures will positively or negatively impact on performance, standards compliance, and flexibility across an organization.

- Weigh-up the benefits and drawbacks of the large-scale agile framework and how they may alter business operations.
- Destroy the barriers to agile behaviours.
- Incentive systems should be revised to promote global optimization.

Plan-driven or traditional organizations adopting agile portfolio management should figure out ideas for cultivating an organizational culture shift.

7.5 Top-down Versus Bottom-up Implementation of Large-Scale Agile Frameworks

- Determine whether a large-scale agile framework promotes a top-down or bottom-up implementation approach.
- Strike a clear balance between enabling top-down and bottom-up transformation.
- Provide continuous education or training opportunities at all staff levels including executives, project leaders, and software developers.
- Continually support and reflect on implementation activities from top and bottom.
- Consider starting small and let the word spread.

Some believe the transformation toward agile needs to be done holistically and radically, changing structures, cultures, and traditional practices at once to accommodate the agile philosophy. Others advocate for a more incremental approach.

7.6 Over-Emphasis on 100% Framework Adherence over Value

- Determine whether the organization's agile transformation prioritizes adherence to specific agile frameworks or whether the overall success of the method is better for business.
- Identify which transformational factors will influence adherence over value, such as standards compliance, speed, cost, technology, or customer requirements.
- Plan for the optimal degree of transformation with the large-scale agile framework as per your organizational goals and objectives.

7.7 Lack of Evidence-Based Use of Large-Scale Agile Frameworks

- Build evidence (e.g., metrics) to support the use of a particular large-scale agile framework to transform your organization.
- Regularly test scalability at a more sustainable pace to learn your way through the transformation process, e.g., through transformational "small wins".
- Identify and contextualize issue to offer guidance on agile large-scale transformation and establish best practice.

7.8 Maintaining Developer Autonomy in Large-Scale Agile Frameworks

- Engage with the people to assess their overall satisfaction in relation to autonomy in the workplace provided by the large-scale agile framework.
- Carry out regular audits to ensure awareness and adaptation of a large-scale agile framework remains transparent and relevant within and across projects and teams.
- Explore whether new policies, such as "bring your own device" would improve autonomy and facilitate a smooth large-scale agile transformation.
- Allow "master" teams to customize/tailor their practices.

7.9 Misalignment Between Customer Processes and Large-Scale Agile Frameworks

- Consider involving customer stakeholders during the selection of a large-scale agile framework to increase transparency, cooperation, and alignment.
- Examine how the choice of a large-scale agile framework will provide the organizations with some flexibility to cater for growing dynamic customer needs.

The top challenge categories mentioned were agile difficult to implement, integrating non-development functions, change resistance and requirements engineering challenges.

7.10 Ensure People and Process Issues Do Not Steal the Show

- Staffing some roles are more important than others, e.g., product owner roles need to work on the first day.
- First programme increment (PI) requires extra effort.
- Scaling to large and distributed settings.
- Backlog management is not just like in Scrum.

The data from industry highlights that coaching teams as they learn by doing, ensuring management support, and customizing the agile approach carefully could support the recommendations made by research. This is supported by industry practices where the 14th State of Agile (2020) survey highlights the challenges experienced when adopting and scaling agile as the following top ten:

1. General organizational resistance to change
2. Not enough leadership participation
3. Inconsistent processes and practices across teams
4. Organization culture at odds with agile values
5. Inadequate management support and sponsorship
6. Lack of skills/experience with agile methods
7. Insufficient training and education
8. Lack of business, customer, product owner availability
9. Pervasiveness of traditional development methods
10. Fragmented tooling and project-related data/measurements

Most frameworks identified in Chapter 4 do deliver guidance on designing and implementing their framework based upon experiences from other customers and their own concepts. The scaled agile framework used to (e.g., version 4.0) focus on implementation with a focus on value (value streams) and the agile release trains as means to deliver the value. This should be supported by a Lean-agile implementation rollout strategy (PI roadmap). The second part is preparing to the launch of the first agile release train followed by the execution. At some point the implementation will also include the portfolio layer.

Exercise 7.2 Implementation of Agile Portfolio Management

Discuss how you would implement agile portfolio management in your organization, which challenges, or pitfalls, would be the most concerning, and what you think the organization should do to mitigate the risks of implementing agile portfolio management in your organization. If you do not work in an organization where agile portfolio management could be relevant, discuss this exercise based upon one of the cases found in Chapter 9.

_____

_____

_____

Answers: There is not one right answer.

Chapter 8

Tailoring Agile Portfolio Management

Figure 8.1 Overview.

Tailoring your cloth makes all the difference.

This chapter is about why it is important to adjust the portfolio management approach; a bit like a tailor sews clothes according to individual measures, we plan and carry out our agile portfolio according to individual goals/measures for the organization. It is also equally important to tailor the project portfolio management approach; the focus here is the agile portfolio management approach, however most of the ideas and concepts could also be applied to project portfolio management. Some might argue it is even more important for project portfolio management as it is more process- and documentation-centric, so gains from proper tailoring would most likely be high.

Since each agile portfolio is unique, it is important to understand that an organization's agile portfolio management processes are likely to need to be tailored to ensure agile portfolio success. Agile portfolio adaptations or tailoring consider that agile portfolio management processes are not "one size fits all", which means that there will be many times where processes need to be adjusted to ensure the agile portfolio's success. In English, agile portfolio adaptations are called "tailoring", and in many ways it is reminiscent of working as a tailor, which requires dexterity, a sense of colour, and a good sense of form. As an agile portfolio executive or product owner, these are a different set of competencies, but they must still help the customer/ agile portfolio to choose the right model and fabric. The tailor takes measures and prepares a pattern that must be cut, sewn, and worked according to. Most agile portfolio management approaches are not "standard"; a tailor's customers also have other measures apart from standard measures, where it may be necessary to sew a sample model in canvas and adapt it before it is cut into the right and expensive fabric. As an agile portfolio executive or product owner, you may carry out preparatory work, perhaps an analysis, experiment, short iteration, or proof of concept. A good tailor sews in both thin and thick materials. The tailor primarily uses sewing machines, but also sews by hand if necessary. An agile portfolio executive or product owner will work with various agile portfolio management frameworks; sometimes they may work with a plan-based portfolio, hybrid, agile, or a combination. No two clients/organizations or agile portfolios have completely standard strategy goals and none of them are exactly alike. They are unique, signifying agile portfolios and the tailor's best creations. When organizations make agile portfolio adjustments or tailor the portfolio, it is because what the organization must do is different from what other organizations have just done or what the frameworks was designed to do, e.g., the scope or quantity of what the agile portfolio should contain and do is vastly different. One agile portfolio may contain banking software due to legacy issues, while another portfolio is a major web-shop and distributor. Yes, they are both software developers, so a large part of the same toolbox can be used, but they are two quite different agile portfolios, so they must be approached in their own unique ways. It is not much different from a tailor's customers/organization who want either an entire winter wardrobe or just a small black dress for a big party in the family.

"The great strength of tailoring lies in getting materials to work together, to adapt the model to even the most difficult body, to hide weaknesses and highlight others. This strength is also the weakness of the subject, as the process becomes very individual and time consuming".

Agile portfolios must be individually tailored to get the best possible result and, in the process, likely save time on unnecessary tasks, meetings, roles, and artefacts. The scope of the task determines the amount of resources needed to solve it, how the organization approaches it, the uncertainties associated with the work, and ultimately the price and outcome for the customer/organization. As indicated, the complexity of the agile portfolio or task is of great importance for how the organization approaches it. It can be about how many processes people in the organization must go through.

A tailor may have to make the cut, adjust, sew, and design, while the agile portfolio manager's or product owner's processes are about funnel, analysis, design, and implementation, but the message is the same. No matter what task needs to be solved, it is often beneficial to reduce the complexity of the work, which could be helped by looking at the processes.

Tailoring is one of the professions that is difficult to outsource abroad, as it is a process that requires testing and adjustments along the way before you can deliver the finished product. Agile portfolios are not much different, are they? If a dress was a dress and all women had the same size, the same taste, economy, and the like, then maybe; but fortunately, that is not the case. This also applies to agile portfolios. Sometimes organizations have a lot of funds, resources available, limited time, towering expectations from the stakeholders for the quality and several uncertainties associated with the work processes; other times the opposite may be true. That is why it is important to adapt your agile portfolio. When you, as a tailor or an agile portfolio manager or product owner, adapt your working methods to the specific tasks, it is also due to a desire to be efficient. People and organizations want to use the resources properly; they may be scarce, but in the end, it is a matter of not wasting resources, which in the worst case could reduce the value of our work when too much energy is spent on wasted flows. With an efficient use of resources, people and organizations can achieve the maximum value. Resources for a tailor are material, machinery, people, and time, which is not much different than for an agile portfolio manager; however, with a different kind of material, machine, and competency. A tailor works from the four cornerstones, while the agile portfolio product owner may work with a different set of activities, but the situation is roughly the same. The tailor and the agile product owner both want to increase momentum, want to finish faster at a lower price.

Agile portfolio adaptations or tailoring help organizations remove everything that is unnecessary: something people do not need to do, whether it is meetings, processes, roles, artefacts people must fill out or the like. Maybe workers can skip something and improve the product at the same time? It does not necessarily make sense to follow all the processes, use all the materials and tools, if fewer can do it? It is about being effective; agile portfolio adjustments/tailoring help us stay focused on what creates value. How often have you not followed a process, attended a meeting, completed an artefact or suchlike because you just followed the process? Or you may have experienced that others did not follow your processes because it did not benefit them or the work they do. It might have been a hindrance to their work if they had had to follow the process at hand.

Albert Einstein should have said: "If you are out to describe the truth, leave elegance to the tailor".

You will not get the perfect dress or agile portfolio without agile portfolio tailoring. The tailor has his or her finger on the pulse in terms of fashion and design. Customers/organizations not only demand good craftsmanship, but also that the tailor understands fashion and design. This also applies to the agile portfolio manager or product owner, although they are not always equally fashion-conscious. An agile portfolio executive or similar needs to know what good design is in order to handle the agile portfolio in a good and mature way, which may or may not be the good way for others to handle their agile portfolios. Organizations may be creating something unique, but so are other organizations and the contexts are not the same. The tailor's great strength lies in making the materials work together, adapting the model to even the most difficult body, hiding weaknesses and highlighting others. But the work can be difficult and there is a risk that the creation may not end up as expected, and the customer/organization will be dissatisfied with the result. Agile portfolio managers or product owners need to adapt the agile portfolios so that they can handle the most difficult agile portfolios themselves, reduce the weaknesses and utilize the strengths, but it is not easy.

Therefore, it is crucial that organizations use tailoring to reduce the risk of creations going wrong. Organizations can do this by reducing complexity, making the task visible, removing unnecessary processes, spending time on something that creates value, and, in general, ensuring that workers do nothing just for the sake of others or the processes, roles, or artefacts. When you tailor your work to optimize the processes, it is also about making the necessary decisions. If you choose to continue as before, or as you usually do, you will not make the necessary decisions, which will have a cost: the cost of not making a choice. Agile portfolio tailoring is therefore a welcome opportunity to make the right decisions about how we choose to handle precisely this task. Not deciding is also a decision to let go and do as we usually do, which is rarely the right decision. It can be a difficult decision, where the tailor asks his master and the agile portfolio manager his executive group.

For many, it is difficult to know when to adjust one thing or another so that it does not become too much or too little, which can also have unintended consequences. That is why it is important to apply the experience of the organization: someone else's or one's own. Many other people or organizations may have been in a similar situation where your organization can learn from what went well or what went less well. It can therefore be an advantage to gain some experience, as exercises make perfect, but, by learning from others, some of the mistakes may be avoided or significant progress can be made with less effort. Organizations can get the experience everywhere if the organizations are open to input. It can be networks where people share their worst mistakes, sparring with colleagues, professional literature, or completely their own experiences. Experience is something that makes us good if we know how to learn and not make the same mistakes repeatedly.

Albert Einstein should have said: "He who has never made a mistake has never tried anything new".

As an agile portfolio executive or product owner, all agile portfolios are unique; maybe it is about the same kind of software, but the customers/ organizations are different, the situations are different, the resources on the agile portfolio are different, so agile portfolios are never the same, they are unique in their own way. The context varies. Whether it is a tailor's or agile portfolio product, it is created with creativity, talent, and craftsmanship, and the brain is used when drawing on techniques and experience. In this work, the dialogue with the customer/organization and the other stakeholders is also particularly important. They are not the same stakeholders every time. Stakeholders have different needs; some do not see the need for the creation, while others have been waiting for it for a long time. The management of the stakeholders should be done continuously and proactively, so that they become committed partners, but this does not happen by itself. The agile portfolio tailoring helps us to find the right level for how/when stakeholders should be addressed. If organizations do too much, they waste others' time and resources, if organizations do too little, it can create conflicts; so it is important to find the right level of stakeholder engagement. If organizations just do as organizations usually do, the organization will hardly hit the right level. There may be stakeholders who want a weekly meeting with a general agenda, written status on the main lines each month, or just a phone call if there are problems. This means that you as an agile portfolio manager can easily have five to ten important stakeholders who want to collaborate in different ways.

Another agile portfolio may include other stakeholders. This just increases the need for agile portfolio tailoring or customizations. Organizations may also be in the situation of having to prepare a product/creation in collaboration with other companies. For a tailor, this could be like working with a clothing factory. Here the clothes are sewn and sent back to the tailor, who then tries the clothes on the customer and makes the necessary corrections. But what if the clothing factory only works with certain materials, has many long delivery times and the like? This naturally has an impact on the tailor's work, where the materials cannot be adapted, and the clothes are not finished early due to the long delivery times. But the opposite could also be the case, so that fast delivery times could create space for other tasks. As an agile portfolio manager who works with several vendors, that helps the organization deliver the final product. Their abilities and willingness also matter as to how much the organization can adapt the agile portfolio. Maybe there is a contract between the parties which prescribes an incredibly special process the organization must go through, from which the organization cannot deviate. Suddenly, the degree of our agile portfolio tailoring is dependent on others, which of course should be reduced, but this is not always possible.

When organizations adapt our agile portfolios, it may sound a bit like the organization wants to save time, resources, omit some processes and the like, but that is only part of the truth. An agile portfolio tailoring can also have the opposite effect, i.e., more time, more resources, more meetings, better use of roles, higher quality of the artefacts and more processes, if that is what is needed for the agile portfolio to create in the right way. Whether you work as a tailor or an agile portfolio manager or product owner, everyone wants to work with the exact, necessary process and maximize the value of the agile portfolio. It can mean more, or less, of something. Organizations may obtain an even higher quality of product by using more resources and processes, though organizations may be able to save time by reducing the initial work if it provides little value.

Let us say that Denmark as a nation developed their very own space rocket. Yes, Denmark has tried some of this work in collaboration with NASA, but there is still a lot that is new in the task and Denmark wants to be sure that it goes well, as a space flight is critical with people on board. In this situation, the Danish management will probably adapt the national agile portfolio to such an extent that the space organization adds a lot of extra processes, extra tests, makes use of the latest tools and the like, so the organization gets to examine every single step on the journey, while upgrading Microsoft Office to the cloud will probably be a somewhat smaller task, which also contains several known elements. In some workplaces, there is not much room for agile portfolio tailoring. Organizations do things this way and that is what the organizations always have done because its works. In other companies, the opposite may be true. The size of the company may to some extent have an impact on this, as the larger company often needs a greater degree of formalization than a smaller company. A large company could create space for agile portfolio tailoring, while the small company must do as the boss does. The difference is very often what is at stake in the company culture, the way we talk and interact with each other. Is it okay to make mistakes in radical agile portfolio adaptations or is it safer just to follow the processes even if they create truly little value for the agile portfolio and we thereby waste the company's resources? How often has agile portfolio tailoring been articulated on your work or agile portfolio? It is not necessarily the culture of the company that is all decisive for our agile portfolio adaptations; it can also be the culture of the agile portfolio.

Agile portfolio tailoring is a change for many, where there will be supporters and opponents, as things now must be done differently. People know what they have. It is therefore crucial that organizations create a culture in the agile portfolio where everyone can contribute with agile portfolio adaptations and where everyone and everything can be challenged and accepted if changes can provide value. Besides culture, another important concept is maturity. Very squarely said, a higher degree of maturity will often mean a higher degree of readiness for agile portfolio tailoring, while a lower degree of maturity may decrease the willingness for agile portfolio adaptations. Mature companies and agile portfolio participants will often be receptive to improvements and have experience with these for better or worse, while the less mature company or agile portfolio managers will try to maintain the current situation. When you make agile portfolio adjustments, the organization takes a risk. Organizations know what they have and who usually does what; now it is changed into something completely different to make it even better and with the realization that if the organization does as it usually does, it will not succeed with agile portfolio management. It obviously requires a willingness to change the status quo, but often one will be willing to take a risk if organizations can cover us if things go wrong, e.g., preparedness, new later tests, and the like. This may mean that someone does not want to take chances and do as they usually do. You cannot get criticism for that as an organization, no, but the organization hardly gets praise or becomes a high performer, as it can be done much better.

As a tailor, you can face an agile portfolio that requires collaboration with other craftsmen and artists who work in other ways and with other materials such as gold and silver. If it is to be good, we need to find a common way of working, even though we typically do things differently. As an agile portfolio manager, you can come from a world where everything must be planned down to the smallest details and executed in a certain order, while others rely more on collaboration, simple processes, and the ability to adapt to the situation and the changes that will occur. Agile portfolio tailoring is important because it builds bridges between several ways of working, which is also necessary to get the best result. When an organization has been working on something for a long time, it will often find a good way to work with things. Others may also work this way. In the literature it may be referred to as a kind of "best practice". Even though the organization has found a really good way to work, it does not mean that it is always the right way to do things. The incredibly good way of working should be challenged and adapted in the agile portfolio in question if it can create added value.

Agile portfolio tailoring/adaptations or standard frameworks should challenge the status quo regardless of the situation. In the worst case, the organization will be confirmed in this being the right way; also for the agile portfolio. Agile portfolio adaptations often affect resources, time, quality, risk, and finances. There are different, and often competing, constraints. The importance of each limitation differs from agile portfolio to agile portfolio. If time is of the essence, the organization should consider whether it can make adjustments that can reduce the duration of the agile portfolio initiatives, perhaps by adding additional resources so that it does not affect quality. If price is the most important thing, perhaps the time should be extended if it can mean cheaper internal resources rather than buying expensive external resources. If quality is paramount, the organization will probably be able to do something extra to lift it. It is difficult to carry out agile portfolios on time, within budget, and to the expectations of stakeholders/organizations. Here it is important to note that the latest research shows that there is a clear connection between agile portfolio tailoring and agile portfolio success. You have a greater chance of agile portfolio success if you tailor your agile portfolios, while agile portfolios that are not customized will have a lower chance of agile portfolio success. Think about it! In the summary below you will find a list of reasons why it is important to make agile portfolio tailoring. The items on the list are not in order of priority, but these are all contributing reasons why agile portfolios should be tailored. Agile portfolio adaptation/tailoring:

- Is imperative as no two agile portfolios are alike
- Considers both large and small agile portfolios, which must be handled differently
- Contributes to reducing the complexity of the agile portfolio
- Means that we continuously optimize our resource use and thereby reduce waste and contribute to increasing progress
- May be affected by the collaboration with others
- Is about creating the exactly necessary process and maximizing the value of the agile portfolio
- Involves making active choices rather than letting go
- Applies the experience
- Reduces the risk of the agile portfolio.
- Is influenced by the culture and maturity of the company and the team
- Builds a bridge and creates space for different approaches
- Should always challenge the way we work, regardless of whether or not they are already good processes
- May have an impact on what agile portfolio tailoring should be made. Some are more important than others
- Can increase the possibility of agile portfolio success

8.1 The Process of Tailoring the Agile Portfolio Management Framework

It is not enough to have the best approach in the world to agile portfolio management itself if it is not implemented successfully and continuously improved. The approach to agile portfolio management must be continuously tailored/adapted, where the steps should, to a greater or lesser degree, follow the model outlined in Figure 8.2.

8.2 Step One: Initially Tailoring Based Upon the Organization

The first step is to develop and select the processes, artefacts, roles, meetings, techniques, and practices that make up the elements of an organization's agile portfolio management approach. Often, this agile portfolio

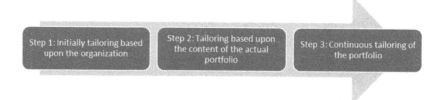

Figure 8.2   The process of tailoring the agile portfolio management framework adapted from Whitaker (2014).

management approach will be based on one or more frameworks (see Chapter 4 for details). Once this initial step is completed, the organization will have a baseline or framework for future use. This means that the organization now has an approach and way of doing things, so that the organization can continuously deliver successful agile portfolios and provide real bottom-line value for the organization. For many organizations, this work will be an agile portfolio. If the organization simply chooses a standard agile portfolio management approach, e.g., a framework such as SAFe, DAD, or LeSS, without making agile portfolio tailoring at this stage, then too many adaptations will be left to the next steps, which may mean that the adaptations do not hit the right level or become quite different from agile portfolio to agile portfolio, whereby the organization's good approach to agile portfolios management can become difficult to achieve.

8.3 Step Two: Tailoring Based Upon the Content of the Actual Portfolio

The first step in the process was about adapting the agile portfolio management approach to the organization, while this second step is about adapting the approach or agile portfolio model to the current content of the agile portfolio. This involves selecting the processes, artefacts, roles, meetings, techniques, and practices that are relevant to the current agile portfolio. Here, it often works well if the organization prepares checklists of mandatory and optional items that can be customized (see next sections for more details). In working on agile portfolio tailoring at this stage, checklists can often be helpful in classifying agile portfolios as: very simple; simple; medium; and complex using a matrix (Whitaker, 2014) as in Figure 8.3. Then tie the model (cf. Figure 8.3) and the checklist together so that there are

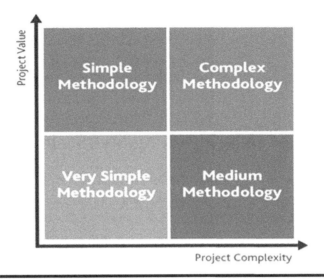

Figure 8.3   Tailoring the methodology.

recommended processes, artefacts, roles, meetings, techniques, and practices for each category of the agile portfolio.

This second step is not about adding new or unique elements, but instead is about refining the existing agile portfolio approach so that it fits perfectly with the agile portfolio in context. A key concept is the idea that we adapt so that elements such as the processes, artefacts, roles, meetings, techniques, and practices are best suited to the purpose and provide the highest value and that we do not do anything that does not contribute value to this. In many organizations, it will provide value if the agile portfolio manager discusses the current agile portfolio adjustments with the agile portfolio office or PMO and subsequently with the agile portfolio executives, to ensure that you hit the right level.

8.4 Step Three: Continuous Tailoring of the Portfolio

The third and final step in the process confirms that the agile portfolio management approach has made the right agile portfolio adjustments and continuously optimizes the adjustments throughout the agile portfolio life cycle. It is a combination of checking that the combination of selected elements is still appropriate and that the agile portfolio is not adapted too much or too little, otherwise it must be corrected. Agile portfolio customizations are an iterative process that is implemented throughout the agile portfolio life cycle.

This is where the agile portfolio retrospective and similar meetings can be of great value. In this connection, the experiences that are shared with the agile portfolio office or PMO must be collected, as well as secure checklists and other things that are continuously adapted to the latest experiences.

8.5 The Effect of Tailoring on Agility@Scale

If you recall, Chapter 2 introduced some of the consequences of agility at scale. These consequences, whether continuous planning or transparency, can and should be tailored. Currently we have discussed tailoring in broad terms but what does it really mean? These are the common items that can be tailored:

- Terminology and language
- Processes
- Tools and techniques
- Documents/artefacts
- Meetings and rituals
- Roles and responsibilities
- The degree of principles applied
- The degree of reporting

These are the areas discussed in Chapter 2:

- 2.1 Understanding Complexity Theory and System Thinking
- 2.2 Adaptability vs. Predictability
- 2.3 Lean Thinking and Lean Portfolio Management
- 2.4 Continuous Planning
- 2.5 From Silos to Collaboration and Increased Interaction
- 2.6 Managing for Innovation (Culture and Work Environment)
- 2.7 Transparency

Now we combine the areas to be tailored with the possibilities of tailoring. This is done in Table 8.1. Table 8.1 uses the following terminology: Y = Yes, would work in many situations; N = Not – Not recommended in most situations, M = Maybe – Could work but it really depends on the situation. The table is intended to give a high-level overview of the possibilities. To make this work you need to examine each field such as "Documents/artefacts" and

Table 8.1 Tailoring Agility@Scale

Tailoring/ Agility@Scale	Terminology and Language	Processes	Tools and Techniques	Documents/ Artefacts	Meetings and Rituals	Roles and Responsibilities	Principles	Reporting
Understanding complexity theory and system thinking	Y	Y	Y	Y	Y	Y	Y	Y
Adaptability vs. predictability	Y	Y	Y	Y	Y	Y	Y	Y
Lean thinking and Lean portfolio management	Y	Y	Y	Y	Y	Y	Y	Y
Continuous planning	Y	Y	Y	Y	Y	Y	Y	Y
Collaboration	Y	Y	Y	Y	Y	Y	Y	Y
Managing for innovation	Y	Y	Y	Y	Y	Y	Y	Y
Transparency	N	Y	M	Y	Y	M	Y	Y

"Continuous planning", then examine the various documents before making the final tailoring.

Each aspect of agility@scale can be increased or decreased using tailoring. Let us examine transparency. The terminology and language of each component can be adapted to the use of the organization. Processes, meetings, and rituals can be increased/decreased or changed to foster transparency. What kind of meetings are you having? Who is taking part? Is transparency a topic during the portfolio retrospective? Is there a role responsible for transparency? Perhaps more/fewer people should be invited to the meetings? What artefacts are used? More/fewer boards? Are principles really applied or are we just talking about flow, value, and such Lean principles? What tools and techniques are we using? Do the tools and techniques provide more/less transparency? Some organizations have too much reporting, so meetings, participation, and artefacts might do or not.

8.6 Tailoring the Agile Portfolio Management Approach

Think about what agile portfolio management is all about. The topics discussed in Chapter 3 are illustrated in the next exercise, Exercise 8.1. Tailoring is not a one-size-fits-all approach and it does not contain one right or wrong solution. It should be based upon the context, framework, maturity, stakeholders' need, and suchlike, as discussed in the previous sections. Organizations can tailor all the topics covered in Chapters 2 and 3 but the degree, and whether the organization wants to increase or decrease something, depends on the context, so it is not easy to provide general advice for all to follow.

Exercise 8.1 Tailoring Agile Portfolio Management

Think about your agile portfolio management approach when you do the exercise, then consider each topic bullet list and how/why it should be tailored in your organization. Some topics are easier to tailor than others, e.g., ceremonies, roles, artefacts, use of techniques, i.e., prioritization, estimating, and suchlike, are more straightforward, while finding the right level for tailoring portfolio inclusion, reporting, or cost of delays are more complicated. Agile portfolio management is discussed in Chapter 3:

- 3.1 Agile Principles
- 3.2 Explaining Roles and Responsibilities
- 3.3 Agile Level of Governance

8.7 Tailoring the Agile Portfolio Management Framework

In this section, one of the frameworks from Chapter 4 is applied and it is showed how you can do the actual tailoring. In this case the framework recipes for agile governance in the enterprise (RAGE) has been selected as it is simple, so it would be clear what and how to tailor it.

Recipes for agile governance in the enterprise (RAGE) applies three primary levels of granularity for the work of an organization: portfolio, programme, and project. The portfolio governance process contains three roles, two ceremonies, and four artefacts which an organization can at least tailor. These are illustrated in Table 8.2 as generic tailoring. When tailoring, it is important to ask all the "W-like" questions such as Who, What, When, Why, and How.

Table 8.2 illustrates a generic tailoring of recipes for agile governance in the enterprise (RAGE) where you should question everything to find the right levels. In the next example (see Table 8.3) the framework recipes for agile governance in the enterprise (RAGE) is applied again but this time illustrating more precisely how it could be tailored to a given organization. In this example (Table 8.3), one organization is less mature and one more mature to illustrate the differences and choices then could be made regarding the tailoring of recipes for agile governance in the enterprise (RAGE) in various organizations. In this case the content to support the more mature organization has been increased and an attempt has been made to keep

Table 8.2   Generic Tailoring of Recipes for Agile Governance in the Enterprise (RAGE)

Content	What Does It Mean	What to Tailor?
Portfolio owner	This role has authority over initiative selection and prioritization. Most business units have only one portfolio manager	Responsibilities?
Area product owner	The sole authority over product requirements for the product, and the intended content of the release	
Programme manager	Works closely with teams' Scrum masters or project managers to ensure that cross-team collaboration is effective in achieving the product's release goals	
Portfolio grooming meeting	Area product owner gets feedback on quality and completeness of business cases. Programme manager provides effort estimate, but often after follow-up consultation with Scrum masters and Scrum teams	How often is the meeting held? Duration of the meeting? Who takes part in the meeting? Topics covered during the meeting? Preparation for the meeting?
Portfolio planning meeting	Each area product owner describes business cases for initiatives. All discuss to clarify understanding, and possibly adjust estimates. Portfolio owner adds items to decision matrix, makes decisions about whether/when to start new initiatives. Portfolio owner may also decide to terminate ongoing initiatives	How often is the meeting held? Duration of the meeting? Who takes part in the meeting? Topics covered during the meeting? Preparation for the meeting?
Business case	Business justification	What content to be included? Iterative developed or one-time? Who does benefit realization? Is it really needed? Who updates it? What do we use it for?
Agile charter	Mandate	What content to be included? Is it really needed? Who updates it? What do we use it for?
Decision matrix	Multicriteria analysis	Use it? When to use it? Which factors to include?
Portfolio backlog	Backlog management	Prioritization (which tools and techniques?) Estimation (which tools and techniques?) Information in the backlog? Who grooms/refines it? IT-supported e.g., JIRA

Table 8.3 Specific Tailoring of Recipes for Agile Governance in the Enterprise (RAGE)

Content	Less Mature Organization	More Mature Organization
Portfolio owner	Keep as described	Add responsibilities – more on business justification
Area product owner	Keep as described	Keep as described and see how it works
Programme manager	Keep as described	Remove – extra layer of waste
Portfolio Scrum master	Do not use	Add new role – facilitating and removing impediments on the portfolio level
Portfolio grooming meeting	Keep as described but 2 hours weekly	2 hours, bi-weekly (keep as described – see how it works)
Portfolio planning Meeting	Keep as described but 1 day weekly	1 day, quarterly (keep as described – see how it works)
Portfolio review	Do not use	Add new meeting – 4 hours monthly – status of in-flight initiatives
Portfolio retrospective	Do not use	Add new meeting – 2 hours quarterly – performance metrics and experiences
Business case		Develop it iterative. Start with strategic alignment
Agile charter		Remove it, it is covered by the business case
Decision matrix	Use few criteria	Use many criteria
Portfolio backlog		Use affinity estimation and ranking based upon effort/value for prioritization
Impediments log	Do not add it yet – wait and see how it goes	New artefacts for the portfolio Scrum master

it simple for the less mature organization, but that is not always the case and the recommended solution here serves to illustrate the "more" or "less" approach to tailoring an agile portfolio management framework.

Some people may still argue that you should adopt a framework with minimal customization; however, that is rarely a recommended approach as contexts may vary a lot. Also, keep in mind the organizations "selling" frameworks, such as in this case, Cprime, have extensive knowledge of the frameworks which should be a factor in one way or another.

> **Exercise 8.2 Action Plan for Tailoring Your Agile Portfolio Management Approach**
>
> Write your personal action plan for tailoring agile portfolio management.
>
> _____
> _____
>
> Answers: No right or wrong answers.

Chapter 9

Case Studies on Agile Portfolio Management

Figure 9.1   Overview.

This chapter contains a wide range of case studies on some degree of agile portfolio management where most of them have been conducted and published within the last five years and a few are older. The case studies contain real life data which has been published and elaborate some of the challenges, solutions, and suchlike to be found for agile portfolio management. These case studies serve to highlight important knowledge and ways for practitioners, researchers, and students to apply critical thinking on possible solutions, approaches, what-to-do, and advice: How would you turn this around and what would you have done differently in the case? Why do you think this went as it did?

Here is a list of the case studies:

- 9.1 Case study (2018) – Ocuco Ltd
- 9.2 Case study (2016) – An Empirical Study of Portfolio Management and Kanban in Agile and Lean Software Companies

- 9.3 Critical thinking case study (2019) – Managing the Agile Scalability to Implement Agile Project Portfolio Management
- 9.4 Case study (2018) – Large-Scale Agile Transformations at Ericsson
- 9.5 Case study (2011) Supporting Scaling Agile with Portfolio Management at Paf.com
- 9.6 Case study (2019) Agile Software Integration at Telfor
- 9.7 Case study (2015) Is Agile Portfolio Management Following the Principles of Large-Scale Agile in the Finish Broadcasting Company Yle
- 9.8 Case study – Agile Portfolio Management Challenges in the Swedish Automobile Industry
- 9.9 Case study (2011) – Agile Kanban IT project Portfolio at Getty Images

9.1 Case study (2018) – Ocuco Ltd

9.1.1 Background

Ocuco Ltd is a medium-sized Irish-based software company that develops practice and lab management software for the optical industry. Ocuco Ltd employs approximately 300+ staff members in its software development organization, including support and management personnel. Ocuco Ltd's annual sales approach €20 million from customers internationally. The development takes place across nine countries such as Canada, France, Ireland, Norway, Poland, and UK which all were represented in the survey results from 36 participants. The organization implemented SAFe at all levels.

9.1.2 Team Level

There are nine teams at Ocuco Ltd. Of these, only one team is fully colocated in the home office; the other teams are globally distributed across seven countries. Ltd development teams use Scrum to develop their software, with two-week sprints. Each team consists of seven to nine4 members comprising the product owner, a senior developer (who also acts as a technical lead), developers, quality assurance (responsible for testing), and a Scrum master (who also acts as a project manager). There are also some cross-trained team members who work on multiple products; programme management facilitates this resource sharing during "Scrum of Scrums" meetings at the programme level.

To access to what extent scaled agile framework (SAFe) practices can be implemented in a global SME the SAFe self-assessment was employed. The SAFe self-assessment addresses five team level areas, namely: product ownership health, programme increment (PI)/release health, sprint health, team health and technical health; the self-assessment questionnaire includes five questions assessing each of these areas. Some of the statements from the assessment were:

> "We do not really use User Stories. We do a lot of prioritization and negotiation. We do a slightly more defined conversation/ specification and communicate directly with developers". As a rationale for not using user stories, a developer explained: "This is a customer focused project. There is little user story development in it. All we have are big, long documents and specifications. However, they [product owners] did a good job in prioritizing and negotiating with the customer".

The grooming session ensures that items on the backlog are sufficiently described and estimated. Then, they can be considered at the sprint planning meeting for implementation during the next sprint. A team usually performs a grooming session once in each sprint. Since teams are distributed, we have observed that product owners use screen shots, mock-ups, and requirement specifications to enhance team understanding during the grooming session.

One of the developers explained how the grooming session starts, and the exchange between the team and the customer:

> grooming [comprises] cleaning up the requirements and making sure that they are clearly understood and there are no questions or grey areas. There is some cleaning involved with regards to the requirements … Then if we need any information from the customer themselves then we turn it back to them, saying, we need this information.

Product owner teams have staff members onshore for discussions with clients, and offshore for disseminating information to development teams.

In Ocuco Ltd, the product manager spends one or two weeks on-site with customers going through their plan and business processes to document their requirements. Then, the product owners translate those requirements into an "epic" comprising features or "tickets" to be implemented, in collaboration with the product manager; these are placed on the backlog. It has been agreed by most of the team members that geographic separation has both advantages and disadvantages. One of the technical leads at the remote office observed:

> It would helpful if everybody were in the same room but in our case … we have the advantage of people in different time-zones. They are given some work that I am doing now then they will be working on it during the day.

Then the [onshore] DBA can handover to me in the next morning". In contrast, the product owner mentioned: "The difficulty is that, when I am here on-site, I only get a couple of hours in the morning to deal with Dublin stuff".

The motivation of Ocuco Ltd is to become a global organization, developing software globally for a global market by using benefits of global software development but one of the product owners identified that geographic separation is massively hindering his project. He cannot talk to the people he needs to talk to urgently. Due to global development difficulties, the product owner has considered moving to another project that has a team in the same time zone.

Though teams "often" calculate velocity to plan for the upcoming sprint, due to lack of accurate estimation, teams cannot always meet the sprint goals: "We are often behind on doing the estimates, not taking the needed time or missing information enough to do a proper estimate". A project manager identified that "over commitment" and quality assurance "speed" are hindering the team in meeting the sprint goals. However, a developer said: "It is a bit up and down, sometimes we succeed. It is like it has become common to always introduce new 'critical' issues into the current sprint, instead of letting them wait for the next sprint planning".

Team members are self-organized, respect each other, "always" help each other to complete sprint goals, manage interdependencies, and stay in-sync with each other. A product owner states: "Teams work well together, and everyone is providing their part to making the best product. We just don't always agree, which is good!" The retrospective meeting is meant to be a qualitative method to measure the Scrum team's performance in a sprint by asking (1) what went well, and (2) what did not work well. This meeting helps the team to ensure that all team members contribute equally and helps to encourage "self-organization". "I can only recall one retrospective during the last two years, it was done after a release and not after each sprint".

9.1.3 Programme Level

The program level at Ocuco Ltd is distributed across seven countries. The research identified five important roles at this level: product manager, architectural lead, quality assurance (QA) lead, project manager, and director of development, who oversees the programme level. Each project manager is responsible for an individual team and is also the Scrum master at team level.

SAFe prescribes seven areas at the programme level, namely planning readiness, programme increment (PI) planning event, PI execution, PI results, inspect and adapt (I&A), stakeholders' engagement, and portfolio alignment to access programme level. Of these, the researchers found inspect and adapt reported "occasionally" in practice, and the rest of the areas are "often".

In Ocuco Ltd, the programme management team "often" performs some elements of PI planning events, which are supported by the director of development: "We don't have a formal PI planning event, but we do have elements of this done informally". As a way forward, programme management decided to develop an agile release train (ART), where each team participates at the end of each sprint to sync with other teams.

In SAFe, inspect and adapt (I&A) is a significant event that is held at the end of each programme increment (PI), where all programme stakeholders participate with the agile teams. This event consists of three parts: the PI system demo, quantitative measurement, and retrospective. The teams "often" perform I&A workshops at the end of each PI. However, the director of the development said, "We don't do this yet. That is also supported by a Project Manager: … I haven't attended a PI Planning event in a long time". As the study identified, the PI planning event has not been implemented at the program level, and because of that teams do not need to perform I&A workshop.

9.1.3.1 Portfolio Alignment

The programme vision and roadmap provide a view of the features to be developed and reflect the needs of stakeholders. Programme portfolio management (PPM) holds the primary responsibility to align the portfolio with the program level to guide programme execution and governance. In the studied organization, PMO "often" aligns the programme vision and roadmap with the strategic themes and portfolio vision. This is consistent with one of the project manager's comments: "Product manager, chief executive officer (CEO), chief technical officer (CTO) and director of development are meeting periodically, I have only attended the last portfolio review and it seems to start working on the agile direction at portfolio level". Regarding whether governance adheres to Lean–agile principles, this same project manager also mentioned: "In my opinion it has only started, but there is a complete shift in culture that still has to happen".

9.1.4 Portfolio Level

There are eight areas in portfolio level, namely programme portfolio management (PPM) team, strategy and investment funding, governance, programme management, portfolio metrics, budgets, value streams, and portfolio Kanban. Of these, governance and programme management are "often" implemented in practice, while the rest are not. The portfolio level is distributed in five countries, but most of the portfolio team members are based at the headquarters in Dublin.

9.1.4.1 Programme Portfolio Management (PPM) Team

In SAFe, programme portfolio management (PPM) represents the people who have the highest-level strategy and fiduciary decision-making responsibility. PPM also participates in the establishment and communication of strategic themes that guide the enterprise's investments and strategy, determine the relevant value streams, and allocate budgets (Table 9.1).

The values in the table are as follows: 0 – Never, 1 – Rarely, 2 – Occasionally, 3 – Often, 4 – Very Often, 5 – Always (Table 9.2).

However, in Ocuco Ltd, the PPM team "occasionally" support demand management and continuous value flow. The CTO mentioned:

> We don't do demand management but rather that it is not particularly done as part of the portfolio process. The demand management we do is more at the resource and project management and resource balancing. The portfolio drives what needs doing and it

Table 9.1 Programme Portfolio Management (PPM) Team

Question	Median 1	Mode 1
Q1. Effectively supports demand management and continuous value flow	2	0,2
Q2. Facilitates lightweight, epic-only business cases	1.5	0,2
Q3. Supports decentralized rolling-wave planning	1	0
Q4. Fosters agile estimating and planning	2	1,2,3
Q5. Drives product and solution strategy; effectively manages investments	3.5	4
Q6. Uses objective, fact-based measures and milestones to evaluate the performance of agile release trains (ARTs)	0.5	0

Table 9.2 Strategy and Investment Funding

Question	Median1	Mode1
Q1. Strategic themes have been created and are used to connect the portfolio vision to the enterprise business strategy	3	3
Q2. Strategic themes guides investments and the enterprise architecture needed to support customer and business needs	2.5	2
Q3. Strategic themes are used as decision-making filters in the portfolio Kanban system	1.5	1,2

is the management of the execution which then makes it happen, including resetting the timelines to match production capability.

In respect to epic in portfolio level, the CTO also mentioned: "We aren't really epic-based at the PPM level, it is more about projects/deliverables/contracts, from which epics are produced within the team environment after the fact". The PPM "occasionally" fosters agile estimating and planning. As a rationale of that, a PPM member mentioned:

We do plan and estimation, but it isn't specifically done at the PPM level outside of general broad estimates and timelines. But it is the word "fosters" which is important here. The PPM doesn't specifically or actively "foster" estimation and planning, outside of it being part of the accepted strategic direction to embrace agile.

9.1.4.2 Strategy and Investment Funding

The purpose of strategy and investment funding in SAFe is to support implementation of the business strategy through programmes that develop and maintain the company's value-added products and services. The studied organization "often" use strategic themes to connect the portfolio vision to the enterprise business strategy.

The values in the table are as followed: 0 – Never, 1 – Rarely, 2 – Occasionally, 3 – Often, 4 – Very Often, 5 – Always.

Governance functions still exist in agile otherwise there would be no portfolio-level feedback on investment spend. In comparison to other areas at the portfolio level, governance seems to be one of the strongest areas at Ocuco Ltd. The decision-making process at this level is "very often" decentralized, as reported in Table 9.3. This has the effect of making distributed development easier through provision of autonomy to global teams.

9.1.5 Home Office vs. Remote Office Work

During this study, the researchers have observed some mismatches between the qualitative and quantitative data. The data has also allowed us to compare the perceived knowledge between home office and remote team members at the team, programme, and portfolio levels.

At the team level, we can see that there are three areas where home office team members state that they perform "very often" compared to remote team members who "often" perform these activities. Product ownership health and team health are reported equal by both home office and remote team members. According to Ocuco Ltd's director of development:

> Ocuco Ltd realized our product owners were being pulled in different directions by their multiple responsibilities, and as a result their teams were drifting away from the product road map. So Ocuco Ltd. decided to hire additional staff so the product owners could focus solely on product ownership and keep the long-term product vision in focus.

Interestingly, at program level, the researchers have found that, the adoption rate of SAFe by remote team members is higher than home office team

Table 9.3   Governance

Question	Median 1	Mode 1
Q1. Decisions are decentralized when they are frequent, time-critical, and do not have global economies of scale	4	4
Q2. Release management assists and adjusts scope, communicates expectations internally and externally, and provides necessary governance authority	4	4
Q3. Centralized control is used for decisions that are infrequent, not time-critical, and have global economies of scale	3.5	3,4
Q4. The programme portfolio management (PPM) team is respected as having the highest fiduciary decision-making authority for its programmes	3.5	3,4
Q5. The PMO is agile and provides operational support to the programme portfolio management (PPM) team	3	3,4
Q6. Each agile release train (ART) programme vision and roadmap is aligned with the portfolio vision and strategic themes	3	2,3,4
Q7. Epic owners work with product and solution management to split epics into capabilities and features and to prioritize them into the respective backlogs	3	3
Q8. Each value stream reports objective fact-based KPIs and milestones	1.5	1,2
Q9. Guidelines have been established to direct programme epics to an individual value stream or ART or to the portfolio Kanban, depending upon its estimated size	2	2

members. Home office team members think inspect and adapt have never been adopted. However, remote team members think they perform this workshop "often". But the researchers have observed there is a mismatch between quantitative and qualitative data set, as a remote project manager said: "At the programme level, there are other people doing it [inspect and adapt] or is it the project manager that is providing. But collectively at the PMO meeting we are not doing this exercise or very informally".

The remote portfolio personnel indicate that they have adopted more SAFe practices at this level compared to home office portfolio personnel. Both home office and remote personnel think governance has been "often" adopted in both cases. However, a remote managing director admitted,

"SAFe is not fully implemented in all countries". That also echoes the voice of the operation manager at home office:

> I think it is just we have adopted items that we feel work well for us, such as the Scrum. We do not do it 'cause it's agile. We just feel it makes sense to meet every morning and discuss what is going on, so people do not work in isolation. So, I think we have adopted principles but not necessarily under the guise of we are going agile.

Finally, the improvements can be seen if teams at different level become more familiar with their roles. This is especially true for global team members. On the other hand, people may try harder to please (and inflate what they do in the survey), because they know they are being measured.

9.1.6 Overall Conclusion

The research question was to examine to what extent SAFe practices can be implemented in a global SME. The self-assessment results provide a mixed message. On the one hand, the quantitative results indicate that Ocuco Ltd has been able to implement SAFe at the team level but has not so far successfully done so at the programme and portfolio levels.

On the other hand, the comments from participants seem to suggest that the numbers do not tell the whole story: while the team level numbers indicate many practices are performed "very often" or "always", comments indicate some teams never perform certain practices. This is echoed at the programme level, where for example responses indicate inspect and adapt is performed "occasionally" but the director of development said it is not performed at all (yet).

The portfolio-level assessment presents a third perspective: respondents at the portfolio level seemed to be overly critical of their progress on SAFe implementation. It appears that respondents answered the survey questions according to an extremely strict comparison of their activities to SAFe. The researcher's observations and interviews at the portfolio level suggest that Ocuco Ltd does perform many of the activities assessed by the SAFe self-assessment, but in a different way and using different terminology than SAFe. For example, in the strategy and investment funding area, respondents rated Ocuco Ltd's use of "strategic themes" in guiding investment as somewhere between "occasionally" and "often". But the researchers have observed that Ocuco Ltd. is quite disciplined in their approach to investing in product development, although they do not use the term "strategic theme".

Finally, some SAFe practices may simply not apply to SMEs. For example, Ocuco Ltd's portfolio-level respondents rated their implementation of practices related to value streams as quite low. This may reflect the fact that value streams, as conceived in SAFe, are optional, as they are targeted toward large organizations: "The value stream level is optional in SAFe. Enterprises that build systems that are largely independent, or that can be built with a few hundred practitioners, may not need the constructs of this level, in which case they can operate from the 'collapsed view,' which is called three-level SAFe".

In software development, teams tailor their practices based on the metrics used to measure their system and evaluate their performance. By applying self-assessment, a software organization can understand its current process maturity, identify practices to improve, and identify practices that are missing. But an overemphasis on quantitative results of such self-assessments may obscure the true picture. As we have shown, the numbers do not always match the underlying truth.

A strength of the SAFe self-assessment instrument is that it asks respondents to write comments that illuminate the values they assign to questions. This provides insight into why different metrics have given values. Also, the SAFe self-assessment is intended to be a team exercise: while team members may complete the assessment individually, they are encouraged to discuss the results as a group. This promotes deeper understanding than the numbers alone can provide. Considering this observation, the SAFe self-assessment instrument should not be viewed as a management reporting tool, because the values must be filtered through the lens of the qualitative comments that explain why levels are reported as they are.

9.1.7 Literature

Razzak, M.A., Richardson, I., & Noll, J. (2018) *Scaling Agile across the Global Organization: An Early-Stage Industrial SAFe Self-Assessment.* ACM/IEEE 13th International Conference on Global Software Engineering.

9.2 Case study (2016) – An Empirical Study of Portfolio Management and Kanban in Agile and Lean Software Companies

9.2.1 Background

The group of researchers from the university of Oulu in Finland researched among other questions what tools and methods are used to manage

Table 9.4   Participation

Company ID	Primary Domain	No. of Employees in the Company	Roles of Interviewees (Years in Company)
A	Computer security	> 900	Director of External R&D Collaboration (8 yrs) Senior Manager for Quality of Operations (4 yrs)
B	Software and systems (specializing in embedded systems)	> 1000	1. Head of Quality and Environment, and Strategy Process Facilitator (12 yrs)
C	IT services and consultancy	> 75	1. CEO and Co-Founder (13 yrs)
D	Telecom network	> 45,000	1. Business Improvement Manager (> 20 yrs)
E	IT and product engineering services	> 14,000	1. Senior Solutions Consultant (> 9 yrs)
F	Telecom network	> 25,000	1. Internal Coach for Agile and Lean Organizational Transformation (> 20 yrs)
G	Services and consultancy	> 250	1. Agile, Lean, and Kanban Consultant Coach (2.5 yrs)

portfolios in Lean and agile software companies, how portfolio management in agile and lean software companies differs from traditional portfolio management, and what the role and potential is for the use of Kanban in portfolio management for agile and lean software companies. The research method was a mixed method with a literature review and interviews. The companies who took part are illustrated in Table 9.4.

9.2.2 The Approach

Traditional project portfolio management does not take into consideration the operability of agile and Lean operations since it often involves a centralized decision-making process with detailed annual plans giving an impression of waterfall milestones. On the other hand, the agile portfolio management, that are used in agile and Lean software companies, tends to focus on decentralized decision-making with light-weighted planning of product and service development activities. Table 9.5 illustrates the main goal of a traditional project portfolio management and the methods applied in these companies.

Table 9.5 Main Goals of Project Portfolio Management

Main Goal of Portfolio Management	Portfolio Management Methods	A	B	C	D	E	F	G
Maximize the value of the portfolio	Cost–benefit analysis	X			X	X		
	DCF		X					
	PBP		X					
	EVA				X			X
	NPV					X		X
	Cash flow			X				
	Scoring models, checklists, e.g., lead time, value throughput	X	X	X	X	X	X	X
	Product experimentation		X			X	X	
Ensure balance among portfolio offerings	Strategic buckets (key focus areas)	X	X	X	X	X	X	
	Business roadmap	X	X					
	Kanban	X	X	X	X	X	X	X
	Bubble diagram, burndown charts, cumulative flow diagrams	X				X	X	
	Ad hoc process, matrix							X
Achieve strategic alignment of the portfolio	Strategic goals	X	X	X	X	X		X
	Product roadmap	X	X					
	Kanban	X	X	X	X	X	X	
	Key performance indicators (KPI)			X	X			
	PowerPoint and videos to communicate strategy					X		
Pick the right number of offerings	R&D capacity pipeline analysis	X	X			X		
	Capacity or capability planning		X		X	X	X	X

9.2.3 Overall Conclusions

The findings of this study revealed that agile and Lean software companies used some of the traditional portfolio management tools and methods, but the emphasis was different from that described in the portfolio management literature. The main distinguishing factors were that agile and Lean software companies employed tools and methods that emphasized getting immediate feedback from customers and immediate delivery of offerings to evaluate the value maximization of the portfolio. Agile and Lean companies strongly advocate frequent interaction with customers and gaining immediate feedback on products through the quick delivery of functionality. This aspect increases the probability of reducing the risk of uncertainty and maximizes value for the customer and the company.

From the studied companies, the researchers have identified and drawn three implications of portfolio management in agile and Lean software development. First, the selected agile and Lean software companies actively employed tools and methods that helped facilitate customer feedback. Moreover, agile, and Lean approaches in software development and delivery served to lower the level of investment risk for the companies. This is because, instead of relying on financial models to evaluate value maximization, companies relied on the immediate delivery of products to solicit customer feedback and quickly ascertain the value of products. Financial models, as portfolio management tools, require long periods of time to compute, and to confirm their estimations after product delivery. In addition, it was found that incremental delivery and the ability to make changes at any time during product development further increased a company's ability to quickly respond to emerging opportunities.

Second, agile, and Lean approaches allowed companies to have more frequent and decentralized decision-making points, in contrast to traditional portfolio management processes, which are often plan-driven and centralized.

Third, the traditional literature on portfolio management methods and tools does not take into consideration customer interaction to the extent required in agile and Lean software companies. Generally, these findings have important implications for traditional portfolio management processes, which tend to incorporate preplanning activities on a large scale with minimum flexibility, or which use complex methods and tools.

For portfolio management, a variety of methods and tools are adopted and adjusted according to the context. The findings highlight that agile and Lean software companies rarely use financial models for their offerings at the portfolio level. Portfolio management tools and methods need to be dynamic and adaptable to process changes within the company. Agile, Lean, and Kanban adoption in companies has changed the nature of collaboration, coordination, and communication in software development projects. This also illustrates a shift toward more collaborative and coordinated portfolio management processes with greater transparency, trust, and frequent interaction.

For the studied agile and lean software companies, business strategy played a significant role and was a crucial tool for managing the portfolio. This puts emphasis on the means used to communicate the business strategy clearly across the entire company as well as its active renewal. For better portfolio management, the business strategy needs to be actively reviewed and clearly communicated across the entire company. Additionally, the software companies interviewed use Kanban at the portfolio level, which brings more visibility to the workflow and clarity with respect to high-priority activities measured against resources.

This study contributes to the body of knowledge on portfolio management and agile and Lean software product management by providing empirical evidence on tools and methods used to manage a portfolio of offerings. The findings highlight that agile and Lean software companies have a different emphasis than that described in the traditional portfolio management literature.

9.2.4 *Literature*

Ahmad, M.O., Lwakatare, L.E., Kuvaja, P., Oivo, M., & Markkula, J. (2017) An empirical study of portfolio management and Kanban in agile and lean software companies. *Journal of Software: Evolution and Process* 29, e1834.

Bhattacharya, S., Krishnan, V., & Mahajan, V. (1998) Managing new product definition in highly dynamic environments. *Management Science* 44, 50–64.

Stettina, C.J., & Hörz, J. (2015) Agile portfolio management: An empirical perspective on the practice in use. *International Journal of Project Management* 33, 140–152.

9.3 Case study (2019) – Managing the Agile Scalability to Implement Agile Project Portfolio Management

9.3.1 *Background*

This case study is based upon the Master of Science Thesis "Managing the Agile Scalability to implement Agile Project Portfolio Management – A Case Study within the Automotive Industry" by Charlott Kapic in 2019 at the KTH School for Industrial Engineering and Management in Stockholm, Sweden. The main research question of the thesis was to examine "How can a mature industrial company become more agile in their PPM".

9.3.2 The Approach

The organization in the study is a global manufacturing company within the automotive industry. The company designs, develops, and manufactures heavy vehicles. The majority of its business is built on hardware technology, but the expansion of its software department has increased rapidly in recent years. The company's methods and processes are deeply rooted in the waterfall model. Throughout its many years of existence, the company has been able to develop products in a sequential process without many iterations.

The idea of working agile within the R&D department emerged at the team level. Inspirations to work agile were originally taken from the company's IT department, a department that does not belong to R&D and is placed in a completely different building. Since the concept of agile has its origin within software departments, it became naturally for the people working within IT to adopt it first.

The scaled agile framework has not formally been announced by top management to be implemented at the company. An attempt to use this approach has been done within one of the strategic units, which specifically works with the development of new technology. The framework has recently been adopted to a certain extent and adjusted to fit the company's processes. It was initiated as a pilot. The adoption includes the creation of a development flow that runs in parallel with the product development process.

9.3.3 What Went Wrong?

The organization in the study adopted SAFe but kept the traditional project portfolio management approach. Some of the problems experienced were:

■ Resource conflicts are often related to information known in projects and that does not reach the portfolio level.
■ "Hidden" projects that are consuming the same resources as the product development projects, which are unknown to higher management.
■ Project managers have not always been consulted when employees have been spending their time on work with other purposes than that of the original project. As project managers do not acquire complete

and reliable information, it becomes increasingly difficult for them to determine the accurate status of a project, thus the project portfolio becomes much more challenging to manage.

■ Information regarding projects resources were suffering as resource transparency decreased.
■ Poor resource estimations were evidenced.
■ Resource allocation syndrome. Poor project scheduling, over commitment (i.e., too many projects in relation to available resources), and opportunistic project management behaviour are some of the causes of this syndrome.
■ Projects were started before the required resources are available.

The adaptation of SAFe is summarized in Table 9.6 where black indicates low performance while grey is high performance.

9.3.4 Literature

Kapic, C. (2019) *Managing the Agile Scalability to Implement Agile Project Portfolio Management – A Case Study within the Automotive Industry.* KTH Industrial Engineering and Management, Sweden.

9.4 Case study (2018) – Large-Scale Agile Transformations at Ericsson

9.4.1 Background

The Ericsson research and development (R&D) product development programme was located on five sites, on two continents. By 2011 15 development teams and more than 200 people worked in the programme.

Previously, the company has been successful in implementing agile at small scale where the team have had the opportunity to work agile as they saw fit. The good experiences became part of the corporate strategy which puts more emphasis toward agile adoptions. At the same time, another key motivator for working differently was the dissatisfaction with the current way of working – Ericson had a long history of working plan-based. An additional factor was a need in the market to deliver more quickly. The product, a XaaS platform and a related set of services, was acquired by Ericsson

Table 9.6 Performance

Theme	Explanation	Performance
Feedback the fuel learning	Use rapid feedback on all results	○
Synchronization	Collaborative groups solve problems than individuals	○
Sequence of project execution	Identify what must be done in parallel and what must be done in sequence to maximize throughput of the portfolio	●
Even workload	Create an even workload	●
Scale using fractals	Scale agile incrementally	◐
Understanding of agile	The personnel's understanding of what agile specifically means to the company	●
Importance of agile	The personnel's perception of the importance of agile	◐
Knowledge-building	Storing and leveraging of obtained knowledge	○
Work traceability	Vertical traceability of work items, from team level to portfolio level	●
Work culture	Tensions within the working environment The employees' willingness to sharing	○
Educated staff	Knowledge within agile among employees	○
Employee empowerment	Listen to employees at lower level Value is created in the front line	◐

in 2011 where 30 to 40 people worked on it; at that time the product was released every eight weeks, which Ericsson was not yet able to change.

It was clear to Ericsson that they needed to adopt agile to improve time-to-market and the overall competitiveness of the company with the goal of implementing continuous feature delivery.

This case study is based upon 45 semi-structured interviews in the period 2013 to 2014, combined with literature research and documentation used during the transformation by the case company.

9.4.2 The Approach

Ericsson initiated the agile transformation with a pilot including a highly skilled, all-star agile team which went remarkably well. This led to an experimental approach with a stepwise implementation. The implication was that a common framework for the whole organization was not used. The stepwise implementation was implemented in three steps: agile, common ground, and continuous integration/deployment. The first step, agile, had focus on building pilot cross-functional teams. When this was working, a full-scale roll-out was conducted. To support the teams, there was a competence pool to supplement the teams. Each team was specialized in a certain business flow or domain which was governed by a product-owner–like role. It was clear that team interchangeability was limited as specialization was needed. The second step in the agile transformation was creating a common ground and value, where values such as one organization, passion to win, fun, step-by-step, customer collaboration were designed. The last step in the agile transformation was the emphasis on continuous integration/deployment to speed up on the deliveries by the teams.

The transformation faced varies challenges, some being:

- Change resistance in a waterfall organization which was challenged by agile teams and way of working (leadership team with agile mindset)
- Technical debt
- No common framework (community of practice was implemented)
- Lack of training and coaching
- Lack of automation
- Cross-site team
- All the team cannot do all features or components (specialized business flows)
- Way of working – agile teams in a waterfall organization
- Defining the product owner role
- Breaking down requirements
- Backlog challenges (change to a common backlog)

9.4.3 Literature

Passivaara, M., Behm, B., Lassenius, C., & Hallikainen, M. (2018) *Large-Scale Agile Transformation at Ericsson*. 11 January.

9.5 Case study (2011) – Supporting Scaling Agile with Portfolio Management at Paf.com

9.5.1 The Background

Paf (Ålands Penningautomatförening), founded in 1966, is a public association that operates gaming activities on the autonomous Åland Islands, onboard Ålandic and Finnish ships, and on the Internet.

One department at Paf, Paf.com, introduced portfolio management to help support scaling agile software development. The reason was that Paf .com had experienced problems with long time-to-market due to: thrashing, which was caused by frequently changing priorities due to an ad hoc prioritization process and handovers; lack of visibility into projects entering and progressing in the development pipeline; no structured way of starting projects being enforced company-wide; and too many parallel projects getting started. The company had worked with multiple Scrum teams for years, many using Scrum by the book.

9.5.2 The Approach

The first steps toward portfolio management were taken when the content of every release was internally prioritized according to business value. Gradually this began to work but then four new problems were discovered:

- Lack of visibility on "projects" about to enter the development pipeline
- The maturity of the planning of the "projects" entering the development pipeline
- Prioritization of projects was ad hoc rogue
- "Business critical" projects were induced "under the hood" by some managers

Paf completed a merger with Eget. In the spring of 2009, the management of Paf was still not happy with the inefficiency and handovers in the organization inherited from the merger of Paf and Eget.

In the spring of 2009, the PMO and QA proposed a model (Figure 9.2) for managing the portfolio of projects in a structured way. It was called Pamp and it combined elements from Stage-Gate models, the open unified process, and project management body of knowledge (PMBoK). The main goal of Pamp was to clarify a business need and increase the visibility for each project in Paf.com.

The project model was supplemented with a portfolio backlog process which was first drafted in 2008 and in the beginning of summer 2009 the current version (shown in Figure 9.3) was taken into use. The process addresses the problem of managers inducing "business critical" projects "under the hood".

The Pamp model and backlog process seemed to do the trick for Paf. The original 200 projects were reduced to 30 and from those 30 projects, only 5 to 10 at a time are indicated as high priority, making the priorities clear to the whole organization. This drove the way work was organized and accepted by the teams, and the team members refused to take work of lower priority, instead of ending up in a thrashing mode of constantly changing priorities.

To summarize the initial positive results, it seems that the problems that were tackled by introducing Pamp and portfolio management have been

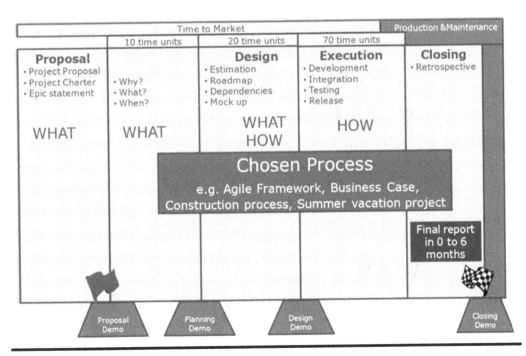

Figure 9.2   Paf model for projects.

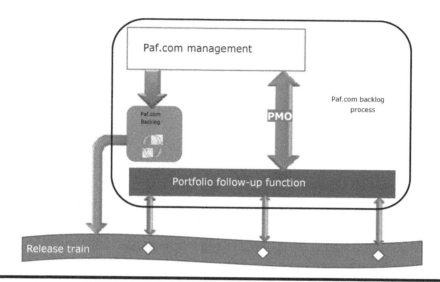

Figure 9.3 Current version.

solved quite satisfactorily. However, it is still too early to conclusively say how much time-to-market has improved.

9.5.3 Literature

Rautiainen, K., Schantz, J.V., & Vahaniitty, J. (2011) Supporting Scaling Agile with Portfolio Management at Paf.com.

9.6 Case study (2019) – Agile Software Integration at Telfor

9.6.1 The Background

The case study was conducted in the first half of 2019 at an Austrian mobile network operator who needed to integrate a COTS fault management system into an operation support system by a hybrid approach.

9.6.2 The Approach

Initially the project was divided into four phases. The first phase started in April 2015 with the investment in the COTS fault management system to be integrated and the concept to develop the remaining functionalities. March

2016 Phase 2 started with focus on go-live features and extensions. The two first phases of the project were mainly predictive/plan-based in their approach which was mainly due to the need for external integrators. With the start of Phase 3 a major Scrum company roll-out was completed which changed the development in the complex environment to a Scrum team. Scrum had been implemented without any form of tailoring or adaptation to the organization. This was not working out well. By the start of Phase 4 the Scrum team was changed to a Kanban team. The two-week sprints were changed to monthly sprints. The team was expanded to 14 people and supported by a second product owner type. The Scrum master was no longer needed as the team was using Kanban, not Scrum, now.

The company was struggling with an untailored Scrum implementation that did not meet the requirements of the complex environments of telecommunications. The initial Scrum team was hardly able to complete the work in two weeks which led to untested work being done just in time. When teams got really busy, which was most of the time, agile was bypassed and team members went back to old waterfall routines by dividing the work and doing it alone. This being a new team, it lacked a team lead or more senior people which was worsened by the product owner role having no budget responsibilities, meaning things were rarely settled in time to do the actual work.

9.6.3 Literature

Hirner, H., Lavicka, M., Schefer-Wenzl, S., & Miladinovic, I. (2019) *Agile Software Integration in Telecommunications – A Case Study*. IEEE.

9.7 Case study (2015) – Is Agile Portfolio Management Following the Principles of Large-Scale Agile in the Finish Broadcasting Company Yle

9.7.1 The Background

Yle is a public service broadcasting company in Finland. Yle have four national TV channels, six radio channels and 25 regional radio programmes. They have been using agile portfolio management for years as part of their web and mobile development.

9.7.2 *The Approach*

This case study examines whether the usual identified benefits in literature for agile portfolio management and for large-scale agile development was identified in the case company.

The usual benefits (identified in the literature) of agile portfolio management are:

- Epics: Avoid a long queue of development items that will get outdated. Specify the new epics just-in-time when needed. Focus on value derived from each epic.
- Prioritization: Clear visibility and communication of what needs to be implemented. Generically, the fractal backlog structure helps development teams to identify what is the larger entity that the stories under development will comprise of. A change of priorities in the portfolio backlog enables the company to quickly change its strategic direction.
- Epic owner: Each epic has an epic owner who is responsible for making all the decisions regarding the contents of that epic. An epic owner remains the same from the idea until the epic is ready, and participates in all negotiations and meetings considering the epic, this process resulting in a lot of tacit information.
- Enterprise architect: Architecture is a business decision. What architecture solutions are used impacts the return on investment, i.e., the payback of each investment decision made. Thus, enterprise architects analyze and make decisions regarding the possible future architecture solutions, e.g., what cloud solution, database, or framework a company should use.
- Programme portfolio management: Programme portfolio management is a group of senior managers, strategy planners, and directors that make portfolio decisions and prioritize the portfolio backlog.
- Strategic themes: Strategic themes express the intent to which direction the enterprise would like to develop its portfolio, i.e., what kind of new strategies it will implement in the future. Epics are derived from strategic themes.
- Portfolio metrics: Portfolio metrics measure the enterprise's performance on the highest level. They can include measures like employee engagement and market share/development.

These benefits were all identified in the case company and supplemented by additional benefits of transparency and visibility.

The second part of the study focused on the principles of large-scale agile development where the following 21 benefits, listed below, were identified in the literature:

- The content is the king
- Co-creation
- Feedback is the fuel to learning
- Business agility
- Use of automation as leverage
- Scale using fractals
- Avoid combinatorial explosions
- Sequence for maximal throughput
- Appreciate deep knowledge
- Work levelling
- Simplicity
- Situationally
- Control process not items
- Growth mindset
- Listen to employees, they know all the problems
- Detect and use patterns
- Cost innovation
- Utilize tacit knowledge
- Learning happens between teams
- Fast is better than perfection
- Prevent problems when small

Of the 21 principles only "Feedback is the fuel to learning" and "Business agility" were not detected or identified at the case company. In this case study there seems to be a remarkably high relation between the identified benefits and principles in the literature and what benefits are obtained by the case company and principles applied throughout the organization.

9.7.3 *Literature*

Laanti, M., & Kangas, M (2015) *Is Agile Portfolio Management Following The Principles of Large-Scale Agile?* Conference paper. ResearchGate.

Table 9.7 Analytical Themes

Analytical themes	PPM performance	APPM importance	APPM performance
Formalization	▼ Red	► Yellow	▼Red
Strategic alignment	▲ Green	▲ Green	► Yellow
Resource allocation	▲ Green	▲ Green	▼ Red
Identification and selection	▲ Green	▲ Green	▼ Red
Prioritization	► Yellow	▲ Green	▼ Red
Communication and decision-making	► Yellow	► Yellow	► Yellow
Number of projects	▼ Red	▲	▼ Red
Balance	▼ Red	▲	▼ Red
Cultural alignment	► Yellow	► Yellow	▼ Red

Table 5. *Overview of findings the performance and importance of the analytical themes at the case company, categorized as low(red), moderate(yellow), high(green).*

9.8 Case study (2018) – Agile Portfolio Management Challenges in the Swedish Automobile Industry

9.8.1 The Background

This study in the Swedish automobile industry examines the main challenges to becoming more agile in project portfolio management for a traditional company in the automotive industry. The paper examines varies analytical themes such as formalization, strategic alignment, among others. The organization's project portfolio management performance is then aligned with the analytical themes using grey as good, light grey as decent, and black as satisfactory. The importance of agile portfolio management is then aligned with the same themes (see Table 9.7) and supported with the current state of agile portfolio management performance which highlights some of the challenges the organization have been facing.

9.8.2 Literature

Isakovic, O.B.E (2018) *Agile Project Portfolio Management Challenges – An Exploratory Case Study of Product Development Projects in the Automotive Industry.* Degree Project in Industrial Management, second cycle. Stockholm, Sweden.

9.9 Case study (2011) – Agile Kanban IT project Portfolio at Getty Images

9.9.1 Background

This case study was developed by Rally Software in December 2011 and published by IDC Customer Spotlight. The company Getty Images was having an operational challenge as one-off approaches with poor visibility into the status of an agile Kanban IT project portfolio led to inaccurate project information and delayed delivery to the business with ineffective collaboration and little or no prioritization possible.

9.9.2 The Approach

Gaining accurate, timely information about key project and portfolio progress is business critical. It is also one of the toughest things we do as business and development leaders. Even more challenging is knitting together rapidly changing agile projects and programmes to gain the dynamic benefits of agile approaches to software and business development while providing coherent portfolio management. Few companies have succeeded in moving beyond static, up-front timelines and roadmaps to manage work dynamically with agile teams "pulling" in the work rather than having it "pushed" out to them. Getty Images provides an excellent example of a way to make the transition.

Getty Images offers products and services for creative professionals and communicators by leveraging a collection of 80,000,000+ stock photographs and editorial images and 50,000 hours of film, video, music, and multimedia content. Getty Images' client base includes small and large businesses that rely on imagery as part of their work. Core target markets include entertainment, advertising, graphic design, print and online media, and corporate marketing and sales for this 2,000-employee organization headquartered in Seattle.

Software projects drive company success, and the company's project and programme management group work closely with its executive team to align technology with strategic business goals. One team of programme managers (PMs) partners with specific line-of-business (LOB) stakeholders to break down ideas and formulate business cases to help ensure that they are working on the right things in the right order. Separate, coordinated project management staff focus on IT execution and delivery. The company's senior director of planning and programme management, Nina Schoen, coordinates this effort. Although the programme management teams collaborate with the information technology team, they are not "technical managers". Getty Images' programme management organization (PMO) sits as close to the business as possible.

The technology team at Getty Images transitioned to agile and Lean practices approximately three years ago, creating 20+ scrum teams with approximately 200 application developers. The transition provided great benefits, allowing most of all for improved time-to-market. The transition, however, quickly highlighted the need for agile planning methods. The desire from the business was to improve predictability and visibility and to make better sense of the endless queues of work. To help solve this problem, Getty Images chose to work with Rally Software as a beta customer on the development of Rally Portfolio Manager. This way, Getty Images could be intrinsically involved in creating product capabilities that would support intuitive portfolio management for Getty Images' Kanban needs, as well as enterprise rollups of agile and another programme and project information.

9.9.3 Implementation: Dealing with Predictability and Workload Visibility

Getty Images tried a variety of tools for transitioning to Lean and agile development. In early 2010, an agile product that it initially used ran out of capability as Getty Images scaled its scrum projects to the enterprise. As the company evaluated alternatives, it decided to focus on principles of methodology and workflow rather than fixed, time-boxed process approaches. What Getty Images liked about Rally's ALM platform and products was the flexibility it offered to manage the project work the way they needed to, based on weekly assessments of team readiness rather than arbitrary, unrealistic commitments, and enabled them to change approaches as their workflow needs evolved.

Over time, the agile transition for application development became quite successful. The next area of focus quickly became demand and portfolio management. Getty Images executives, business owners, and technology management wanted to focus on improving the prioritization process, visibility into technology work, and predictability. The programme management organization (PMO) had built some homegrown tools and processes to manage demand, prioritization, and create visibility, but they often fell short.

Seeking a solution and prior to bringing in Rally Portfolio Manager, Getty Images evaluated high-end IT project portfolio management tools, but agile and Kanban support from those products was limited or non-existent, and enterprise IT PPM tools were too expensive for the company's budget and the product capabilities were overkill for the company's needs.

Initially, Getty Images' teams were unable to find software that would solve their problem to give them both the management they needed and the flexibility their IT development teams wanted. Since Getty Images was already using Rally for development, it became interested in participating in a new, beta agile portfolio management solution that Rally Software was developing. Over the past year, this joint development effort resulted in Rally Portfolio Manager, a solution which now enables Getty Images to manage all efforts on Kanban boards with visibility into more accurate, current project portfolio status for the PMO and the business. The company has been able to do away with structured quarterly timeline commitments, giving project teams the flexibility to pull in new project work dynamically as they complete core initiatives.

Planning is now dynamically updated with real-time project status. This reflects current project "reality" being useful in managing and communicating to help direct business demand, replacing former static roadmap approaches with dynamic planning. This approach has been so successful on the IT side that Getty Images is now moving these capabilities to other business-oriented areas.

"Our big accomplishments are pulling projects into development when they're ready for more, in separating planning from delivery, and managing prioritization by line of business through our use of Rally", said Schoen. "Recently, our marketing team also adopted Rally, moving beyond just IT". She added that business executives are using Rally's AgileZen (www.agilezen.com) board to make information visible to their peers since the user interface is easy to digest and will be incorporated into Rally Portfolio Manager.

> A lot of technical tools are so complicated that you get lost in the weeds. With AgileZen, the eye focuses on what is most important. Tagging lets you see and filter by data elements, which are easy to maintain and update. Using a Kanban board to manage work makes it easier to see problems and progress.

Schoen manages allocation of technology resources across the company's LOBs (such as marketing and e-commerce) so that they do not compete with one another for projects, while individually each group prioritizes in a focused way.

Getty Images' teams recently eliminated hard timeline commitments in project roadmaps. Although the company plans, at a high level, what work will be accomplished, at a detailed level, it commits only to work that's about 60 days out and reviews those commitments at a regular cadence, using the workflow that Rally helps it automate. "We've gotten rid of false notions of delivery time frames, and it's a beautiful thing", said Schoen, who manages planning work on the company's Kanban board with Rally Portfolio Manager now.

The teams focus on what they call "minimum viable features" to break down the initiatives into core chunks of business value and to prioritize them, but the IT teams do not pull in additional work until they are ready to take on more.

> This prevents business churn later and is much more efficient. Our reporting shows that we are delivering much more to the business because we have separated out the planning churn from delivery and allowed the team to focus on what's most important, she added.

9.9.4 Challenges: Evolving Agile Portfolio Management

Although the company had already been doing agile projects, making adoption consistent was a necessity and took additional organizational effort. Overall, Getty Images' staff found the process of partnering with Rally Software to create Rally Portfolio Manager to be exhilarating and engaging. They were able to be on the cutting edge with Rally Software to support the team in creating the features and functionality most important to addressing their business needs. They knew what they were signing up for and were fully committed to the joint development process. While this process brought key benefits to Getty Images (and saved the company the considerable effort and challenge of creating its own Kanban-based portfolio management tool), it also brought the usual challenges of dealing with unfinished code that was a "work in progress".

Getty Images is looking forward to improvements in the portfolio dashboard presentation for the executive teams as the product evolves. The teams at Getty Images found that the advantages of participating in the development process far outweighed the challenges of dealing with alpha and beta code for Rally's new product. Because the teams were able to tailor the features to address their needs and workflow demands, user uptake also benefited, and Rally Software is now launching production-quality software with Rally Portfolio Manager that Getty Images has incorporated into its development and business strategy.

9.9.5 Literature

IDC Customer Spotlight (2011) Agile Kanban IT project Portfolio at Getty images. *Rally Software*, December.

Exercise 9.1 What Did You Learn in School Today?

What did you learn from discussing the varies cases? Compare/contrast. Any overall trends/insights? What would you do different in the various cases? Why are some cases going well while others are struggling?

_____
_____
_____
_____
_____

Answers: No right or wrong answers.

References

Agile Alliance (2001) Manifesto for agile software development. Retrieved from Agilemanifesto.org.

Agile Alliance (2012) Information radiator. Retrieved from http://www.Agilealliance .org.

Agnostic Agile (2021) Introduction. Retrieved from https://www.agnosticagile.org.

Ahmad, M. O., Lwakatare, L. E., Kuvaja, P., Oivo, M., & Markkula, J. (2017) An empirical study of portfolio management and Kanban in agile and lean software companies. *Journal of Software: Evolution and Process*, 29(6), e1834.

Alleman, G. (2011) Agile and EVM? Herding blog. Retrieved from http://herdingcats. typepad.com/my_weblog/2011/05/Agile-and-evm.html.

Alqudah, M., & Razali, R. (2016) A review of scaling agile methods in large software development. *International Journal Advanced Science Engineering Information Technology*, 6(6).

Ambler, S. (2012) *Disciplined Agile Delivery: A Practitioner's Guide to Agile Software Delivery in the Enterprise*. IBM Press, Boston. ISBN-13: 978–0132810135.

Ambler, S., & Lines, M. (2017) *An Executive's Guide to Disciplined Agile: Winning the Race to Business Agility*, Volume 1. CreateSpace Independent Publishing Platform.

Ambler, S., & Lines, M. (2020) *Choose Your WoW: A Disciplined Agile Delivery Handbook for Optimizing Your Way of Working*. Project Management Institute, Chicago.

Anderson, D. J. (2010) *Kanban: Successful Evolutionary Change for Your Technology Business Paperback*, Blue Hole Press; Illustrated edition (April 7, 2010).

Anderson, D. J. (2012) *Kanban – Successful Evolutionary Change for Your Technology Business*, Blue Hole Press; Illustrated edition (April 7, 2010).

Archer, N., & Ghasemzadeh, F. (1999) An integrated framework for project portfolio selection. *International Journal of Project Management*, 17(4), 207–216. portfolio selection and management. In Morris, P., & Pinto, J. K. (2007) *The Wiley Guide to Project, Program & Portfolio Management*. John Wiley & Sons Inc., Hoboken, NJ, pp. 94–112.

Artto, K. A. (2001) *Management of Project-Oriented Organization—Conceptual Analysis. Project Portfolio Management: Strategic Management Through Projects.* Project Management Association, pp. 5–22.

Artto, K. A., & Dietrich, P. H. (2004) Strategic business management through multiple projects. In: *Wiley Guide to Managing Projects*, P. W. G. Morris, & J. K. Pinto (Eds.), John Wiley and Sons, Hoboken, NJ, pp. 144–176.

Axelos (2011) *Management of Portfolios.* Norwich, Axelos.

Beck, K. (2000) *Extreme Programming Explained: Embrace Change.* Longman Higher Education.

Beck, K. (2007) A theory of programming. *Dr. Dobb's Journal*, November.

Bernstein, E., Bunch, J., Canner, N., & Lee, M. (2016) Beyond the Holacracy hype. The overwrought claims—And actual promise—Of the next generation of self-managed teams by. *Harvard Business Review.* July–August 2016 issue, 38–49.

Bhattacharya, S., Krishnan, V., & Mahajan, V. (1998) Managing new product definition in highly dynamic environments. *Management Science*, 44(11–part), 50–64.

Bittner, K., Kong, P., & West, D. (2018) *The Nexus Framework for Scaling Scrum.* The Professional Scrum Series. Prentice Hall.

Blichfeldt, B. S., & Eskerod, P. (2007) Project portfolio management – There's more to it than what management enacts. *International Journal of Project Management*, 26, 357–365.

Bradley, G. (2010) *Benefit Realisation Management: A Practical Guide to Achieving Benefits through Change.* Routledge, London.

Burrows, M. (2014) *Kanban from the Inside.* Chicago, Blue Hole Press.

Carvalho, C. (2010) *Dimensions for the Analysis of PPM Adapted for NPOs Source.*

Chao, R., & Kavadias, S. (2008) A theoretical framework for managing the new product development portfolio: When and how to use strategic buckets. *Management Science*, 54(5), 907–921.

Christenson, D., & Walker, D. H. T. (2004) Understanding the role of "Vision" in project success. 35(3), 39–52, September 1, Issue published.

Clegg, S., Killen, C. P., Biesenthal, C., & Sankaran, S. (2018) Practices, projects, and portfolios: Current research trends and new directions. *International Journal of Project Management*, 36(5), 762–772.

Cockburn, A. (2001) *Agile Software Development.* Melbourne, Addison-Wesley Professional.

Cockburn, A. (2004) *Crystal Clear: A Human-Powered Methodology for Small Teams: A Human-Powered Methodology for Small Teams.* Melbourne, Addison-Wesley Professional.

Cockburn, A. (2007) *Agile Software Development: The Cooperative Game.* Melbourne, Addison-Wesley Professional.

Cohen, M. (2005) *Agile Estimating and Planning.* New Jersey, Prentice Hall.

Conboy, K. (2009) Agility from first principles: Reconstructing the concept of agility in information systems development. *Information Systems Research*, 20(3), 329–354.

Conboy, K., & Carroll, N. (2019) Implementing large-scale agile frameworks: Challenges and recommendations. *IEEE Software*. https://doi.org/10.1109/MS. 2018.2884865.

Cooper, R. G., Edgett, S. J., & Kleinschmidt, E. J. (1997a) Portfolio management in new product development: Lessons from the leaders – I. *Research-Technology Management*, 40(5), 16–28.

Cooper, R. G., Edgett, S. J., & Kleinschmidt, E. J. (1997b) Portfolio management in new product development: Lessons from the leaders – II. *Research-Technology Management*, 40(6), 43–52.

Cooper, R. G., Edgett, S. J., & Kleinschmidt, E. J. (1999) New product portfolio management: Practices and performance. *Journal of Product Innovation Management*, 16(4), 333–351.

Cooper, R., Edgett, S., & Kleinschmidt, E. (2000) New problems, new solutions: Making portfolio management more effective. *Research-Technology Management*, 43(2), 18–33.

Cooper, R. G., Edgett, S. J., & Kleinschmidt, E. J. (2001) *Portfolio Management for New Products*, 2nd edition. Perseus, Cambridge, MA.

Cooper, R. G., Edgett, S. J., & Kleinschmidt, E. J. (2002) Optimizing the stage-gate process: What best-practice companies do – II. *Research-Technology Management*, 45(6), 43–49.

Cooper, R. G., & Sommer, A. F. (2016) Agile–Stage-Gate: New idea-to-launch method for manufactured new products is faster, more responsive. *Industrial Marketing Management*, http://dx.doi.org/10.1016/j.indmarman.2016.10.006.

Cottmeyer, M. E. (2011) *Large Scale Program and Portfolio Management with Scrum and Kanban*. Paper presented at PMI® Global Congress 2011—North America, Dallas, TX. Project Management Institute, Newtown Square, PA.

Cram, W. A., & Brohman, M. K. (2010) *Beyond Modes: A New Typology of ISD Control*. Icis, Paper.

Daniel, E. M., Ward, J. M., & Franken, A. (2014) A dynamic capabilities perspectives of IS project portfolio management. *The Journal of Strategic Information Systems*, 23(2), 95–111.

Demarco, T., & Lister, T. (2003) *Waltzing With Bears: Managing Risk on Software Projects. Dorset House*, http://www.systemsguild.com/riskology.

Desharnais, J. M., Buglione, L., & Kocatürk, B. (2010) *Using the COSMIC Method to Estimate Agile User Stories*. Boaziçi University, Istanbul -Turkey. Publish by ACM.

Diebold, P., Schmitt, A., & Theobald, S. (2018) *Scaling Agile – How to Select the Most Appropriate Framework XP '18 Companion*, XP '18: Proceedings of the 19th International Conference on Agile Software Development: CompanionMay 2018, May 21–25, Article No.: 7, Pages 1–4, https://doi.org/10.1145/3234152. 3234177.

Dietrich, P., & Lehtonen, P. (2005) Successful management of strategic intentions through multiple projects — Reflections from empirical study. *International Journal of Project Management*, 23(5), 386–391.

Dikert, K., Paasivaara, M., & Lassenius, C. (2016) Challenges and success factors for large-scale agile transformations: A systematic literature review. *Journal of Systems and Software*, 119, 87–108, September.

DORA State of DevOps Research Program (2020) Google cloud. Retrieved from http://www.devops-research.com.

DSDM Consortium (2014) *The DSDM Agile PMO*. Kent, DSDM Consortium.

Elatta, S. (2013) Agile estimating and planning. Retrieved from http:/www.agiletraining.com.

Elonen, S., & Artto, K. (2003) Problems in managing internal development projects in multi-project environments. *International Journal of Project Management*, 21(6), 395–302.

Eskerod, P. (1996) Meaning and action in a multi-project environment. Understanding a multi-project environment by means of metaphors and basic assumptions. April 1996. *International Journal of Project Management*, 14(2), 61–65.

Fenech, B. (2014) *Project Portfolio Management Essentials*. Australia, PPMIntelligence.

Fowler, M., & Highsmith, J. (2001) The agile manifesto. *Software Development*, 9(8), 28–32.

Freeman, R. E., Harrison, J. S., & Wicks, A. C. (2007) *Managing for Stakeholders: Survival, Reputation, and Success*. Yale University Press, New Haven, CT.

Fricke, S., Shenhar, A., Technol, S., & Bloomington, M. (2000) Managing multiple engineering projects in a manufacturing support environment. *IEEE Transactions on Engineering Management*, 47(2), 258–268.

Gartner (2004) *Building Brilliant Business Cases*. Gartner, Inc, EXP Premier.

Geiger, G. (2007) IT-Sicherheit als integraler Bestandteil des Risik omanagements im Unternehmen. In: *Managementhandbuch der IT-Sicherheit*, T. Gründer, & J. Schrey (Ed.), Erich Schmidt Verlag, Berlin.

Greenleaf, R. K. (1996) *On Becoming a Servant-Leader*. Josey-Bass Publishers, San Francisco.

Grundler, A., & Westner, M. (2019) *Scaling Agile Frameworks VS*. Traditional Project Portfolio Management: Comparison and Analysis International Conferences Internet Technologies & Society 2019 and Sustainability, Technology and Education 2019.

Grundy, T. (2000) Strategic project management and strategic behaviour. *International Journal of Project Management*, 18(2), 93–103.

Heifetz, R. A., & Laurie, D. L. (1997) The work of leadership. *Harvard Business Review*, December 2001.

Highsmith, J. (2002) *Agile Software Development Ecosystems*. Addison–Wesley, Boston, MA.

Highsmith, J., Luu, L., & Robinson, D. (2020) *EDGE: Value-Driven Digital Transformation*. Addison-Wesley.

Hillson, D. (2004) *Effective Opportunity Management for Projects: Exploiting Positive Risk*.

Hirner, H., Lavicka, M., Schefer-Wenzl, S., & Miladinovic, I. (2019) *Agile Software Integration in Telecommunications – A Case Study*. New York, IEEE.

HM Treasury (2012) Delivering public value from spending proposals – Green book guidance on public sector business cases using the five case model. Retrieved January 2017 from gov.uk.

Hoda, R., Kruchten, P., Noble, J., & Marshall, S. (2010) *Agility in Context*. OOPSLA/ SPLASH'10, October 17–21. Reno/Tahoe, Nevada.

Hodgkins, P., & Hohmann, L. (2007) *Agile Program Management: Lessons Learned from the VeriSign Managed Security Services Team*. IEEE Agile Conference, pp. 194–199.

Horlach, B., Schimmer, I., & Drews, P. (2019) *Agile Portfolio Management: Design Goals and Principles*. Twenty-Seventh European Conference on Information Systems (ECIS2019). Conference Paper. Stockholm-Uppsala, Sweden.

IDC Customer Spotlight (2011) Agile Kanban IT project Portfolio at Getty images. *Rally Software*, December.

IIBA (2012) A guide to the business analysis body of knowledge. Retrieved from www.iiba.org.

Isakovic, O. B. E. (2018) *Agile Project Portfolio Management Challenges - An Exploratory Case Study of Product Development Projects in the Automotive Industry*. Degree Project in Industrial Management, Second Cycle. Stockholm, Sweden.

Jeffery, M., & Leliveld, I. (2004) Best practices in IT portfolio. *MIT Sloan Management Review*, 45(3), 41–49.

Jeffery, M., & Wilson, D. C. (2004) Best practices in portfolio management. *Sloan Management Review*, 45(3), 41–49.

Jenner, S. (2012) *Managing Benefits: Optimizing the Return from the Investments*. Stationery Office, London.

Johnson, D. W., & Johnson, R. T. (1999) *Learning Together and Alone. Cooperative, Competitive, and Individualistic Learning*, 5th edition. Allyn & Bacon, Boston, MA.

Jonas, D., Kock, A., & Gemünden, H. G. (2013) Predicting project portfolio success by measuring management quality—A longitudinal study. *IEEE Transactions on Engineering Management*, 60(2), 215–226.

Joyce, D. (2009) *Kanban for Software Engineering*. UK, BBC.

Kalenda, M., Hyna, P., & Rossi, B. (2018) Scaling agile in large organizations: Practices, challenges, and success factors. *Journal of Software: Evolution and Process*, 30(10), 1–25.

Kalliney, M. (2009) *Transitioning from Agile Development to Enterprise Product Management Agility*. IEEE Agile Conference, pp. 209–213.

Kallman, A., & Kallman, T. (2017) *Flow*. Morgan James, Forthcoming.

Kapic, C. (2019) *Managing the Agile Scalability to Implement Agile Project Portfolio Management - A Case Study Within the Automotive Industry*. KTH Industrial Engineering and Management, Sweden.

Kendall, G., & Rollins, S. (2003) *Advanced Project Portfolio Management and the PMO: Multiplying ROI at Warp Speed*. J. Ross, Fort Lauderdale, FL.

Killen, C. P. (2008) *Project Portfolio Management for Product Innovation in Service and Manufacturing Industries*. Macquarie University, Sydney, p. 464.

Kim, Gene (2013) *The Phoenix Project: A Novel about IT, DevOps, and Helping Your Business Win.* Kindle Edition. Portland, IT Revolution Press.

Knaster, R., & Leffingwell, D. (2017) *SAFe Distilled.* Scaled Agile, Inc.

Kniberg, H. (2011) The multitasking name game. Retrieved from http://www.crisp.se.

Kniberg, H., & Ivarsson, A. (2012) *Scaling Agile@ Spotify with Tribes, Squads, Chapters & Guilds,* Sweden.

Kopmann, J. (2013) *The Realization of Value in Multi-Project Environments: Developing a Framework for Value-Oriented Project Portfolio Management.* Paper presented at EURAM European Academy of Management Conference, June 26–29. Istanbul, Turkey.

Krebs, J. (2009) *Agile Portfolio Management.* Microsoft Press, Washington.

Laanti, M., & Kangas, M. (2015) *Is Agile Portfolio Management Following The Principles of Large-Scale Agile?* Conference Paper. Researchgate.

LaBrosse, M. (2010) Project portfolio management. *Employment Relations Today,* 37(2), 75–79.

Laloux, F., & Wilber, K. (2014) *Reinventing Organizations: A Guide to Creating Organizations Inspired by the Next Stage in Human Consciousness.* 1st edition. Millis, MA, Nelson Parker.

Larman, C., & Vodde, B. (2008) *Scaling Lean and Agile Development: Thinking and Organizational Tools for Large-Scale Scrum.* Upper Saddle, NJ, Addison-Wesley, ISBN-13: 978-0321480965.

Larman, C., & Vodde, B. (2009) *Scaling Lean and Agile Development,* Melbourne, Addison-Wesley Professional.

Larman, C., & Vodde, B. (2016) *Large-Scale Scrum - More with LeSS.* Pearson Education, Crawfordsville.

Larman, C., & Vodde, B. (2019) *LeSS Framework.* Retrieved from http://less.works/. [Accessed December 20, 2019].

Larman, G. (2003) *Agile and Iterative Development: A Manager's Guide,* 1st edition. Melbourne, Addison-Wesley Professional.

Leffingwell, D. (2017) *Reference Guide.* USA, Scaled Agile, Inc.

Levine, H. A. (2005) *Project Portfolio Management: A Practical Guide to Selecting Projects, Managing Portfolios and Maximising Benefits.* Jossey & Bass, San Francisco.

Liker, J. K. (2004) *The Toyota Way: 14 Management Principles from the World's Greatest Manufacturer.* New York, McGraw-Hill. ISBN 978-0-07-139231-0.

Lockard, R. (2019) *Secrets from the Agile Manifesto Authors on Flow.* Publish by Contino.

Mahadevan, L., Ketinger, W. J., & Meservy, T. O. (2015) Running on hybrid: Control changes when introducing an agile methodology in a traditional "waterfall" system development environment. *Communications of the Association for Information Systems,* 36, 77–103.

Marchwinski, C., & Shook, J. (2003) *The Lean Enterprise Institute. 3. Lean Lexicon.* Brookline.

Martinsuo, M., & Kilen, C. P. (2014) Value management in project Portfolio: Identifying and assessing strategic value. *Project Management Journal*, 45(5), 56–70.

Martinsuo, M., & Lehtonen, P. (2007) Role of single-project management in achieving portfolio management efficiency. *International Journal of Project Management*, 25, 56–65.

Maruping, L. M., Venkatesh, V., & Agarwal, R. (2009) A control theory perspective on agile methodology use and changing user requirements A control theory perspective on agile methodol use and changing user requirements. *Source: Information Systems Research Information Systems Research*, 20(3), 377–399. http://doi.org/10.1287/isre.l090.0238.

McFarlan, F. W. (1981) Portfolio approach to information systems. *Harvard Business Review*, 59(5), 142–150.

Menke, M. (2013) Making R&D portfolio management more effective. *Research-Technology Management*, 56(5), 34–44.

Meskendahl, S. (2010) The influence of business strategy on project portfolio management and its success — A conceptual framework. *International Journal of Project Management*, 28(8), 805–817.

Mikkola, J. (2001) Portfolio management of R&D projects: Implications for innovation management. *Technovation*, 21(7), 423–435.

Milanov, G., & Njegus, A. (2012) *Analysis of Return on Investment in Different Types of Agile Software Development Project Teams. Informatica Economica*, 16(4).

Mitchell, R. K., Agle, B. R., & Wood, D. J. (1997) Toward a theory of stakeholder identification and salience: Defining the principle of who and what really counts. *Academy of Management Review*, 22(4), 853–886, October.

Moe, N. B., Šmite, D., Šāblis, A., Börjesson, A.-L.,. & Andréasson, P. (2014) Networking in a large-scale distributed agile project. In: *Proceedings of the 8th ACM/IEEE International Symposium on Empirical Software Engineering and Measurement*, p. 12.

Mohammad, A. R., Richardson, I., Noll, j., Canna, C. N., & Beecham, S. (2018) Scaling agile across the global organization: An early stage industrial SAFe self-assessment. In *ICGSE '18: 13th IEEE/ACM International Conference on Global Software Engineering*, May 27–29. Gothenburg, Sweden; ACM, New York, 10p. https://doi.org/10. 1145/3196369.3196373.

Morris, P., & Jamieson, A. (2005) Moving from corporate strategy to project strategy. *Project Management Journal*, 36(4), 5–18.

Müller, R., Martinsuo, M., & Blomquist, T. (2008) Project portfolio control and portfolio management performance in different contexts. *Project Management Journal*, 39(3), 28–42.

Nolan, R., & McFarlan, F. W. (2005) Information technology and the board of directors. *Harvard Business Review*, 83(10), 96–106.

Passivaara, M., Behm, B., Lassenius, C., & Hallikainen, M. (2018) *Large-Scale Agile Transformation at Ericsson, Empirical Software Engineering* January 11, 23, 2550–2596. https://doi.org/10.1007/s10664-017-9555-8.

Paasivaara, M., Lassenius, C., & Heikkilä, V. T. (2012) Inter-team coordination in large-scale globally distributed scrum: Do scrum-of-scrums really work? In: *Proceedings of the ACM-IEEE International Symposium on Empirical Software Engineering and Measurement*, pp. 235–238.

Patanakul, P., & Milosevic, D. (2005) Multiple-project managers: What competencies do you need? *Project Perspectives*, 2005, 28–33.

Pellegrinelli, S. (1997) Programme management: Organising project-based change. *International Journal of Project Management*, 15(3), 141–149.

Pennypacker, J., & Dye, L. (2002) Project portfolio management and managing multiple projects: Two sides of the same coin. *Managing Multiple Projects*, New York, 1–10.

Pohl, K., & Rupp, C. (2011) *Requirements Engineering Fundamentals: A Study Guide for the Certified Professional for Requirements Engineering Exam - Foundation Level*. San Rafael, CA, Rocky Nook.

Poppendieck, M., & Poppendieck, T. (2003) *Lean Software Development: An Agile Toolkit*. Upper Saddle, New York, Addison-Wesley Professional.

Poskela, J., Dietrich, P., & Artto, K. (2003) Organizing for managing multiple projects–a strategic perspective. In: *Proceedings of the 17th Nordic Conference on Business Studies*, Reykjavik, Iceland, pp. 14–16.

Power, K. (2014) A model for understanding when scaling agile is appropriate in large organizations. In: *International Conference on Agile Software Development*, pp. 83–92.

Project Management Institute (2017a) *A Guide to the Project Management Body of Knowledge (PMBOK® Guides)*, 6th edition. Project Management Institute, Newtown Square, PA.

Project Management Institute (2017b) *The Standard for Portfolio Management*, 4th edition. Project Management Institute, Newtown Square, PA.

Puppet and Dora (2017) *The State of DevOps Report*. Retrieved from http://www.devops-research.com.

Putta, A., Paasivaara, M., & Lassenius, C. (2018) Adopting scaled agile framework (SAFe): A multivocal literature review: Extended abstract. In: *XP '18 Companion: XP '18 Companion*, May 21–25, Portugal Porto, Jennifer B. Sartor, Theo D'Hondt, & Wolfgang De Meuter (Eds.), ACM, New York, Article 4, 6p. https://doi.org/10.1145/3234152. 3234164.

Rautiainen, K., Schantz, J. V., & Vahaniitty, J. (2011) Supporting scaling agile with portfolio management. Retrieved from Paf.com.

Rautiainen, K., & Vähäniitty, J. (2011) *Towards Agile Product and Portfolio Management*, Aalto University, pp. 2–30.

Razzak, M. A., Richardson, I., & Noll, J. (2018) Scaling agile across the global organization: An early stage industrial SAFe self-assessment. In *ACM/IEEE 13th International Conference on Global Software Engineering*.

Reinertsen, D. G. (2009) *The Principles of Product Development Flow*. Burlington, Celeritas Publishing.

Ries, E. (2011) *The Lean Startup*. Penguin books, London, Crown Publishing Group.

Rigby, D. K., Sutherland, J., Takeuchi, H., John, T. S., & Org, H. (2016) How to master the process that's transforming management. *Harvard Business Review*, no. 5 (May): 40–50.

Rolland, K. H., Fitzgerald, B., Dingsoyr, T., & Stol, K.-J. (2016) Problematizing agile in the large: Alternative assumptions for large-scale agile development. In: *Proceedings of the International Conference on Information Systems*, Dublin, pp. 1–21.

Rother, M., & Shook, J. (1998) *Learning to See Value Stream Mapping to Create Value and Eliminate Muda*. Brookline, Lean Enterprise Institute.

Rubin, K. S. (2013) *Essential Scrum*. Upper Saddle River, NJ, Addison-Wesley.

Sanchez, H., & Robert, B. (2010) Measuring portfolio strategic performance using key performance indicators. *Project Management Journal*, 41(5), 64–73.

Schindler, M., & Eppler, M. J. (2003) Harvesting project knowledge: A review of project learning methods and success factors. *International Journal of Project Management*, 21(3), 219–228.

Schwaber, K. (2004) *Agile Software Development with Scrum*. Microsoft Press, California.

Schwaber, K., & Beedle, M. (2001) *Agile Software Development with Scrum*, 1st edition. Prentice Hall PTR, Upper Saddle River, NJ.

Sebestyén, U. (2017) *Agile Multi-Project Management: Portfolio Management, Resource Management and Product Management*. May 30.

Shalloway, A. G. B., & Trott, J. R. (2010) *Lean-Agile Software Development: Achieving Enterprise Agility*. Addison-Wesley, Boston, MA.

Sharp, H., & Robinson, H. (2008) Collaboration and co-ordination in mature eXtreme programming teams. *International Journal of Human-Computer Studies*, 66(7), 506–518.

Shenhar, A. J. (2004) Strategic project leadership. Toward a strategic approach to project management. *R and D Management*, 34(5), 569–578.

Shenhar, A. J., Dvir, D., Levy, O., & Maltz, A. (2001) Project success: A multidimensional strategic concept. *Long Range Planning*, 34(6), 699–725.

Sidky, A. S. (2007) *A Structured Approach to Adopting Agile Practices: The Agile Adoption Framework*. PhD thesis. Virginia Tech. (SolutionIQ, 2014).

Smite, D., Moe, N. B., Floryan, F., Levinta, G., & Chatzipetrou, P. (2020) Spotify guilds. *Communications of the ACM*, 63(3), March, 63.

Smits, H. (2006) *5 Levels of Agile Planning: From Enterprise Product Vision to Team Stand-Up*. Whitepaper. Rally Software Development Corp.

Sommer, A. F., Hedegaard, C., Duskoska, I., & Jensen, K. S. (2015) Improved performance through Agile/Sage gate hybrid. *Research-Technology Management*, 58, 34–45.

Srivannaboon, S., & Milosevic, D. (2006) A two-way influence between business strategy and project management. *International Journal of Project Management*, 24(6), 493–505.

Stellman, A., & Greene, J. (2011) *Applied Software Project Management - Estimation*. Boston, O'Reilly.

Stettina, C. J., & Hörz, J. (2014) Agile Portfolio management: An empirical perspective of practice in use. *International Journal of Project Management, International Journal of Project Management* 33(1) April, DOI:10.1016/j.ijproman.2014.03.008.

Stettina, C. J., & Hörz, J. (2015) Agile portfolio management: An empirical perspective on the practice in use. *International Journal of Project Management*, 33(1), 140–152.

Sutherland, J., & Schwaber, K. (2012) *Software in 30 Days: How Agile Managers Beat the Odds, Delight Their Customers, and Leave Competitors in the Dust*, 1st edition. New York, Wiley.

Sweetman, R. O., & Conboy, K. (2018) Portfolios of agile projects: A complex adaptive systems' agent perspective. *Project Management Journal*, 49(6), 18–38.

Sweetman, R. O., O'Dwyer, & Conboy, K. (2014) Control in software project portfolios: A complex adaptive systems approach. In: *Agile Methods: Large-Scale Development, Refactoring, Testing, and Estimation*, vol. 199, T. Dingsøyr, N. B. Moe, R. Tonelli, S. Counsell, C. Gencel, & K. Petersen (Eds.), Springer Verlag.

Takeuchi, H., & Nonaka, I. (1986) The new new product development game. *HBR*, January-February.

Teller, J., & Kock, A. (2013) An empirical investigation on how portfolio risk management influences project portfolio success. *International Journal of Project Management*, 31(6), 817–829.

Teller, J., Unger, B. N., Kock, A., & Gemünden, H. G. (2012) Formalization of project portfolio management: The moderating role of project portfolio complexity. *International Journal of Project Management*, 30(5), 596–607. https://doi.org/10.1016/j.ijproman.2012.01.020.

Thiry, M. (2001) Sensemaking in value management practice. *International Journal of Project Management*, 19(2), 71–77.

Thiry, M. (2002) Combining value and project management into an effective programme management model. *International Journal of Project Management*, 20(3), 221–227.

Thompson, K. (2013) *Recipes for Agile Governance in the Enterprise*. Cprime.

Uludag, Ø., Kleehaus, M., Xu, X., & Matthes, F. (2012) *Investigating the Role of Architects in Scaled Agile Frameworks*.

Unger, B. N., Kock, A., Gemunden, H. G., & Jonas, D. (2012) Enforcing strategic fit of project portfolios by project termination: An empirical study on senior management involvement. *International Journal of Project Management*, 30(6), 675–685.

University of London (2014) *Guide to Risk Management*.

Vähäniitty, J. (2010) *Chapter 3: The Gap in the Literature in Towards Agile Product and Portfolio Management*, V. Heikkilä, K. Rautiainen, & J. Vähäniitty (Eds.), Aalto University, Espoo, pp. 38–51.

Vähäniitty, J., Rautiainen, K., & Lassenius, C. (2010) Small software organizations need explicit project portfolio management. *IBM Journal of Research and Development*, 54(2), Issue on Business Value through Software Development, 12p.

Varadarajan, P., & Clark, T. (1994) Delineating the scope of corporate, business, and marketing strategy. *Journal of Business Research*, 31(2–3), 93–105.

Voss, M., & Kock, A. (2013) Impact of relationship value on project portfolio success—Investigating the moderating effects of portfolio characteristics and external turbulence. *International Journal of Project Management*, 31(6), 847–861.

Version One (2020) The 14th annual state of Agile. Retrieved from stateofagile.com.

Walker, O., & Ruekert, R. (1987) Marketing's role in the implementation of business strategies: A critical review and conceptual framework. *Journal of Marketing*, 15–33, 51.

Wang, C. L., & Rafiq, M. (2009) *Organizational Diversity and Shared Vision: Resolving the Paradox of Exploratory and Exploitative Learning. European Journal of Innovation Management* 12(1) January, DOI:10.1108/14601060910928184.

Whitaker, S. (2014) The benefits of tailoring: Making a project management methodology fit. *PMI*, September.

Wiegers, K. (2003) *Software Requirements 2*. Microsoft Press, California.

Williams, L. (2012) What agile teams think of agile principles. *Communications of the ACM*, 55(4), 71–76.

Womack, J. P., & Jones, D. T. (2003) *Lean Thinking: Banish Waste and Create Wealth in Your Corporation*, 2nd edition. Free Press, Detroit.

Womack, J. P., Jones, D. T., & Roos, D. (2007) *The Machine That Changed the World: The Story of Lean Production, 2007 Updated Edition*. Free Press, Detroit.

Wu, S.-C. W. (2011) *Running Head: Traditional and Agile EVM Process*. Boston University. School of Management, Boston.

Glossary of Terms and Acronyms

A

Acceptance criteria: The criteria that a system or component must satisfy in order to be accepted by a user, customer, or other authorized entity.

Acceptance test-driven development (ATDD): a collaborative practice where users, testers, and developers define automated acceptance criteria early in the development process.

Active listening: Techniques to listen well.

Activity network diagrams: A graphic representation of the logical relationship among the project schedule activities.

Adapt: Fourth phase of the agile project management (APM) delivery framework.

Adaptability: The ability of a system to adapt to changing market conditions and customer demands to be better fit for its purpose.

Adaptive leadership: Leadership which deals with changes and problem-solving.

Adaptive planning: See **Progressive elaboration**.

Adaptive software development: Popular agile methodologies.

Affinity estimating: An estimation method to generate high level estimates.

Agile modelling (AM): A practice-based methodology for effective modelling and documentation of software-based systems.

Agile manifesto: The manifesto for agile software development created in Utah 2001.

Agile methodologies: Frameworks and process which are based on Agile Manifesto, i.e., Scrum.

Agile smells: Ways to describe and quickly recognize and diagnose common problems so that a remedy may be pursued.

Agile Software Development Manifesto: A document created in 2001 that lays out the guiding principles of agile project management.

Agile themes: Describe a collection of stories, an iteration, or release.

Agile tooling: Agile tooling is a generic term for the range of tools agile teams applies to foster communication.

Analogy: Technique for estimation.

B

Backlog: A listing of product requirement and deliverables to be completed, written as stories, and prioritized by the business to manage and organize the project's work.

Belbin team roles: Technique to identify people's behavioural strengths and weaknesses.

Benefit–cost ratio: Is the ratio of the present value (PV) of benefits to the present value of costs.

Benefit management: The identification, quantification, definition, analysis, planning, tracking, realization, and optimization of benefits.

Burndown charts: Showing the relationship between two variables.

Burn rate: The rate at which resources is consumed.

Burnup charts: Showing the relationship between two variables.

Business case: A documented economic feasibility study used to establish validity of the benefits of a selected component lacking sufficient definition and that is used as a basis for the authorization of further project management activities.

Business value: A concept that is unique to each organization and includes tangible and intangible elements, through the effective use of project, programme, and portfolio management disciplines, organizations will possess the ability to employ reliable, established processes to meet enterprise objectives and obtain greater business value from their investment.

Brainstorming: Rapid technique to gather ideas.

C

Cause-and-effect diagram: See **Root-cause analysis**.

Change control board: A formally chartered group responsible for reviewing, evaluating, approving, delaying, or rejecting changes to the project, and for recording and communicating such decisions.

Change control process: Whereby modifications to documents, deliverables, or baselines associated with the project are identified, documented, approved, or rejected.

Change control tools: Manual or automated tools to assets with change and/or configuration management. At a minimum, the tools should support the activities of the CCB.

Change log: A comprehensive list of changes made during the project.

Change request: A formal proposal to modify any document, deliverable, or baseline.

Chartering (agile): The project charter is a formal document to authorize the project.

Code of ethics and professional conduct: Standards for what is honourable and right.

Collocated team: When teams collocate because it maximizes their ability to communicate.

Communication management: The process of managing communication.

Communication management plan: A component of the project, programme, or portfolio management plan that describes how, when, and by whom information about the project will be administered and disseminated.

Communication methods: A systematic procedure, technique, or process used to transfer information among project stakeholders.

Complex adaptive systems (CAS): A theoretical lens for understanding agile being capable of adapting to the external environment.

Compliance: Adherence to standards or regulations.

Cone of uncertainty: A term describing the difficulty of estimating early due to unknowns and how that should improve over time.

Configuration management: a subsystem of the overall project management system.

Configuration management system: See **Configuration management**.

Conflict resolutions: Methods to solve conflicts.

Constructive agile estimation algorithm (CAEA): An algorithmic approach for estimation of cost, size, and duration of project.

Continuous deployment: In its purest form, continuous integration means that all code changes are checked in and the entire system is built and tested at the end of each day.

Continuous improvement: Also about maintaining agile project teams to ensure efficiency, effectiveness, individual integrity, and professionalism.

Continuous integration: Concept to check out code and ensure it runs and nothing is broken.

Control limits: Process behaviour chart used to determine whether a process is in a state of statistical control or not.

Control schedule: The process of monitoring the status of project activities to update project progress and manage changes to the schedule baseline to achieve the plan.

Climate for learning: An organization with a climate for learning views learning as an investment that is needed for growth, not as a necessary evil, undertaken only when required.

Close: Final phase of the agile project management (APM) delivery framework.

Crashing: A technique used to shorten the schedule duration for the least incremental cost by adding resources.

Critical path: The sequence of activities that represent the longest part through a project, which determines the shortest possible duration.

Critical chain: A schedule method that allows the project team to place buffers on any project schedule path to account for limited resources and project uncertainties.

Crystal methods: Popular agile methodologies.

Culture: Learned, shared, and enduring orientation patterns in a society.

Cumulative flow diagram: Visualizes the work status.

Customer-valued prioritization: Prioritization by value for customers.

Cycle time: The time between two successive deliveries.

Cynefin framework: Conceptual framework used to aid decision-making.

D

Daily plan: Like the daily Scrum.

Daily Scrum: A Scrum event. It is a daily meeting for approximately 15 minutes, which is organized to keep track of the progress of the Scrum team and address any obstacles faced by the team.

Daily standup: See **Daily Scrum**.

DEEP: An acronym describing desirable attributes of a product backlog: (d)etailed, appropriately, (e)stimable, (e)mergent, and (p)rioritized.

Delphi: An estimating technique which ask a range of experts for an estimate. See also **Wideband Delphi**.

Definition of done: The quality of the software to be defined as working software.

Disaggregation: Splitting a story or feature into smaller, easier-to-estimate pieces.

Disciplined agile (delivery): Agile framework acquired by PMI and develop by Scott Ambler and Mark Lines.

Discounted cash flow (DCF): Converts future cash flow into present-value cash flow.

Distributed team: A team where its members are distributed in varies locations, often around the globe.

Dynamic systems development method: An agile project management and delivery framework that aims to deliver the right solution at the right time.

E

Earned value management (EVM): A methodology that combines scope, schedule, and resource measurements to assess project performance, and progress.

EDGE: Framework by Jim Highsmith. Linda Luu, and David Robinson.

Elapsed time: The amount of time it takes to complete a story.

Emotional intelligence: Focused on people and forging strong and supportive relationships.

Empowerment: The process of individuals that enables them to take action, control work, and make decisions autonomously.

Enterprise environment factors: Conditions, not under the immediate control of the team, that influence, constrain, or direct the project, programme, or portfolio.

Enterprise Scrum: Agile framework developed by Mike Beedle.

Envision: First phase of the agile project management (APM) delivery framework.

Epic (stories): A very large story that may span iterations.

Erg-seconds: Information transmission used to detect and transfer ideas.

Escaped defects: Defects escaped quality controls and found by the customer.

Estimation: Time or resource required.

Expert judgement: A method to ask someone who is familiar with, and knowledgeable about, the application area, and the technologies, to provide an estimate.

Explore: Third phase of the agile project management (APM) delivery framework.

Extreme characters: See **Personas**.

Extreme Programming: A popular agile methodology.

F

Facilitation methods: The process of helping participants learn from an activity.

Fast tracking: A schedule compression technique in which activities or phases normally done in sequence are performed in parallel for a least a portion of their duration.

Feature: Synonymous with **Story**.

Feature-driven development: A popular agile methodology.

Feedback techniques: Techniques which demonstrate part of the solution to the business at an early stage but still in a quick and easy format.

Fibonacci numbers: 0,1,1,2,3,5,8,13,21,34,55,89,144.

Financial models (for portfolio selection: Net present value (NPV), Present value (PV), Return on investment (ROI), Intern rate of return (IRR), Discounted cash flow (DCF), Real option analysis (ROA), Payback period (PBP), Benefit–cost ratio (BCR), Profitability index (PI), and suchlike.

Fishbone diagram: See **Root-cause analysis**.

Five-level of planning: High-level description of the planning phases.

Five principles of Lean thinking: Value, value-stream, flow, pull, and perfection.

Five "Whys" technique: A form of root-cause analysis.

Flow: The state of optimal performance achieved by applying a clear, consistent, persistent, and unified vision at all levels of an organization.

Force-field analysis: Decision-making technique.

Functional requirement: A requirement concerning a result of behaviour that will be provided by a function of the system.

Future value: The value of an asset at a specific date.

G

Governance: Levels of planning and cycles of control.
Ground rules: Rules about expectations on the project.

H

Hersey–Blanchard Situational Leadership Theory: Leadership depends upon each individual situation.
High performing agile teams (HPT): Teams that constantly satisfy the needs of customers, employees, investors, and others in their area of influence.
Huddles: A variant of the daily standup.
Hybrid approach: A combination of various software development models, e.g., waterfall and the spiral model.
Hybrid portfolio management: A combination of various software development models, e.g., waterfall and the spiral model on the portfolio level.

I

Ideal time: The time is takes to complete an assignment, story point, or task without hindrances of any sort.
Ideal agile team space: See **Team space**.
IKIWISI: Short for I Know It When I See It.
Incremental development: The process of delivering the most valuable elements of a system first.
Information radiator: Is the generic term for any of a number of hand-written, drawn, printed, or electronic displays.
Inspection: Scrum pillar with emphasis on timely checks and differences.
Innovation games: Games used for gathering ideas and elicit requirements.
Internal rate of return (IRR): A way of expressing profit as an interest rate earned.
INVEST: Acronyms for creating effective writing user stories.
Investment selection: the periodic activity involved in selecting a portfolio, from available project (and programme) proposals and projects (and programmes) currently underway, that meets the organization's stated objectives in a desirable manner without exceeding available resources or violating other constraints.

Ishikawa diagram: See **Root-cause diagram**.
Iteration planning: Planning of iterations.

K

Kanban: A change management method.
Kanban board: Highly visible agile metrics on information radiators.
Kano classification: Technique using dissatisfiers, satisfiers, and delighters to prioritize requirements.
Knowledge sharing: The process of disseminating things learned and skills acquired by individuals for the benefits of the team.

L

Lags: The amount of time whereby a successor activity can be advanced with respect to a predecessor activity.
Large-scale Scrum (LeSS): Agile framework developed by Craig Larsen and Bas Vodde.
Lead: The amount of time whereby a successor activity is required to be delayed with respect to a predecessor activity.
Lead time: The time between the initiation and delivery of a work item.
Lean software development: An agile methodology.
Little's Law: A way to analyze queues from the cumulative flow diagram.

M

Management of portfolios: Global standard for portfolio management developed by Axelos
Meyers–Briggs Type Indicators (MBTI): Team selection theories based on the work of Jung.
Milestones: A significant point or event in a project, programme, or portfolio.
Minimal marketable features (MMF): Features are decomposed into the smallest marketable units of useful deliverable business value.
MoSCoW prioritization: Technique to prioritize requirements.

Multiple levels of planning: The five level of planning from product vision to daily planning.

N

Negotiation: Process of reaching the best results.

Net present value (NPV): A way of factoring in the time-value of money to calculate a project's worth.

O

Organization process assets: Plan, processes, policies, procedures, and knowledge bases that are specific to and used by the performing organization.

Open team space: See **Team space**.

Optimal team size: Application of probably project team size.

Osmotic communication: Ongoing sounds around the team.

P

Pair programming: All production codes are written by two programmers.

Parametric estimating: An estimation model, which is based on correlation of cost and variables such as weight, size, type of assembly.

Parkinson's Law: States that an activity takes as much time as you allow it to.

Parking lot chart: Graphical report highlighting features.

Participatory decision models: Decision models for shared ownership.

Payback period (PP): Is the number of months it takes to recoup the initial investment.

Perspective-based readings: Is a kind of validation technique that adopts different perspectives to check the requirements and is typically applied in conjunction with other review techniques.

Plan-Do-Check-Act cycle: Quality management cycle by W. H. Deming.

Product backlog: This is the prioritized list of all features and changes that have yet to be made to the system desired by multiple actors, such as customers, marketing and sales, and project team.

Prioritization: Business prioritization of what to do.

Programme evaluation and review technique (PERT): Estimation techniques which give three estimates with uncertainties in considerations.

Progressive elaboration: The iterative process of increasing the level of detail in the project management plan as a greater amount of information and more accurate estimates become available.

Personas: Made-up pretend users.

Planning poker: Agile estimation methods.

Portfolio artefacts: All the various kinds of documents, logs, or deliverables.

Portfolio backlog: See **Product backlog**.

Portfolio ceremonies: Meetings, rituals, and suchlike.

Portfolio Kanban: See **Kanban** and **Information radiator**.

Portfolio metrics: See **Software metrics**.

Portfolio product owner: See **Product owner**.

Portfolio Scrum master: See **Scrum master**.

Portfolio selection: See **Investment selection**.

Portfolio retrospective: See **Sprint retrospective**.

Predictability: The degree to which a correct prediction of a system's future can be made.

Present value (PV): A way of factoring in time-value of money to calculate a project's worth.

Problem and opportunity analysis: A way of identifying problems and opportunities.

Process decision programme charts: The model is used to understand a goal in relation to the steps for getting to the goal.

Process tailoring: The process of adapting the processes to the team's needs.

Product: An artefact that is produced, is quantifiable, and can be either an end item in itself or a component item.

Product backlog: A Scrum artefact. This is the prioritized list of all features and changes that have yet to be made to the system desired by multiple actors in Scrum.

Product owner: A Scrum role. Voice of the customer.

Product road map: An overview that shows an overall plan with each planned release and the relevant features associated with those releases.

Product vision statement: An elevator statement for the product, describing what is it, who would need it, the key reasons someone would pay for it, and what differentiates it in the market.

Profitability index (PI): Also known as profit investment ratio (PIR) and value investment ratio (VIR), it is the ratio of payoff to investment of a proposed project.

Progressive elaboration: The iterative process of increasing the level of detail in the project management plan as greater amount of information and more accurate estimates become available.

Project: A temporary endeavour undertaken to create a unique product, service, or result.

Project charter: A document issued by the project initiator or sponsor that formally authorizes the existence of a project and provides the project manager with the authority to apply organizational resources to project activities.

Project goals: Achieving a desired outcome (performance goal) at a specific end date (time goal) employing a specific number of resources (resource goal).

Project management: The application of knowledge, skills, and techniques to execute projects effectively and efficiently.

Project management constraints model: The project management constraints are scope, time, cost, risk, quality, and resources.

Project portfolio management: A group of projects that are carried out under the sponsorship and/or management of a particular organization.

Project portfolio optimization: The project portfolio is the process of base-lining the risk and benefits profile of a sequenced strategic investment portfolio, applying what-if analysis to generate alternative portfolio scenarios, comparing the risk and benefits profiles of the alternative scenarios, and choosing the most optimal strategic investment portfolio based on a balance of risk versus reward over the life of the project portfolio.

Project portfolio prioritization: The process of individual evaluation, comparative analysis, and ranking projects and programmes relative to each other and it is central to maximizing the value of the portfolio as it favours projects and programmes with the highest contribution.

Project portfolio sequencing: The process of applying a sequencing logic (or algorithm) to establish the order in which mandatory requirements and prioritized investment vehicles (projects, programmes, and other work) shall be undertaken in a desirable manner without exceeding available resources or violating other constraints.

Project portfolio risk management: The process of reviewing risk across the portfolio with a view to identifying threats to overall portfolio performance and benefits.

Project portfolio stakeholder engagement: Identification and analysis of the relevant stakeholders.

Project scope: The features and functions that characterize a product, service, or result.

Project scope description: The documented narrative description of the project scope.

Proxies: Customer representatives.

Q

Quality checklists: A structured tool used to verify that a set of required steps have been performed.

Quality metrics: A description of a project or product attribute and how to measure it.

Quality requirement: A requirement that pertains to a quality concern that is not covered by functional requirements. Also called a nonfunctional requirement.

R

RACI: A common type of responsibility assignment matrix that uses responsible, accountable, consulted, and informed statuses to define the involvement of stakeholders in project activities.

Recipes for agile governance in the enterprise (RAGE): Agile framework developed by Cprime.

Refactoring: A disciplined technique for restructuring an existing body of code, altering its internal structure without changing its external behaviour.

Relative prioritization/ranking: The process of selecting few items with higher priority over others based upon customer value.

Relative sizing: Agile estimating methods of estimation of scales.

Release planning: Planning of releases with deliverables of features, benefits, and value to the customers.

Requirement: A condition or capability to which a system must conform.

Requirement documentation: A description of how individual requirements meet the business need for the project.

Requirement management plan: A component of the project or programme management plan that describes how requirements will be analyzed, documented, and managed.

Requirements traceability: Refers to the ability to describe and follow the life of a requirement, in both a forwards and backwards direction.

Requirement traceability matrix: An S grid that links product requirements from their origin to the deliverables that satisfy them.

Responsibility assignment matrix: A grid that shows the project resources assigned to each work package.

Retrospective: A look back in time and analysis of the situation in order to make improvements.

Return on investment (ROI): Demonstrate what return an organization makes by investing in a percentage.

Risk: An uncertain event or condition that, if it occurs, has a positive or negative effect on one or more project objectives.

Risk-adjusted backlog: Value-generating business features and risk-reduction actions.

Risk appetite: The degree of uncertainty an entity is willing to take on, in anticipation of a reward.

Risk-based spikes: Quick experience used to help the team answer a question and determine a path forward.

Risk burndown graphs: A chart where the risk to project success associated with each feature is displayed.

Risk-management plan: A component of the project, programme, or portfolio management plan that describes how risk management activities will be structured and performed.

Risk register: A document in which the result of risk analysis and risk response planning are recorded.

Roll-calls: A variant of the daily standup.

Root cause: The underlying cause of the problem which, if adequately addressed, will prevent a recurrence of that problem.

Root-cause analysis: A cause-and-effect diagram, Ishikawa diagram, or fishbone diagram is a process for identifying contributing/causal factors that underlie variations in performance associated with adverse events or close calls.

Rolling wave planning: See **Progressive elaboration**.

Running tested features: Metric that forces agility.

S

Scaled agile framework (SAFe): Agile framework developed by Dean Leffingwell.

Scope: The sum of the products, services, and results to be provided as a project. See also **Project scope** and **Product scope**.

Scrum: A popular agile methodology.

Scrum master: A Scrum role. Liaison between the product owner and the team.

Scrum values: Focus, openness, respect, commitment, and courage.

Self-assessment: Stimulate learning and change, as well as enthusiasm for development.

Servant leadership: A philosophy and set of practices that enriches the lives of individuals, builds better organizations, and ultimately creates a more just and caring world.

Shu-Ha-Ri: Describes the progression of learning.

SMART: Acronym for creating effective goals (specific, measurable, achievable, relevant, and time-sensitive).

SMITH: Acronym used in communication short for simple, minimal, influential, transient, and highly visible.

Software metrics: Measurement of the software product and the process by which it is developed.

Speculate: Second phase of the agile project management (APM) delivery framework.

Splitting user stories: General guidance to make each story provide a vertical slice, some piece of user value, through the system.

Spotify model: A people-driven, autonomous approach for scaling agile that emphasizes the importance of culture and network.

Sprint: A Scrum event. Sprints are 30 days in length. It is the procedure of adapting to the changing environmental variables (requirements, time, resources, knowledge, technology etc.) and must result in a potentially shippable increment of software.

Sprint backlog: The list of features that is currently assigned to a particular sprint. When all the features are completed a new iteration of the system is delivered.

Sprint planning meeting: A Scrum event. A sprint planning meeting is first attended by the customers, users, management, product owner and Scrum team where a set of goals and functionality are decided on.

Sprint retrospective: A Scrum event. Reflection on the process and room for improvements.

Stage-Gate model: The Stage-Gate model (also referred as phase-gate process) is a project management methodology used to drive a project from idea to launch in a structured way, including several decision-making points.

Strategic alignment: Strategy alignments focus on strategic vision/planning, aligning all work in the backlog to the strategy.

Strategic alignment measure: Return on investment, costs, risks, required resources, available resources, time frame, strategic fit (most important), level of impact, constraints, and suchlike.

Standard for portfolio management: Global standard for portfolio management developed by the Project Management Institute.

Stakeholder: A person, a group, or an organization that is actively involved in the project or whose interests may be positively or negatively affected by the results achieved by or the completion of the project.

Stakeholder analysis: A technique of systematically gathering and analyzing quantitative and qualitative information to determine whose interests should be taken into account throughout the project.

Stakeholder management: A process to identify, assess, and manage stakeholders.

Stakeholder register: A project document including the identification, assessment, and classification of the project stakeholders.

Stakeholder salience: Stakeholder identification by power, legitimacy and urgency.

Statement of work (SOW): A narrative description of products, services, or results to be delivered by the project.

Story maps: A technique to organize and prioritize user stories.

Story points: A measure of complexity.

System boundary: Separate the system to be developed from its environment.

System context: The part of the system environment that is relevant for the definition as well as the understanding of the requirements of a system to be developed.

System thinking: A mental effort to uncover the endogenous sources of system behaviour.

T

Tailoring: The process of adapting the governance to fit with the given context.

Task board: Highly visible agile metrics on information radiators.

TEAM: Short for together, everyone, archives, and more.

Team selection: The process of selecting the right team members for the team.

Team space: Space assigned to the team.

Technical debt: Invisible technical negative value to the project.

Test driven development (TDD): A special case of test-first development.

Test first development: A rapid XP cycle of testing, coding, and refactoring.

Time box: A previously agreed period of time during which a person or a team works steadily towards completion of some goal.

Traceability: The ability to interrelate any uniquely identifiable software engineering artefact to any other, maintain required links over time, and use the resulting network to answer questions of both the software product and its development process.

Transformational leadership: The ability to inspire and motivate people with shared values and sense of purpose.

Twelve principles of agile software: Working values of agile methodologies.

U

User story: Specifying software requirements in a brief statement.

User story backlog: See **Product backlog**.

User story mapping: See **Story maps**.

V

Validation: Ensures that software being developed or changed satisfies functional and all other requirements.

Value-based prioritization: Project justification.

Value management: A systematic method to define what value means for organizations, and to communicate it clearly and provide methods to maximize value across portfolios, programmes, projects, and operations.

Value-stream mapping: Method adopted by agile to analyze an entire chain of processes with goals of eliminating waste.

Value proposition: A promise of vale to be delivered.

Velocity: At the end of each iteration, the team adds up effort estimates associated with user stories that were completed during that iteration.

Verification: Ensures that every step in the process of building the software delivers the correct product.

Version: A particular form of software.

Vision document: A document that defines the high-level scope and purpose of a programme, product, or project.

W

Work breakdown structure (WBS): A hierarchical decomposition of the total scope of work to be carried out by the project team to accomplish the project objectives and create the required deliverables.

WBS directory: A document that provides detailed deliverables, activity, and scheduling information about each component in the work breakdown structure.

Westrum organizational culture: Model of organizational culture developed by sociologist Dr Ron Westrum.

Wideband Delphi: Process that a team can use to generate an estimate.

Wireframes: Lightweight non-functional user interface design.

Work-in-progress (WIP): To limit the amount of work and concentrate on getting the work done.

WIP Limits: A strategy for preventing bottlenecks in software development.

X

XSCALE: Agile framework developed by Peter Mercel.

XP: See **Extreme programming**.

XP values: Simplicity, communication, feedback, courage and respect.

Index